DEVELOPING HOUSING FOR THE WORKFORCE
A Toolkit

Urban Land Institute

ULI–the Urban Land Institute
1025 Thomas Jefferson Street, N.W.
Suite 500 West
Washington, D.C. 20007-5201

Library of Congress Cataloging-in-Publication Data

Developing housing for the workforce : a toolkit.
    p. cm.
   1. Housing—United States. 2. Working class—Housing—United States. I. Urban Land Institute.
   HD7293.D48 2007
   363.5'96230973–dc22

                                2007009016

ISBN 978-0-87420-929-7

10 9 8 7 6 5 4 3 2 1
Printed in the United States of America

About ULI–the Urban Land Institute

The mission of the Urban Land Institute is to provide leadership in the responsible use of land and in creating and sustaining thriving communities worldwide. ULI is committed to:

• Bringing together leaders from across the fields of real estate and land use policy to exchange best practices and serve community needs;

• Fostering collaboration within and beyond ULI's membership through mentoring, dialogue, and problem solving;

• Exploring issues of urbanization, conservation, regeneration, land use, capital formation, and sustainable development;

• Advancing land use policies and design practices that respect the uniqueness of both built and natural environments;

• Sharing knowledge through education, applied research, publishing, and electronic media; and

• Sustaining a diverse global network of local practice and advisory efforts that address current and future challenges.

Established in 1936, the Institute today has more than 35,000 members from 90 countries, representing the entire spectrum of the land use and development disciplines. Professionals represented include developers, builders, property owners, investors, architects, public officials, planners, real estate brokers, appraisers, attorneys, engineers, financiers, academics, students, and librarians. ULI relies heavily on the experience of its members. It is through member involvement and information resources that ULI has been able to set standards of excellence in development practice.

The Institute has long been recognized as one of the world's most respected and widely quoted sources of objective information on urban planning, growth, and development.

Project Staff

Rachelle L. Levitt
Executive Vice President, Information Group

Dean Schwanke
Senior Vice President, Publications and Awards

Richard M. Haughey
Director, Multifamily Development
Project Director

Nancy H. Stewart
Director, Book Program
Managing Editor

Lori Hatcher
Director, Publications Marketing

Sandra Chizinsky
Otter Creek Editorial, Manuscript Editor

James A. Mulligan
Associate Editor

Anne Morgan
Graphic Design

Betsy Van Buskirk
Art Director

Craig Chapman
Director, Publishing Operations

Karrie Underwood
Adminstrative Manager/Digital Images Assistant

Susan S. Teachey, ON-Q Design, Inc.
Design and Composition

Introduction Author

Richard M. Haughey
Urban Land Institute
Washington, D.C.

Toolkit, Author

Diane R. Suchman
Diane Suchman, LLC
Springfield, Virginia

Case Study Authors

Ken Braverman
The Braverman Company
Burlington, Vermont

Adam Ducker
Robert Charles Lesser
Bethesda Maryland

Clair Enlow
Seattle, Washington

Richard M. Haughey
Urban Land Institute
Washington, D.C.

Jennifer LeFurgy
Metropolitan Institute at Virginia Tech
Alexandria, Virginia

Deborah L. Myerson
Deborah Myerson, LLC
Bloomington, Indiana

Adam Ploetz, A.I.C.P.
495/MetroWest Corridor Partnership
Westborough, Massachusetts

Review Committee

Donald Carter
President
Urban Design Associates
Pittsburgh, Pennsylvania

Bruce Gunter
President/C.E.O.
Progressive Redevelopment, Inc.
Decatur, Georgia

John McIlwain
Senior Resident Fellow
J. Ronald Terwilliger Chair for Housing
Urban Land Institute
Washington, D.C.

J. Michael Pitchford
President
Community Preservation and Development Corporation
Washington, DC

Nicolas Retsinas
Director
Joint Center for Housing Studies
Harvard University
Cambridge, Massachusetts

Michael Stegman
Director for Center for Community Capitalism
Frank Hawkins Kenan Institute of Private Enterprise
University of North Carolina
Chapel Hill, North Carolina

Acknowledgments

So many people contributed to this publication that it's difficult to thank them all here. First, thanks to the developers, architects, planners, and public officials who continually find creative solutions to the vexing affordable housing problem facing most urban areas. Special thanks go to Diane Suchman for her comprehensive review of workforce housing programs. Thanks to the many case study authors who visited the projects; interviewed the developers, architects, and planners; and told the story of these amazing developments. And finally, thanks to the prestigious review committee that guided this publication along the way.

Contents

Contents

Foreword

DURING THE PAST FEW YEARS, there has been a growing awareness of the shortage of affordable workforce housing, and of its impact on families and communities across America. Communities large and small are finding that teachers, police officers, firefighters, emergency workers, nurses, and others who are essential to community life and commerce are unable to live in the localities where they work. As Mary Kate Costello, a new recruit to the Fairfax County, Virginia, fire department said in an interview, "I think it's kind of a shame that . . . we are putting our lives on the line every day for people that we can't afford to live next door to." Each year, more workers face the same dilemma.

Although housing affordable to the workforce is, in fact, being built, it is located, with few exceptions, in outlying suburbs that are often more than an hour's drive from the communities where people work. The impact is manifold. Workers must spend inordinate amounts of time and money to reach their jobs. The long commutes add to traffic congestion and pollution, and decrease efficiency. Children lose the benefit of having teachers live nearby. Businesses have difficulty recruiting and retaining workers—and may ultimately move elsewhere, to be close to

where their workers can afford to live. Finally, in the case of a major emergency, safety can be compromised when police, firefighters, and emergency workers live far away, and are unable to respond to a disaster in time.

Ten years ago, no one had heard of the workforce housing problem; it was first identified by the National Housing Conference during the 1990s boom. Though the problem is of recent origin, it is growing rapidly in severity. Why? For the first time in decades, housing prices are rising faster than inflation—and, driven by the pressure of U.S. population growth, the trend is likely to continue, despite rising interest rates and the inevitable ups and downs of local markets. The United States is adding 30 million people each decade—more than ever before in its history. The result is relentless pressure to accommodate the housing needs of millions of new households each year. This has led, in most communities, to increasing resistance to development. The reasons for trying to restrict development are often sound: the need to preserve farmland, natural habitats, and fragile ecological areas around rivers and bays, for example. Other reasons—such as concern about local home values—may be understandable, but are not always well grounded. But whatever the cause, the effect is

Foreword

to slow housing development and increase housing costs, particular in the cities and developed suburbs located closest to where the jobs are.

As increases in home prices exceed inflation, workforce wages barely keep up with the rise in the cost of living. Recessions, increasing productivity, globalization, and millions of unemployed and underemployed workers all conspire to keep wages flat.

What is to be done? Each community will have to face this challenge with little help from a virtually bankrupt federal government. State and local governments, despite tight budgets and many competing demands, need to mount serious efforts to meet the housing needs of the workforce. Fortunately, there are many tools available. Diane Suchman and Richard Haughey have done an excellent job of identifying and describing these tools. This is the most comprehensive toolkit for workforce housing compiled to date, and is an essential reference for government officials, housing advocates, business leaders, community activists, union leaders, and housing developers—indeed, for anyone concerned with sustaining the social and economic life of their community.

John McIlwain
ULI/J. Ronald Terwilliger Chair for Housing

DEVELOPING HOUSING FOR THE WORKFORCE
A Toolkit

ULI

Urban Land
Institute

DEVELOPING HOUSING FOR THE WORKFORCE
Introduction

Introduction

THIS PUBLICATION IS DESIGNED TO PROVIDE IDEAS,
best practices, and strategies to help the public and private
sectors support the production of housing that is affordable to
moderate-income working households. The intended audience
is public policy makers, elected and appointed government
officials, developers, planners, architects, lenders, investors, and
others interested in increasing the supply of privately developed
workforce housing. The book has three parts: (1) this introduction; (2) a series of case studies, each of which highlights a
recent workforce housing development project and describes
the policies, programs, and financing approaches that made

the project possible; and (3) a toolkit that describes the types of efforts that states and localities have undertaken to support workforce housing, and also provides overviews of successful programs.[1]

The term *workforce housing* did not come into wide use in the United States until the 21st century. Although most people have an intuitive understanding of what workforce housing is, obtaining consensus on a specific definition is difficult because in each market, a number of factors—including income levels, home prices, construction costs, land constraints, and the regulatory environment—conspire to create a unique housing affordability problem. For example, a teacher in San Jose, California, and a teacher in Washington, D.C., might both be unable to purchase a home, but the specific characteristics of the housing options available to them will differ significantly because of the particular housing markets in question.

Overview of the Workforce Housing Problem

In this book, two definitions of workforce housing—one general, and one more specific—will be used. Generally, *workforce housing* refers to housing that is affordable to working households that do not qualify for publicly subsidized housing, yet cannot afford appropriate market-rate housing in their community. More specifically, workforce housing is defined as housing that is affordable to working households with incomes between 60 and 120 percent of the area median income (AMI) for their Metropolitan Statistical Area. The rationale for using 60 percent of AMI as the lower limit is that many affordable-housing programs, including the Low-Income Housing Tax Credit (LIHTC), do not offer public subsidies for households with incomes above this level. Although the cap of 120 percent of

AMI is used by a number of workforce housing programs, it is somewhat arbitrary. The specific definition was used for a national review of workforce housing programs conducted by ULI, and may be entirely inappropriate for particular local markets.

Depending on the characteristics of the local market, a community may choose a different definition of workforce housing. One option, for example, is to set the upper income cap by calculating the annual income required to afford a median-priced home in the community. In a number of metropolitan areas, this income level, when compared with actual area incomes, will reveal a housing market seriously out of balance. For example, the California Association of Realtors reported that in 2005, the median price of a home in the state was $548,400. Assuming a mortgage interest rate of 6.26 percent and a 20 percent downpayment, the annual income required to purchase that home is $133,390. But the 2005 median income in California was $64,113; thus, to afford a median-priced home in the state, a household would have to earn 208 percent of the state median income. So California may wish to define workforce housing as housing that is affordable to households earning between 60 and 200 percent of the state median income.

Although such an analysis may be used to set the upper threshold for the definition of workforce housing, it begs the question of whether workforce housing is rental or for-sale housing. A community with balanced housing options provides housing opportunities—both rental and for-sale—for people in all stages of the life cycle. In fact, both rental and for-sale housing play an important role in the health of a community's economy. Any effort to determine the appropriate proportions of rental and for-sale housing should be based on an assessment of community needs and the existing composition of the housing supply.

Before moving on to a more detailed consideration of the workforce housing problem, it is important to return for a moment to the broad definition of workforce housing offered earlier: generally speaking, the target market for workforce housing consists of households that do not qualify for subsidized housing, but that cannot afford appropriate market-rate housing. The use of the word *appropriate* in this definition is significant. In many localities, market-rate housing that is affordable to working households does in fact exist, but it is often in substandard condition, or located in unsafe neighborhoods with poor schools—or both. Alternatively, affordable market-rate housing can sometimes be found in what have become known as "exurban" locations—that is, areas that are at a significant distance from employment centers. The question is, are these housing options "appropriate" for the workforce?

This book assumes that the answer to this question is no. The level of risk associated with substandard housing, unsafe neighborhoods, and poor schools, and the negative consequences of exurban development make both options inappropriate and unsustainable as solutions to the workforce housing problem.[2] This should not be construed to mean, however, that urban revitalization and the construction of suburban workforce housing have no place in addressing affordable-housing needs. The revitalization of declining neighborhoods can play a significant role in the creation of workforce housing for a portion of the target market—for example, young professionals who are willing to be urban pioneers. Similarly, the ongoing decentralization of employment centers will create opportunities for workforce housing development near emerging suburban employment centers.

Ideally, efforts to address the workforce housing problem will yield a wide variety of housing options for households with a wide variety of incomes—and these housing options will be located in close proximity to employment centers and mass transit. Thus, the creation of a healthy jobs-housing balance is part of the assumed goal.

A Problem or a Crisis?

With homeownership in the United States hitting all-time highs—almost 70 percent of Americans now own their homes—many question whether there is indeed a workforce housing problem, let alone a crisis. While statistics on homeownership may be encouraging, they mask a number of troubling issues. First, those who are fortunate enough to own their homes are seriously concerned about rapidly appreciating home prices. A recent survey conducted by the National Association of Realtors, for example, reported that one-third of respondents were worried that because of rising monthly payments—especially property taxes and energy costs—they would be forced to sell their homes and buy less expensive ones.[3] There is evidence that such fears may be warranted. With the slowing housing market and the explosion of adjustable-rate mortgage products, the rate of loans entering into foreclosure in the third quarter of 2006 was the highest since the fourth quarter of 2004.[4]

More worrisome are households characterized by the National Housing Conference (NHC) as having "critical housing need." A household with critical housing need is a household that lives in severely dilapidated conditions or spends more than 50 percent of its income on housing. The NHC estimates that 14.1 million households—that is, one in eight households—is in critical housing need. Of these households, the NHC estimates that 5 million are low- to moderate-income working families—households in which at least one person works a full-time job, and earns anywhere from minimum wage to 120 percent of

AMI. Another attempt to quantify the extent of the problem is *The State of the Nation's Housing 2006,* a report issued by the Joint Center for Housing Studies of Harvard University; according to the report, 35 million households spend more than 30 percent of their income on housing. Moreover, between 2000 and 2004, the number of middle-income households with severe housing-cost burdens shot up by over 700,000, to a total of 3.1 million.[5]

In its groundbreaking study *Paycheck to Paycheck: Wages and the Cost of Housing in America,* the NHC calculated housing affordability for a sampling of workers in the 60 largest urban markets. The study found that neither a janitor nor a retail salesperson (earning average wages for their industries) would qualify to purchase a median-priced home in any of the cities that were analyzed. An elementary school teacher and a police officer would qualify in roughly half the cities, while a licensed practical nurse would qualify in only three cities. Although the elementary school teacher and the police officer could afford the median rent on a two-bedroom apartment in almost all the markets studied, neither the janitor nor the retail salesperson could have afforded to rent the same apartment in any of the cities studied. In about one-third of the cities, the licensed practical nurse would also have been unable to afford the median rent for a two-bedroom apartment.[6]

The report also found that the problem of housing affordability is not limited to large cities: although 40 percent of households with critical housing need reside in central cities, a larger percentage—43 percent—live in suburbs, and 17 percent live in nonmetropolitan areas.[7] The follow-up to the NHC study, *Paycheck to Paycheck: Wages and the Cost of Housing in Counties,* which was developed in partnership the National Association of Counties, undertook a similar analysis for 98 counties and confirmed that the problem of housing affordability extends beyond large urban areas, and encompasses smaller urban areas, large and small counties, and suburban and rural areas.[8] The analysis also included a survey of county officials, 85 percent of whom reported that most new housing in their communities is geared to middle- and upper-income households.[9] Roughly three-quarters of the respondents reported that community opposition and lack of public funds were the main obstacles to workforce housing.[10]

So what do these workers do when they are priced out of their markets? They do what they must in order to find affordable housing options. For many, this means enduring long commutes, or crowding into housing that is not designed to accommodate the number of people who are actually dwelling in it. Some workers do both: they live in crowded conditions, *and* they endure long commutes.[11] The NHC estimates that 4.3 million low- to moderate-income working families who do not technically have critical housing need (that is, do not live in severely dilapidated conditions or spend more than 50 percent of their income on housing) are nonetheless profoundly affected by the cost and conditions of their housing. According to NHC estimates, 1.6 million of these families live in crowded conditions, and another 2.7 million endure one-way commutes of 45 minutes or more. Nearly 200,000 of these families have long commutes *and* live in crowded conditions.[12]

Long commutes are difficult for workers, but they also jam regional transportation networks, creating congestion problems even for those who live close in. For example, the 2005 Urban Mobility Report of the Texas Transportation Institute found that between 1982 and 2003, the time that a typical commuter spent sitting in traffic had increased from 16 to 47 hours per year. Congestion, in addition to being a nuisance, has serious costs: the Texas Transportation Institute estimated that in 2003, traffic congestion caused 3.7 billion hours of delay and wasted 2.3 billion gallons of fuel; taken together, the lost productivity and the wasted fuel had a value of more than $63 billion.[13]

Because exurban locations usually lack the density to support mass transit, cars are the only commuting option, which creates a significant additional expense for working families. And as the exurbs fill up with residents seeking affordable homes, the commutes—which were likely on the edge of bearable to begin with—rapidly move into the realm of the unbearable. Several years ago, workers who lived in Temecula, a suburb 60 miles from downtown San Diego, could make the commute in 60 minutes; today, the commute is two-and-a-half hours—and, without significant public investment, will likely increase to three hours in the near future.[14] The notion that the market can deliver affordable housing in exurbia without any public investment is a fallacy: ultimately, sprawl creates the need for new roads, new schools, new libraries, new fire and police departments, and so on. In a time of rising energy costs and climate change, the sustainability of simply expanding outward has to be questioned.

A recent survey conducted by the National Association of Realtors reported that 42 percent of respondents cited the lack of affordable housing as one of their top three concerns—right behind high energy costs and health care.[15] Surprisingly, 80 percent of respondents supported increasing the availability of affordable homes in their community, and almost 70 percent said that they would be more likely to vote for a candidate who supports affordable housing.

While public support for affordable housing is growing, the response to the problem varies with its perceived severity: some communities would say that they have a workforce housing crisis, others that they have a workforce housing problem, and still others that they don't have a workforce housing problem at all. Certain difficulties are symptomatic of a workforce housing problem: these include regional traffic congestion, limited homeownership opportunities, and housing costs that consume an increasing percentage of take-home pay. A workforce housing problem becomes a crisis when it begins to impact the economic health of the region. Characteristics of a housing crisis include labor shortages and rising labor costs (because workers are choosing to live and work in more affordable markets); difficulty recruiting and retaining both public and private sector workers; and reluctance on the part of firms to relocate in the community, because their workers cannot afford to live there. Although it is difficult to assess the amount of economic development that is bypassing a particular community because of its housing affordability problem, housing is an important element in the economic development equation. In San Diego, for example, the Office of Land Use and Economic Development reports that when police officers quit their jobs, they cite as a "significant reason" the long commutes that they must endure in order to find a house they can afford.[16]

In 30 metropolitan areas, between 2003 and 2006, the cost of a median-priced home more than doubled; in many of these areas, the workforce housing problem has clearly reached crisis proportions. Meanwhile, when adjusted for inflation, the median incomes of working households have remained flat (see Figure 1). In most urban markets, this divergence between incomes and home prices has created housing affordability problems. Although the problems are most severe on the East and West coasts, there are pockets throughout the country that are suffering from an affordable-housing crisis. While

Figure 1 clearly shows the divergence, at the national level, of incomes and home prices, the graph masks the severity of the problem in individual markets. Table 1 lists the 20 least affordable markets in the country and the median price of a home in each.

Between 2000 and 2005, the number of metropolitan areas where the median house price is at least four times the median income increased from ten to 33.[17] Overall, in the state of California, only 14 percent of households can afford to purchase a median-priced home, but the situation is worse in the state's two major urban centers: in Los Angeles, only 11 percent of households can afford a median-priced home, and in San Francisco, only 12 percent. Local governments, schools, and institutions of higher education report recruitment and retention problems. In San Jose, the problem is so serious that high-tech employers have invested millions of their own money to create a housing trust fund for workers. In these and selected other markets in the state, describing the issue as a crisis would not be hyperbole.

Figure 1: Income and Home Prices, 1975–2004

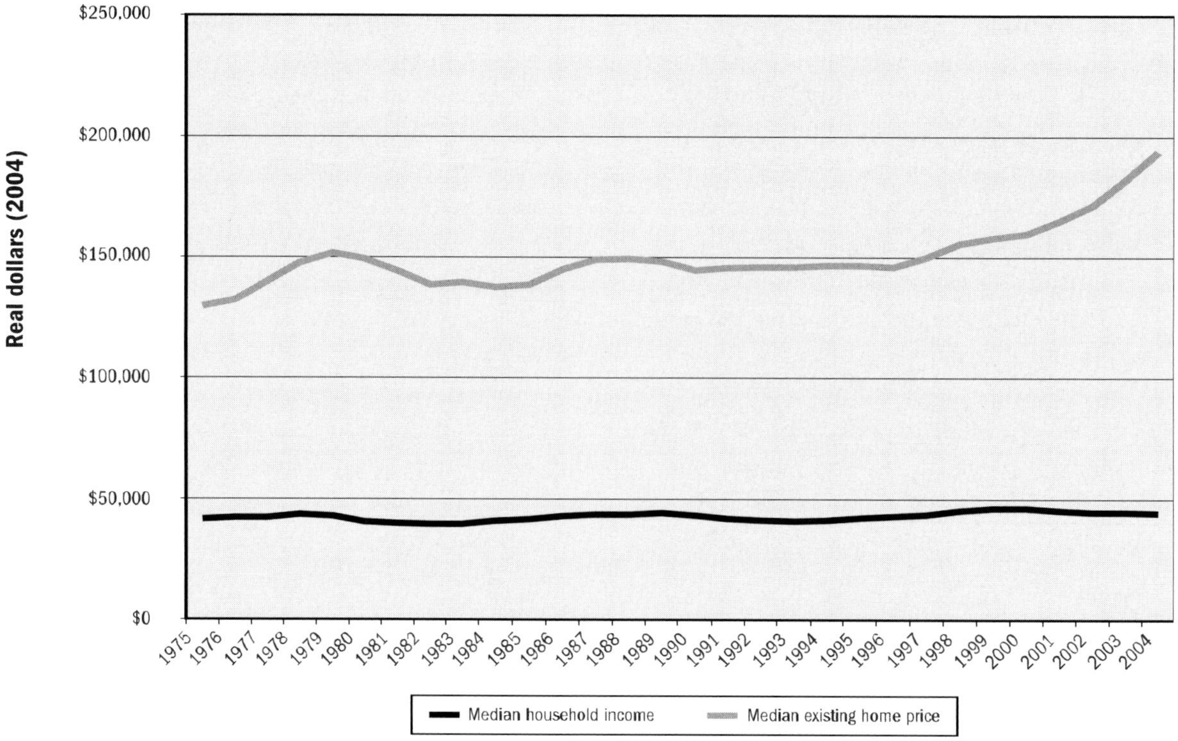

Source: Data from U.S. Census and National Association of Realtors.

Table 1: The 20 Metropolitan Statistical Areas with the Most Expensive Median Prices for Single-Family Homes

Metropolitan Statistical Area	Median Home Price ($)
San Francisco–Oakland–Fremont (California)	720,400
San Jose–Sunnyvale–Santa Clara (California)	746,800
Anaheim–Santa Ana (Orange County, California)	712,600
Honolulu (Hawaii)	625,000
San Diego–Carlsbad–San Marcos (California)	607,300
Los Angeles–Long Beach–Santa Ana (California)	563,900
New York–Wayne–White Plains (New Jersey and New York)	521,400
Bridgeport–Stamford–Norwalk (Connecticut)	471,200
New York: Nassau–Suffolk (New York)	475,300
New York: Northern New Jersey–Long Island (New York–New Jersey–Pennsylvania)	458,500
New York: Newark–Union (New Jersey, Pennsylvania)	405,300
Washington–Arlington–Alexandria (District of Columbia, Virginia, Maryland, and West Virginia)	422,500
Boston–Cambridge–Quincy (Massachusetts and New Hampshire)	390,400
Barnstable Town (Massachusetts)	384,700
Riverside–San Bernardino–Ontario (California)	396,200
New York: Edison (New Jersey)	375,600
Sacramento–Arden-Arcade–Roseville (California)	376,200
Miami–Fort Lauderdale–Miami Beach (Florida)	377,000
Boulder (Colorado)	360,400
Reno–Sparks (Nevada)	357,000

Source: National Association of Realtors, Washington, D.C., First Quarter 2006.

But California's metropolitan centers are by no means the only areas suffering from a housing crisis. In high-cost resort areas, for example, the divergence between AMI and the median home price is even greater. In 2006, the median price for a home on the Hawaiian island of Maui was $690,000, yet the island's economy is based on the traditionally low-paying tourist industry. Similar disparities occur in Colorado's resort communities—in fact, they can be seen in virtu- ally any market that experiences an influx of wealthy residents and retirees yet lacks a diversi- fied economic base.

In an annual report entitled *Out of Reach,* the National Low-Income Housing Coalition analyzes incomes and rental-housing costs to identify the least affordable housing markets in the country. While California represents the extreme, other states, cities, and counties have severe problems. Table 2 summarizes the results of the 2005 report.

Table 2: The Top Ten Least Affordable Jurisdictions, 2005
(in Ascending Order of Affordability)

States	Counties	Metropolitan Areas
Hawaii	Marin County, California	San Francisco, California
California	San Francisco County, California	Stamford-Norwalk, Connecticut
Massachusetts	San Mateo County, California	Oxnard-Thousand Oaks-Ventura, California
New Jersey	Ventura County, California	Orange County, California
New York	Orange County, California	Santa Cruz-Watsonville, California
Maryland	Santa Cruz County, California	Oakland-Fremont, California
Connecticut	Alameda County, California	Boston-Cambridge-Quincy, Massachusetts
Rhode Island	Contra Costa County, California	Westchester County, New York
New Hampshire	Nantucket County, Massachusetts	San Jose-Sunnyvale-Santa Clara, California
Alaska	Westchester County, New York	Easton-Rayham, Massachusetts

Source: National Low-Income Housing Coalition, *Out of Reach 2005* (Washington, D.C.: NLIHC, 2005).

Origins of the Workforce Housing Problem

For both incoming and established members of the workforce, homeownership has been the most important part of the American dream, and has been a strong motivating force for economic achievement. It has also been a powerful vehicle for creating wealth—and, through the mortgage interest deduction, for reducing the tax burden. For many years, at least on the national level, median home prices stayed pretty much in line with incomes—which, for many workers, kept the dream of homeownership within the realm of the possible. Somewhere around 1997, however, income and housing costs began to significantly diverge: as shown in Figure 1, incomes remained essentially stagnant, and home prices increased rapidly.

The workforce housing problem is rooted in this divergence of incomes and home prices. Why incomes have been stagnant and why housing prices have risen so sharply will be debated by economists and politicians for some time to come. But the practical effects are already apparent: for many workers, the American dream of homeownership has become less and less achievable. This shift will have profound implications for American society.

A 2004 article in *Business Week* noted that even in a booming economy, "many of today's economic gains are flowing to profits and efficiency improvements, and the job market isn't tight enough to lift the pay for average workers, much less for those on the bottom."[18] Possibly even more disturbing is the fact that the traditional means of entry to the middle class—one of which is homeownership itself—may be disappearing. During the coming decade, the ten fastest-growing occupations include retail clerks, janitors, and cashiers, jobs that offer little in the way of a career track. Moreover, increases in college costs continue to outpace inflation, fore-closing educational opportunities and compelling workers to remain in occupations where the "career ladder" is essentially nonexistent. James D. Sinegal, the chief executive officer of Costco Wholesale Group, has summed up the problem this way: "If current trends persist, a greater and greater share of the wealth will keep going into the hands of the few, which will destroy initiative. . . . We'll no longer have a motivated working class."[19]

There is already evidence that the middle class is declining in the United States. A recent study by the Brookings Institution shows that in 1970, middle-income neighborhoods made up 58 percent of all metropolitan neighborhoods; by 2000, the percentage had declined to 41 percent.[20] In California, the situation is so dire that Edward Leamer, director of the economic forecasts undertaken by the Anderson School of Management at the University of California at Los Angeles, said, "I don't think we're going to have a middle class" in California.[21]

While stagnating incomes represent one part of the problem, escalating home prices represent the other. Many theories have been offered to explain the rapid increase in housing prices, from supply constraints to excessive development regulations, advances in the processing of mortgage applications, an abundance of foreign and domestic capital, and interest rates that are at historic lows. More than likely, numerous factors converged to create this phenomenon. But whatever the cause, the sharp increase in housing prices has not only made it harder for working families to afford to purchase homes, but has also widened the gap between rich and poor: homeownership is a significant source of wealth generation, from which renters are excluded.

Geographic constraints on new development, such as those in Los Angeles, can play a huge role in housing affordability. Although other areas, such as Phoenix and Las Vegas, may have more land available for development, they, too, may eventually run into other constraints: limitations on the water supply, for example, could increase housing prices. Spikes in demand created by a significant influx of new residents—as in retirement hot spots—may also lead to price increases by throwing off the balance between supply and demand.

Development regulations are another constraint that can alter the supply-demand equation and cause appreciation in home prices. In "The Impact of Building Restrictions on Housing Affordability," Edward L. Glaeser, of Harvard University, and Joseph Gyourko, of the Wharton School at the University of Pennsylvania, argue that significant regulatory constraints on development have artificially constricted housing supply. According to Glaeser and Gyourko, the problem is not national, but has created affordability problems in particular markets: "The evidence suggests that zoning is responsible for high housing costs, which means that if we are thinking about lowering housing prices, we should begin with reforming the barriers to new construction in the private sector."[22]

Why Is Workforce Housing Important?

Housing that is affordable to workers and close to their jobs is essential to the proper functioning of the local economy. Housing costs are one of the determining factors in workers' relocation decisions—and as housing affordability declines, it becomes more difficult to recruit and retain employees. In the tight labor market that results, employers must offer higher salaries in order to attract and retain employees, which increases the cost of doing business. A high cost of doing business, in turn, makes an area less desirable to employers.

Although arguments in support of workforce housing often center around public employees—the teachers, police officers, firefighters, and others who are integral to a community, yet who often cannot afford to live in the communities they serve—the market for workforce housing is actually much broader: it includes young professionals, workers in the construction trades, retail salespeople, office workers, and service workers. These people also play a crucial role in the economic success of a region.

But the consequences of a housing affordability problem reach far beyond the arena of economic development. Studies have shown that as workers are forced to live farther and farther from their jobs, their productivity declines; a likely explanation is that employees are not only putting up with longer drives but with greater regional traffic congestion; as a result, they spend more time stuck in traffic and are more likely to arrive at work late—not to mention tired and frustrated.

Can We Sprawl Our Way Out of This Problem?

One theory about housing affordability is that it can be addressed by sprawling development: in other words, workers can "drive until they qualify," traveling outward from the urban core until they find a neighborhood they can afford. And sprawl has indeed been increasing rapidly. In 1970, only 13 of the country's largest metropolitan areas had more than half their households living at least 10 miles (16 kilometers) from the central business district (CBD). By 2000, that figure had more than tripled, to 46. During the same years, among the largest metropolitan areas, the number of metropolitan areas in which more than one-fifth of households lived at least 20 miles (32 kilometers) from the CBD jumped from 17 to 44. And in six of the largest metropolitan areas, more than one-fifth of households lived at least 30 miles (48 kilometers) from the CBD.[23]

As noted earlier, sprawl entails significant investment in public infrastructure. In addition, as more and more workers are forced into longer and longer commutes, the resulting traffic congestion lowers the quality of life throughout the region. Idling cars create significantly more harmful emissions than moving cars, further damaging air quality. Sprawl destroys open space and agricultural lands, reducing tree cover and increasing the volume, velocity, and temperature of stormwater runoff—which further degrades water quality. Communities must decide whether the infrastructure investment, increased traffic congestion, loss of open space, and air and water pollution are worth it.

Increasing energy costs may settle the issue once and for all. As gas prices rise, the overall affordability of exurbia diminishes. A significant spike in gas prices could wipe out any economic advantage afforded by exurban communities.

Some observers have argued that sprawl is simply the result of market forces—and that the market can therefore solve the affordable-housing problem. But this perspective discounts an important reality: the so-called market is the result of deliberate and extensive governmental intervention in the land development process. Federal, state, and local governments are all, in part, responsible for current development patterns. Governmental interventions—including zoning regulations and practices, home-financing regulations, and control of public infrastructure— have all paved the way for sprawl. Thus, the argument that an attempt to address the workforce housing problem amounts to social engineering or constitutes an "unwarranted governmental intervention" into the market ignores the existing impact of governmental intervention on the market.

Even if communities do decide to prohibit further sprawl, addressing the effects of the sprawl that has already occurred will not be an easy task. The traditional model—in which a single downtown is the employment center for an entire region, and is surrounded by bedroom communities—is outdated. Over the past few decades, dispersed growth has yielded scattered development, with multiple employment nodes. In many major metropolitan areas, the suburbs have more office space than the downtown.[24] The realities of current development patterns mean that creating a jobs-housing balance is more than a matter of building more housing downtown.

The large number of two-income families further complicates attempts to address the workforce housing problem. In the not-too-distant past, the typical family had a father who commuted to a job downtown, while the mother stayed at home with the kids. Today's "typical" family is likely to include two wage earners who work in two different suburban locations. This shift in employment patterns has profound implications for public planning. Providing mass transit, for example, becomes much more complicated when workers are commuting from one suburb to another. And providing affordable and conveniently located housing for these workers becomes difficult as well. Although a given company is likely to employ workers with a broad range of incomes, from custodians to upper-level executives, most of the surrounding communities do not provide housing opportunities that are as diverse.

Finally, workers who spend their entire careers with a single employer have become the exception rather than the rule. Most employees will change jobs many times in the course of their working lives. This degree of employment mobility, coupled with the demographic realities of today's working households, speaks to the need for flexibility and choice in housing options— and confirms the importance of maintaining an appropriate jobs-housing balance.

Introduction

Who Is Responsible for Solving the Problem?

The debate over the causes of the workforce housing problem will continue. Some blame exclusionary zoning practices, which allow only large homes on large lots and prohibit multi-family housing. Others blame increasingly complex entitlement processes, which add time, risk, and costs that ultimately constrain the housing supply. The NIMBY ("not in my backyard") phenomenon has surely reduced the housing supply in many communities, and thus raised the value of the existing housing stock. From the demand side of the equation, some observers blame stagnant incomes and the low minimum wage.

Although there is no consensus on the cause of the affordable-housing problem, political pressure for solutions is building across the country. In response, many communities are bringing together disparate groups who agree that it is in their best interest to find solutions to the affordable-housing problem. Indeed, a growing number of organizations and individuals have made affordable-housing their priority. Governors, local elected and appointed officials, chambers of commerce, and others have made the connection between workforce housing and the regional economy. Organizations including Homes for Working Families, the National Association of Counties, Fannie Mae, the National Association of Homebuilders, and the National League of Cities have created programs and initiatives that are attempting to find solutions to the workforce housing problem—and that are also trying to build the necessary political support for reforms that will encourage the development of more housing for this underserved market.

Such efforts have yielded partnerships—among employers, local governments, school boards, unions, developers, financial institutions, faith-based organizations, community organizations, community development corporations, and others—that have delivered workforce housing. Several of the case studies highlighted in this book are the result of such partnerships.

Although effective partnerships are a crucial means of addressing the workforce housing problem, the bulk of the responsibility remains with local governments. As the federal government continues to decentralize housing policy to the states and municipalities, lower levels of government are struggling to find creative solutions to their affordable-housing problems. Communities across the country have been experimenting with solutions, many of which are covered in this book. Most communities try to leverage as much private investment as possible with their limited public funds. In an effort to encourage the market to create affordable housing, many communities have turned to policies such as inclusionary zoning, which requires developers to create affordable housing as they develop market-rate housing. Such policies usually offer additional density to offset the costs of the affordable housing.

How Can the Problem Be Solved?

At its core, the workforce housing problem appears to be a simple financial equation: given costs and market realities in many areas, the development and construction of housing that is affordable to the workforce is simply not financially feasible. Some form of assistance or incentive is needed to change the equation.

But the calculation gets a lot more complicated when one considers all the factors that could potentially be manipulated to create affordability. The final cost of housing is affected by a host of variables, including land costs, construction costs, densities, the length and complexity of the entitlement process, the size of the units, financing costs, and expected returns. In some communities, providing the land for free—and thereby removing this cost from the development equation—may make the development of workforce housing financially feasible. In the most severely affected markets, all available incentives must be employed.

Communities can use a host of tools to create incentives for the development of workforce housing. These tools should be strategically employed as part of a comprehensive, creative, and flexible effort that takes advantage of every available opportunity to support workforce housing. A strategic and comprehensive approach represents the best hope for solving the workforce housing problem. The remaining sections of this introduction examine the elements of just such an approach.

Creating a Workforce Housing Strategy

Communities seeking to address their workforce housing problem should first accept one simple fact: as complicated as the problem seems to be, it's probably even more so. No single program, policy, or change will solve it. Solutions must be multifaceted, and will require constant assessment and revision to respond to shifting market realities and shifting goals. Communities can choose from a variety of tools, described in this publication, in assembling their strategies. Some of these tools may be more politically viable in some localities than in others. This section describes a series of steps that a community can take to create a successful workforce housing strategy.

Inventory the Current Housing Supply

With the assistance of a good market analyst, a community can create an accurate snapshot of the value and affordability of its existing housing stock. This effort should include an analysis of the rental and for-sale housing ratio, and of the variety (or lack thereof) of housing types in the community.

The assessment of the rental stock should focus on its adequacy for the community's needs. What are the current median rents? What are the highest and lowest rents? What new rental products are in the development pipeline? In the case of for-sale housing, the assessment would address analogous questions: median home values, highest and lowest values, and developments in the pipeline.

The costs and difficulties inherent in constructing new affordable housing have led many communities to take a closer look at preserving the existing stock of affordable housing. Ideally, the assessment of rental and for-sale housing will bring to light some existing housing that can be categorized as workforce housing. In many communities, for example, market-rate garden apartments have provided workforce housing since long before that term even existed. There may also be for-sale homes in middle-income neighborhoods that would be considered workforce housing, or areas with smaller homes and lots that may be affordable to working families.

Although an analysis of the existing affordable-housing stock is often a good starting point for addressing the affordability problem, once existing affordable housing has been identified, a number of additional questions must be considered:

- ■ What is the condition of the existing affordable-housing stock (both rental and for-sale)?
- ■ Is the existing stock at risk of disappearing because of redevelopment or conversion to higher-end housing?
- ■ What can be done to preserve the affordability of the existing housing stock?

- If the existing stock has declined to the point where there is significant vacancy, can it be redeveloped as mixed-income housing?
- Have existing middle-income neighborhoods received adequate public services and infrastructure improvements, or is there deferred maintenance that could be addressed?
- Are there regulations that can be changed to preserve existing affordable housing?
- Within existing affordable neighborhoods, are there opportunities to build new workforce housing on infill lots?

Inventory Public Lands and Structures

A community that wishes to develop an affordable-housing strategy must identify any publicly owned surplus properties that may offer development opportunities. For example, the Casa del Maestro development, in Santa Clara, California, took advantage of a forgotten scrap of school land that was being used as a neighborhood dog park. As described in the case study, that land now offers attractive and affordable rental housing for public school teachers. There are no doubt similar opportunities in other communities.

The inventory should not overlook public land that already has existing structures, or that is designated for planned public development projects. Can existing structures be renovated to provide workforce housing? Abandoned schools, for example, are often well suited for renovation as housing. If the community has an inventory of public parking garages, it may be possible to construct housing above these structures.

Planned public development projects—such as courthouses, libraries, government offices, hospitals, and schools—may also offer opportunities to incorporate workforce housing. One particular advantage of this approach is that if the municipal workers who will staff the facilities can be housed in residential development that is inte-grated into the new buildings, or in housing nearby, the project may help alleviate traffic congestion. If the community is fortunate enough to have mass-transit access, are there public lands in proximity to mass transit that could provide opportunities for workforce housing?

Finally, creating an inventory of public lands and structures can illuminate potential opportunities for public/private development partnerships. Several case studies in this book highlight public/private partnerships in which the public sector provided land for the development of workforce housing.

Public lands and structures offer a number of potential opportunities for workforce housing development, some of which may be easier to take advantage of than others. It is important for the community to ask, What are the obstacles to these opportunities, and how can they be overcome?

Inventory Privately Held Vacant and Abandoned Properties

Land acquisition and assembly represent a major challenge for the development community, especially in the case of workforce housing. By inventorying vacant and abandoned property, a community can reduce some of the risk involved in land acquisition and assembly, and increase the chances that such property will be returned to productive use.

The inventory should also assess the development constraints on these sites. Are there abandoned buildings on the property in need of demolition? Does the property include environmentally sensitive areas? Is the site contaminated by hazardous materials? Who owns the land, and have the owners kept their property tax payments current? Are there any title problems or encumbrances on the property?

The National Vacant Properties Campaign, an initiative that was undertaken to help return vacant and abandoned properties to economically viable use, is a good resource for communities dealing with any issues relating to such properties.[25]

Assess Workforce Housing Needs

Although residents may have a general idea that there is a housing affordability problem in their community, few will be able to pinpoint the depth and breadth of the problem. The initial goal of the housing needs assessment is to help define the target market for workforce housing in the community—a market that is likely broader and more diverse than may have initially been assumed. Further analysis of the target market will help the community determine how to translate housing demand into actual housing products.

The analysis of the community's housing supply should reveal whether the community offers a variety of housing types for a diversity of households with a broad range of incomes. While supply analysis is reasonably straightforward, demand analysis can be much more complicated—principally because the extent of demand is masked by the many things people do to find affordable housing, such as enduring long commutes and living in overcrowded housing. To capture the full extent of the market for workforce housing, regional analysis of demand is likely to be required. Analysis of regional employment generation will help provide a basis for determining the relationship between jobs and housing, both in the community and in the larger region. A full understanding of the demand for workforce housing may also require surveys. In short, extensive information about the extent and the specifics of the demand for workforce housing will be needed to provide factual support and guidance for the creation of a comprehensive workforce housing strategy.

To create the diverse range of housing products that will meet the needs of the target market, it is essential to understand the complexities of that market. For example, the market for workforce housing is likely to include both highly skilled and less-skilled workers, with differing career prospects and differing housing needs. Young professionals working in high-demand fields may start out in the target market for workforce housing, but may soon be able to afford a market-rate home as they move up in their careers. Less-skilled workers may never be able to afford market-rate housing.

Other factors contributing to the complexity of the problem are household size, the number of incomes in the family, and the market in which the households are located. In some markets, for example, two married teachers might be able to afford for-sale, market-rate housing—but, as mentioned earlier, in most markets, a single teacher is unlikely to be able to afford such housing. If both members of a couple have low incomes, the household may not qualify for subsidized rental housing, but it may also be unable to afford appropriate market-rate rental housing.

Changing demographics are yet another influence on the target market. The number of nontraditional households (including men and women living alone; households made up of unrelated people; single-parent households; and households headed by someone other than a parent, such as a grandparent) has been steadily rising for decades. In 2000, nontraditional households made up almost half (48.4 percent) of all households, and are projected to eventually make up the majority of American households. In fact, in 2000, the percentage of households consisting of men or women living alone (26.2 percent) exceeded the percentage of households consisting of married couples with children (23.3 percent), and almost equaled the single largest household group, which consisted of married couples without children (28.2 percent). While much public discussion centers on the difficulties faced by two-income households with children, a larger percentage of the population is trying to figure out how to obtain appropriate housing on just one income.

In sum, the workforce housing problem is much more complicated and nuanced than it may appear at first glance. But the complexity of the target market should not be an excuse for inaction. The bottom line is that in most (but not all) communities, many working people cannot rely on the housing market to provide adequate housing choices.

A community that has conducted a housing needs assessment should be able to answer a number of questions:

- How is workforce housing defined in the community?
- How large is the overall target market for workforce housing?
- Who makes up the target market (for example, municipal employees, service workers, young professionals), and in what proportions?
- What housing types would each of these groups be looking for?
- What are workers doing now for housing? For example, are they commuting long distances, or are adult children living with their parents until they can save the money to buy a home?
- What are the demand-side constraints on workforce housing? For example, do workers lack the downpayments to purchase homes?
- How do residents feel about higher-density development and mixed-use development?
- Are local businesses having difficulty recruiting and retaining workers?

Assess Current Workforce Housing Programs and Policies

A review of existing workforce housing programs and policies should reveal the number of people currently being served, and what income groups they belong to. Determining what is working in the existing programs and what is not should provide a good basis for future strategies. For example, where are the gaps in the existing programs? Could the programs be expanded to include households with incomes above the low and very low range?

It is also important to assess long-range planning and zoning efforts to address affordable housing. Is affordable housing a community priority, and is it addressed in the comprehensive plan? Does the comprehensive plan support a diversity of housing types and densities? Does existing zoning reflect any affordability goals that are stated in the comprehensive plan? Are affordable-housing projects fast-tracked? Is there a linkage in the planning process between job creation and housing?

Assess the Barriers to Workforce Housing Production

Although there are a number of potential barriers to workforce housing production, two of the most common are community opposition and regulatory barriers.

Community Opposition

Because community opposition to workforce housing is an unfortunate reality, one good starting point for any workforce housing strategy is a public relations effort designed to educate residents about the role of workforce housing in maintaining the economic health of the community.

Community resistance to workforce housing is often grounded in misperceptions about the target market. Residents may refer to occupants of affordable housing as "those people"—not realizing that "those people" care for them at the hospital, respond to their 911 calls, teach their children, look after their parents at the senior center, maintain their yards, bag their groceries, and pick up their trash. "Those people" are also the children and parents of community residents. Erasing the stigma associated with affordable housing is the first step in engendering public support for the production of homes for "those people" who are an integral part of making a community function. For example, the advertisements for the Long Island Campaign for Affordable Rental Housing created by the Carlton Group, a student ad agency at the New York Institute of Technology, showed the faces of nurses, teachers, police officers, and others who made up the target market.

Although there are numerous examples of communities in which residents have shot down efforts to provide workforce housing, there are some encouraging signs. A poll conducted by the National Association of Realtors shows growing support for workforce housing, and concludes that the residents who show up at public hearings to voice heated opposition are a vocal minority. In the words of Minneapolis mayor R.T. Rybak, "People are beginning to understand that affordable housing is about having a place for people to live for the people waiting on us in the restaurants, behind the counter at the library, teaching our kids and even providing security."[26]

Regulatory Barriers

In many communities, regulatory barriers—such as impact fees, exclusionary zoning, and environmental protection measures—effectively prohibit workforce housing development. Although many existing regulations support important societal interests, it is important to balance those interests with the need for affordable housing. Any workforce housing strategy should include a review of current regulations to ensure that they allow workforce housing needs to be adequately addressed; however, it is equally necessary to ensure that workforce housing development doesn't come at the expense of other important community interests.

Set Workforce Housing Production Goals

The housing needs assessment should reveal the housing types and price points that would meet the demands of the workforce. Taking into account the current deficiencies in the housing supply, estimated demand, and the segmentation of that demand, a community should be able to translate the housing needs assessment into goals for the preservation of existing housing and the production of new housing.

One of the most important concerns in setting housing preservation and production goals is the balance between affordable rental housing and affordable for-sale housing. The policies and programs that support each type of housing differ significantly, and it is important for the community to be clear about its goals for each housing category. One strategy used in some communities is to require the construction of affordable rental units for households at the lower end of the workforce-housing income scale, and to require the construction of for-sale housing for households at the higher end of the workforce-housing income scale.

Build a Workforce Housing Coalition

Efforts to address the workforce housing problem are likely to encounter opposition from a number of quarters. There may be public opposition to new housing types or to levels of density that have not been constructed in the community before. Such opposition is often rooted in concerns about traffic congestion, school overcrowding, and loss of open space. There may also be opposition from members of the development community who feel that current development regulations created the problem and that more regulations won't solve it. Advocates for low-income housing who are fighting for diminishing governmental resources may view any push for workforce housing as a threat to support for the neediest in the community.

To provide the support that is necessary to overcome opposition and create solutions, it is essential to develop a broad and inclusive coalition of all those who are affected by the shortage of affordable housing: representatives from government, major local employers, small-business owners, the local school system, public safety departments, the development community, citizens' groups, environmental groups, and organizations that support low-income housing.

Organize for Action

Solving the workforce housing problem requires everyone to play a part. Local governments, developers, employers, members of the target market, and community residents can all contribute to a viable strategy to encourage the production of workforce housing.

The local government will likely play the lead role in addressing the workforce housing problem. Local government has the authority to create incentives for workforce housing production, remove regulatory barriers, facilitate community involvement and action, expedite the entitlement and permitting process, and incorporate workforce housing into long-range planning efforts. Local government can also assess the inventory of public lands to identify opportunities for land grants or partnerships in the construction of public facilities that include workforce housing. For-profit and nonprofit developers can partner with

local governments to develop projects that have an affordable component. The local government can assist with the entitlement process and can often provide free or low-cost land.

In the communities with the most serious housing affordability problems, recruiting and retaining private sector employees has become a major concern, and employers have been seeking creative solutions. In Santa Clara County, California, the home of Silicon Valley, major employers have come together and funded the Housing Trust Fund of Santa Clara County; the fund raised $20 million in two years, mostly from donations from private companies. As noted earlier, many companies view the lack of workforce housing as a threat to their continued business success: the companies who are involved in the Santa Clara housing trust fund are among those that have taken steps to address the problem.

Identify Viable Workforce Housing Tools

The viability of various workforce housing tools will depend on a number of factors, including the characteristics of the local housing market and the level of institutional, financial, political, and legal support for workforce housing efforts. A community must also consider potential changes in the housing market and the political climate. For example, regulations designed for a hot housing market may have unintended negative consequences when the market cools.

Create a Flexible, Multifaceted Housing Strategy

No one policy or program will solve the workforce housing problem. A comprehensive approach that incorporates workforce housing into the entire land use planning and entitlement process offers the greatest chance for success. While the tools may vary by market, most communities will probably need some kind of public education component, in order to address misconceptions about workforce housing and to help residents understand why it is needed by the community.

As noted earlier, this book consists of three parts: this introduction, the case studies, and a toolkit of policies and programs currently used to facilitate the construction of workforce housing. The toolkit covers four major topic areas—land acquisition and assembly, planning and regulatory approaches, financing programs, and maintaining long-term affordability—each of which is summarized in this section. The toolkit is not exhaustive, but instead offers illustrative examples of policies and programs. A community can use these examples to determine which tools are most likely to be viable for a particular situation; for example, a community that has limited available land may not benefit from an inclusionary zoning policy, as such policies are usually tied to new development.

Land Acquisition and Assembly

Skyrocketing land costs are a large component of development costs and a big part of the affordability problem. Factors that affect land cost and availability include title issues, encumbrances, tax liens, environmental contamination, and the presence of natural resources.

Granting public land for the development of workforce housing is one of the best ways to make development financially feasible. As noted earlier, an inventory of public lands—for the purpose of finding opportunities for workforce housing—is among the first steps in the development of a comprehensive housing strategy. Several of the communities highlighted in this book used public lands to develop creative solutions to the workforce housing problem—including constructing workforce housing on

surplus school lands, and above a public library. Public land that is already developed may also have potential: there may be opportunities for development above existing public parking garages, or in the air rights above other public buildings, for example.

Ideally, a local government can provide land for the development of workforce housing—but limited availability of public lands, particularly in urban areas, should not foreclose efforts to develop workforce housing. A community has many tools at its disposal to create value and opportunity on private lands. For example, a local government can reduce land costs by assisting with land assembly and taking whatever action is necessary to prepare the land for development or redevelopment. Since remediation of brownfield sites may involve significant costs, cleanup and rehabilitation of existing obsolete buildings is sometimes the better option: such structures can then be returned to productive use as workforce housing or as mixed-use developments with workforce housing components. Because it lowers risk, obtaining clear title to assembled land and removing any liens and encumbrances can also lower land development costs.

Planning and Regulatory Approaches

Through planning and regulation, communities determine what gets built and where. These regulations often limit the supply and location of land for housing and constrain the amount and type of housing. The study by Glaeser and Gyourko, cited earlier, contends that at least in particular markets, such regulation is the source of the housing affordability problem.[27]

Thus, zoning has a direct effect on land values—and more and more local officials are beginning to see this connection. Angelo Kyle, former president of the National Association of Counties, confirms the link between regulation and housing affordability: "We at the local elected official level are the individuals who will allow or disallow the opportunity for affordable housing based on our zoning."[28] A recent study by the Brookings Institution found that "traditional" land use regulations provide fewer housing opportunities for lower-income residents than regulations based on a new paradigm for regulating growth and development. Such regulations "can also directly affect the composition of inhabitants by facilitating rental properties and low-income residents, especially when these regulations are coupled with programs that promote housing affordability."[29]

It stands to reason that just as planning and regulatory initiatives can undermine affordable housing, they can also be used to support it: communities that choose to make the production of workforce housing a priority can encourage it through comprehensive planning, zoning, subdivision regulation, building codes, and building permits. An effective comprehensive plan outlines the goals and objectives for developing workforce housing and creating a jobs-housing balance. The comprehensive plan then becomes the basis for specific regulations designed to reach the goals outlined in the plan.

Planning and regulatory approaches to encourage workforce housing include

■ Inclusionary housing policies and programs;
■ Zoning designed to allow more housing and more housing types;
■ Targeting specific locations;
■ Density incentives;
■ Transfer of development rights;
■ Revisions to building codes and rehabilitation subcodes;
■ Improvements to the development permitting process;

■ Waivers or reimbursement of development fees.

When crafting a workforce housing strategy, it is important to remember that every action involves tradeoffs of some kind. A community must carefully evaluate the costs and risks of any proposed changes in regulations, including unintended consequences. Moreover, because the market can change, often quickly and dramatically, a workforce housing strategy must have the necessary flexibility to address market changes.

Financing Programs

In many communities, workforce housing is simply not financially feasible, and some form of financial incentive will be needed to make it work. Although the federal government has been decentralizing housing policy for decades, a number of programs that are sponsored by the Department of Housing and Urban Development (HUD) and administered by state and local agencies can be used to help finance projects subject to affordability requirements. Although the income limits attached to federal programs are generally too low for the definition of workforce housing used in this book, federal programs can sometimes make possible mixed-income housing projects that include a workforce housing component. The major HUD programs are the Community Development Block Grant program, the HOME Investment Partnership Act, the Section 8 program, and the HOPE VI program.[30] The Low-Income Housing Tax Credit, a major federal financing tool that is administered by state housing finance agencies, provides tax credits to private developers of affordable housing. Although the targeted households earn less than 60 percent of AMI, which is below the targeted income range for workforce housing, some tax-credit projects are mixed-income developments that include moderate-income and/or market-rate units that would be suitable for workforce housing. The federal Historic Preservation Tax Credit program can be used for the rehabilitation of residential and nonresidential properties. Coupled with the LIHTC, the historic tax credit program can be used to provide affordable rental housing in a rehabilitated structure.

As the federal role has diminished, state and local governments have been seeking creative financing options to provide workforce housing. Among the many tools discussed in more detail in the toolkit are housing trust funds, housing linkage programs, bond financing, tax-increment financing, tax waivers and abatements, and public/private partnerships.

Private lenders, including foundations and charitable organizations, play a role in helping to make the development of affordable housing feasible. Groups as diverse as pension funds and unions are potential sources of financing for workforce housing. Some employers have also addressed the workforce housing shortage by establishing creative financing programs for their employees.

While financial assistance is usually needed on the supply side, to encourage the development of workforce housing, it is also needed on the demand side. Potential purchasers of for-sale workforce housing often need homebuyer education, and may benefit from downpayment assistance and from access to low-interest loans. Both private and public organizations provide demand-side services.

Maintaining Long-Term Affordability

A successful workforce housing program should not only address the creation and preservation of workforce housing, but should also ensure the continued affordability of the housing. Unless efforts are made to preserve affordability, market forces in many communities will quickly drive affordable units into the unaffordable range.

The strategies for preserving affordability differ for rental and for-sale housing; those that apply to for-sale housing are more complex. In the case of rental housing, affordability provisions generally last between 15 and 40 years, and are required in order to obtain some sort of public funding. (Another strategy—rent control—is discussed in more detail in the toolkit.)

The most common approach to preserving for-sale housing affordability involves various mortgage controls: in the case of shared-appreciation mortgages, for example, the appreciation that the homeowner can realize is capped at a set amount, which is often based on the Consumer Price Index. Deed restrictions, limited-equity housing cooperatives, and community land trusts can also ensure long-term affordability. These approaches are outlined in the toolkit that follows the case studies.

Assess What Is Working, and Revise What Is Not

Once new programs and policies have been enacted, it is important to evaluate their effects and to address any unintended consequences. As noted earlier, flexibility should be built into new regulations so that market changes and special conditions can be addressed. If an assessment reveals that a program is not working as hoped, it should be changed or eliminated. Similarly, if a program has created unintended negative consequences, the consequences should be addressed, or the program should be changed. For example, affordable-housing requirements often increase development costs, and those costs may be passed on to market-rate buyers who are just outside the target population for the affordable housing, worsening the affordability problem. To avoid this effect, a community may want to consider expanding the range of incomes encompassed by the target market.

The workforce housing strategy should be assessed regularly to monitor its impact on the housing market, including any unintended negative consequences. Continuous assessment enables a community to refine and improve its workforce housing strategy.

Notes

1. This publication is not an exhaustive review of every program but a snapshot of some of the creative solutions communities and developers have created in response to the workforce housing problem. Because of the long lead time required to publish a book, the information is current as of the summer of 2006. Effective programs and policies are constantly changing, and others are discontinued; the authors regret the inclusion of any information that is no longer valid.

2. The relationship between workforce housing and sprawl will be discussed in more detail later in the chapter.

3. National Association of Realtors (NAR), National Housing Opportunity Pulse Survey, 2006.

4. "Foreclosures Are Up on Some Mortgages," *New York Times,* September 14, 2006.

5. Joint Center for Housing Studies, Harvard University, *The State of the Nation's Housing 2006* (Cambridge, Mass.: Joint Center for Housing Studies, 2006), 4.

6. Center for Housing Policy/National Housing Conference, *Paycheck to Paycheck: Wages and the Cost of Housing in America,* vol. 2, issue 2 (2004).

7. Center for Housing Policy/National Housing Conference, *America's Working Families and the Housing Landscape: 1997–2001,* vol. 3, issue 2 (November 2002): 15.

8. Center for Housing Policy/National Housing Conference, *Paycheck to Paycheck,* 2.

9. Ibid.

10. Ibid.

11. An overcrowded residence is defined as one that is occupied by more than one person per room, including kitchens, offices or business rooms, and other finished rooms, but excluding baths, half-baths, laundry or utility rooms, storage rooms or pantries, and unfinished space. Center for Housing Policy/National Housing Conference, *America's Working Families,* 35.

12. Ibid.

13. David Schrank and Tim Lomax, *2005 Urban Mobility Report,* Texas Transportation Institute, Texas A&M University System, May 2005, 1.

14. Noelle Knox, "Buyers in More Markets Find Housing Out of Reach," *USA Today,* June 26, 2006.

15. NAR, Pulse Survey.

16. Knox, "Out of Reach."

17. Joint Center for Housing Studies, *Nation's Housing 2006*, 2.

18. Michele Conlin and Aaron Bernstein, "Working and Poor," *Business Week*, May 31, 2004.

19. Ibid.

20. Jason C. Booza, Jackie Cutsinger, and George Galster, *Where Did They Go? The Decline of Middle-Income Neighborhoods in Metropolitan America* (Washington, D.C.: Brookings Institution Press, June 2006).

21. Knox, "Out of Reach."

22. Edward L. Glaeser and Joseph Gyourko, "The Impact of Building Restrictions on Housing Affordability," *FRBNY Economic Policy Review* (June 2003).

23. Joint Center for Housing Studies, *Nation's Housing 2006*, 3.

24. Robert E. Lang, *Edgeless Cities: Exploring the Elusive Metropolis* (Washington, D.C.: Brookings Institution Press, 2003).

25. How communities can further assist with land acquisition and assembly is discussed in a later section of this chapter.

26. Haya El Nasser, "Most Back Affordable Housing Next Door," *USA Today*, May 23, 2004.

27. Glaeser and Gyourko, "Housing Affordability."

28. El Nasser, "Affordable Housing."

29. Rolf Pendall, Robert Puentes, and Jonathan Martin, *From Traditional to Reformed: A Review of the Land Use Regulations in the Nation's 50 Largest Metropolitan Areas* (Washington, D.C.: Brookings Institution Press, 2006), 1.

30. As of this writing, the future of the HOPE VI is in question.

DEVELOPING HOUSING FOR THE WORKFORCE
Case Studies

Chapter 2

Case Studies

The Bookmark Apartments at the Hollywood Library
Portland, Oregon

Project Information

The Bookmark Apartments at the Hollywood Library are located in a four-story, civic-scale building in Portland, Oregon. The Hollywood Library, a branch of the Multnomah County library system, occupies the ground floor of the mixed-use building, along with 815 square feet (76 square meters) of retail space. The three upper floors are occupied by 47 apartment units, the Bookmark Apartments. A landmark for a redeveloping neighborhood and a model for dense development near transit, the two-part building is designed to make the most of the proximity between the apartments and the library facility, and to meet several broader public goals. The project

■ Brought affordable rental housing into an underserved area;

■ Leveraged money designated for the construction of the library;

■ Benefited from incentives designed to encourage transit-oriented development and housing;

■ Helped create a pedestrian-friendly environment that encourages transit use and decreases the need for automobile use in the immediate area;

■ Set a high standard for energy conservation and sustainable construction for future housing projects and transit-oriented development;

■ Provided a model for public/private partnership in an unusual and complex mixed-use project.

Workforce Housing Information

To help satisfy the need for affordable housing in Portland and meet various funding requirements, 40 percent of the Bookmark Apartments were reserved for households earning 60 percent or less of the area median income (AMI). Based on the AMI in Portland, the income-restricted units were reserved for households with yearly incomes no higher than $31,600 for a two-person household and $39,500 for a four-person household. Rents in the designated units range from $575 for a studio to $625 for a one-bedroom apartment. The rest of the apartments rent at market rate—$795 to $1,295 per month—which is affordable for households earning 80 to 120 percent of AMI.

Site, Surroundings, and History

The Hollywood Library and Bookmark Apartments building (known as Hollywood-Bookmark) is situated in the inner northeast district of Portland, which is bounded by Interstate 84 on the south and the Willamette River on the west. Early development spilled into the area from downtown Portland in the early 20th century. Single-family residential buildup began around 1915, and the area had been substantially developed by 1930.

Convenient to mass transit, public schools, and social services, the inner northeast district is a popular alternative to downtown for households of all income levels. Nearby Sandy Boulevard is a high-use corridor for bus service and bicycles. Local attractions include the historic Hollywood Theatre, health clubs, brew pubs, and cafés.

The Hollywood-Bookmark site is on Northeast Tillamook Street, between Northeast 40th and 41st avenues, at the northern edge of the Hollywood commercial district and about three miles (4.8 kilometers) from downtown Portland. To the north and across Tillamook Street is a row of one-story commercial buildings, and beyond that a single-family residential neighborhood. (There were several single-family homes on the site when the land was assembled by Multnomah County.) One-story bank buildings line the street to the east and west. Behind the building, to the south, are surface parking lots that serve a restaurant and a furniture store.

Planning, Development, and Entitlements

The Hollywood-Bookmark mixed-use building is the product of a partnership between the Multnomah County library system and the principals of Shiels Obletz Johnson, Inc. (SOJ), a Portland-based firm that manages urban development projects involving complex planning issues and combinations of public and private clients. From the beginning, the county and the developer intended the project to be a model for public/private partnership.

In May 1996, county voters approved a $29 million general-obligation bond to fund technology upgrades and construction and repair at branch libraries. The original Hollywood Library had long since outgrown its space in a well-frequented corner near what is now the Hollywood-Bookmark site, and city officials and county commissioners agreed that replacing the existing library presented an ideal opportunity to create mixed-use infill development in a neighborhood well served by transit.

SOJ principals Douglas Obletz and Carter MacNichol are also the managers of Sockeye Hollywood, LLC, an offshoot of SOJ that partnered with the county to develop Hollywood-Bookmark. Thomas Hacker Architects had been chosen, through a competitive process, to redesign 12 libraries for Multnomah County, including the Hollywood Library.

The design and development team held more than ten public presentations and workshops at the existing library; these events involved local neighborhood associations, clubs, government officials and staff, and neighborhood leaders. Overall, there was tremendous support for the project. Early concerns about the height and mass of the proposed building and the amount of off-street parking were allayed through revised plans that reduced the building's height and density. Whereas the original proposal showed between 58 and 61 units in four stories above the library, the completed project has 47 units in three stories above the library. Parking is limited to 28 spaces (0.6 spaces per unit) and is shared by apartment residents and library patrons.

The east and west elevations of the building emphasize height, while the north and south elevations soften the massing by modulating the facade.

Thomas Hacker Architects, Inc.

NORTH ELEVATION

EAST ELEVATION

0   10   20

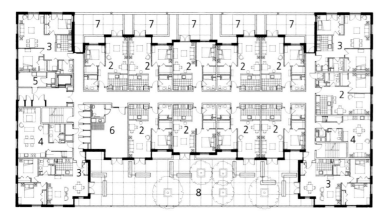

Second Floor Terrace Plan
(Third Floor Similar)

Thomas Hacker Architects, Inc.

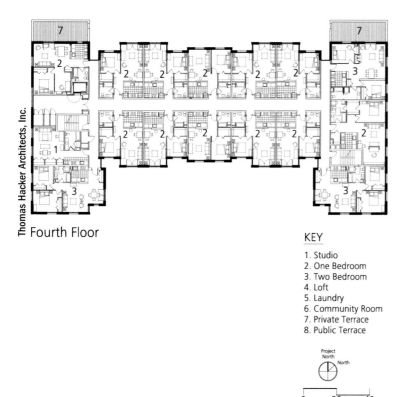

Fourth Floor

KEY

1. Studio
2. One Bedroom
3. Two Bedroom
4. Loft
5. Laundry
6. Community Room
7. Private Terrace
8. Public Terrace

Project
North
North

0   20   40

The H-shaped housing plan provides for private
terraces on the second floor of the north side,
and private terraces and a public courtyard on
the south side.

Financing

Hollywood-Bookmark was developed as two condominium units. The county owns the library. Sockeye Hollywood, LLC, as general partner, has 1 percent ownership of the housing and retail portions of the development. The limited investment partner, 4498 Main Street, Inc., purchased the low-income housing tax credits for the project and has 99 percent ownership of the apartments during the ten-year tax-abatement period. The construction contractor carried separate accounts for each owner, and costs were divided through consultations with the contractor.

U.S. Bank provided 18-month construction financing at a floating rate (the short-term benchmark—London Inter Bank Offering Rate [LIBOR]—plus 200 points). Permanent financing was provided through tax-exempt bonds issued by the city of Portland and privately placed with U.S. Bank. The bonds were issued at 5.99 percent interest with a 30-year amortization and a 20-year term. The $3.85 million loan was based on a 1.15 debt-coverage ratio and an 80 percent loan-to-value ratio.

Additional funding was provided by the Portland Development Commission (PDC), the city's redevelopment arm, in the form of a $1.25 million low-interest loan. Using a pool of proceeds from the sale of tax-exempt bonds, the PDC makes loans on projects that further the specified goals of its redevelopment districts. In this case, the goals met by the project included transit-oriented development, infill development, mixed-income housing, and mixed-use development—all within an area of demonstrated need.

Federal tax credits and local tax-exemption programs were key factors in the project's financial viability. The federal low-income housing tax credit is administered through the state of Oregon, and the city granted the project a transit-oriented development tax exemption through the PDC.

Design and Architecture

The Portland Region 2040 Growth Concept calls for greater density near transit in the Portland metropolitan region. The Hollywood-Bookmark project was conceived as a landmark that would jump-start redevelopment in a mature neighborhood and shape the character of future projects by modeling desirable massing, a strong street presence, high-quality materials, and visual appeal.

The architect, Thomas Hacker Architects, is a Portland-based architecture and design firm with a number of projects in the area, including libraries, museums, and research facilities. The firm had already been selected through a competitive process to design 12 branch libraries and renovations for the Multnomah County Library system, and the Hollywood Library was on this list. GBD Architects, also of Portland, consulted on the layout and finishes for the residential portion of the project.

The ground floor of the Hollywood-Bookmark building is occupied by the 13,000-square-foot (1,208-square-meter) library, an 815-square-foot (76-square-meter) retail space, a lobby for the housing on the upper floors, and a service center. A total of 47 apartments—one studio, two lofts, 33 one-bedroom apartments, and 11 two-bedroom apartments—occupy the second, third, and fourth floors. Behind the building are 28 parking spaces available to residents and library patrons.

All four floors of the building share a masonry and steel palette that emphasizes the civic character of the library and confers a sense of permanence on the entire project. The choice of

Thomas Hacker Architects, Inc.

materials supports the "100-year" construction quality demanded by the county and the developer. Details—such as concrete coping, and windows that are fully recessed to reveal the thickness of the walls—visually reinforce the sturdiness of the construction.

The civic character of the library is reflected in the tall window openings and high ceilings. A "porch," cut into the corner of the floor plan, serves as the entry and welcomes visitors. Prominent signage, made of fabricated steel, arcs out on each side of the corner, proclaiming the building's public nature. The library entrance is on the northeast corner; on the north side, it faces a neighborhood; to the east, it opens to a street that leads to the commercial center. The prominent entry to the Bookmark Apartments is located in the middle of the western side of the building.

The 20-foot (six-meter) floor-to-floor dimension allows for tall windows that provide abundant natural light throughout the library, particularly in the children's area, the reading room, and the meeting room. On the east and west sides of the building, the massing of the housing emphasizes height, whereas along the front facade, on the north (on Tillamook), the bulk

The northern facade is stepped back to three stories to reduce the massing and better articulate the library entrance, which is on the northeast corner.

The 20-foot (six-meter) floor-to-floor dimensions provide for tall windows and an abundance of natural lighting.

Thomas Hacker Architects, Inc.

ern facade are stepped back to three stories, and three-story brick-faced bays rise to meet the four-story building along the northern facade. This reduces the massing and creates the appearance of a three-story building on the north side of the building.

The housing plan is "H" shaped, with courtyards on the second level on the north and south sides. On the north side, the courtyard is divided up entirely into private terraces. The south side includes private terraces and a public courtyard. Planters and privacy screens are used to screen the private terraces from the public courtyard. All the apartments on the third and fourth floors have French balconies.

One-bedroom units occupy the center of the H. The sides of the H include a mix of one- and two-bedroom units, as well as one studio

is softened and modulated. The east and west sides of the building appear as a four-story whole. The corners of the building on the north-

Second-story terraces create valuable outdoor space, pull the housing away from the street, and break up what would otherwise be a monotonous facade.

Thomas Hacker Architects, Inc.

and two lofts. The two-bedroom apartments are located at each corner of the building, with access to light and views in three directions. There are two additional private terraces on the fourth floor, at the northeast and northwest corners of the building, atop the "end blocks" at the building corners. Loftlike ten-foot (three-meter) ceilings throughout the housing section add a critical element of spaciousness to all the apartment units and corridors.

The public areas in Bookmark Apartments have received special attention. At the end of each corridor, tall windows admit natural light and provide a visual connection to the surrounding neighborhood. Individual units are distinguished by recessed alcoves and lights at each door, and further marked by different paint colors. Elevator lobbies are furnished with chairs and plantings.

One of the special construction problems posed by Hollywood-Bookmark was the necessity of protecting the library level from the plumbing in the residential section. To address this issue, a mezzanine crawl space lined with a moisture barrier was constructed; in case of leaks or flooding from above, the space is designed to act like a tub, providing a high level of protection for the book collections below.

In keeping with the city's goals of encouraging transit use and decreasing dependence on cars, the project is designed to foster pedestrian activity. To increase the width of the sidewalk, the building is set back from the property line four feet (1.2 meters); street trees line all three sides. Curb extensions shorten crossing distances and encourage interaction on the sidewalk.

Hollywood-Bookmark is the first building to be certified by Portland General Electric's Earth Advantage program, which has established a set of standards that can increase energy savings by 20 to 40 percent and that help to protect watersheds

Thomas Hacker Architects, Inc.

and ensure indoor air quality. Sustainable features include recycled and composite materials, high-efficiency vinyl windows, high-efficiency appliances, natural-fiber carpets, drought-tolerant plants, and bio-swales for on-site filtration and runoff.

This mixed-use, transit-oriented development is also pedestrian- and bicycle-friendly.

Marketing and Operations

Analysis by an independent real estate appraisal firm showed that the primary market area for the apartment units was the inner northeast district of Portland, which includes several distinct neighborhoods in addition to Hollywood. As noted earlier, the inner northeast district is a popular choice for rental households at all income levels because of its convenience to transit, public schools, and social services. The target market includes empty nesters relocating from single-family homes in surrounding neighborhoods and suburbs; young singles and couples; and older residents who are attracted to nearby medical and social services, including a regional hospital and a very active senior center.

The Bookmark Apartments were not preleased; however, after having been advertised in local newspapers and on the Internet, the building was fully leased, through a local leasing and

Planters, planter boxes, and fencing separate the private terraces from the public courtyard.

Thomas Hacker Architects, Inc.

Experience Gained

Both the housing and the library benefit from being in close proximity within a mixed-use building, and the convenience of transit adds value to both components of the development. The apartments leased quickly, and over 20 percent of residents do not own a car.

The Hollywood Branch Library and its conference room offer an amenity for residents and an attraction to prospective tenants. The library sees 1,500 to 2,000 visitors per day, up from 800 in the old library building.

management company, within three months of opening in the spring of 2002. Since then, occupancy rates have held strong, at 90 to 95 percent in a soft market.

Tenants roughly match the mix identified in the market analysis. A typical unit is occupied by a retired couple that has recently sold a single-family home in which they had lived for many years. Next to the empty nesters, young singles and couples are the second-largest group represented.

The apartment units, with their entrance on the street, provide a lively street presence in the Hollywood-Bookmark block; in addition, because the apartments are so close to other destinations within walking distance, they provide a steady flow of patrons for nearby retail and service facilities.

Integrating housing in a decidedly civic building is a special challenge for a designer. At Hollywood-Bookmark, the architects were able to find common ground for materials and modeling while giving each component a distinct character and keeping costs under control. The devel-

The Hollywood Library and Bookmark Apartments were developed as two condominium units: the county owns the library on the first floor, and the general and limited partners own the apartments on floors two through four.

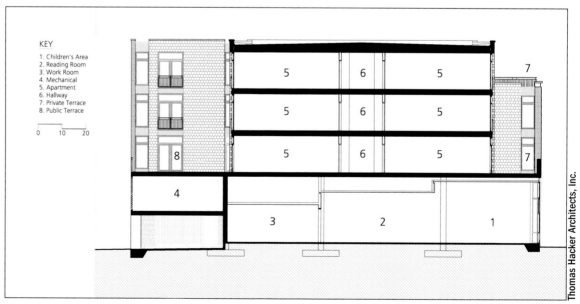

KEY
1. Children's Area
2. Reading Room
3. Work Room
4. Mechanical
5. Apartment
6. Hallway
7. Private Terrace
8. Public Terrace

0   10   20

Thomas Hacker Architects, Inc.

oper did, however, have to revise the original loan request to meet new cost estimates. The request was granted.

Creating a civic landmark project to anchor a neighborhood can jump-start redevelopment. Since the completion of the mixed-use project, a privately developed condominium project has started construction a half-block away.

The keys to building a successful landmark include the following:

- Sensitive, high-quality urban design and architecture;
- Neighborhood support;
- Civic purpose;
- A prominent position on the street;
- High-quality materials and construction.

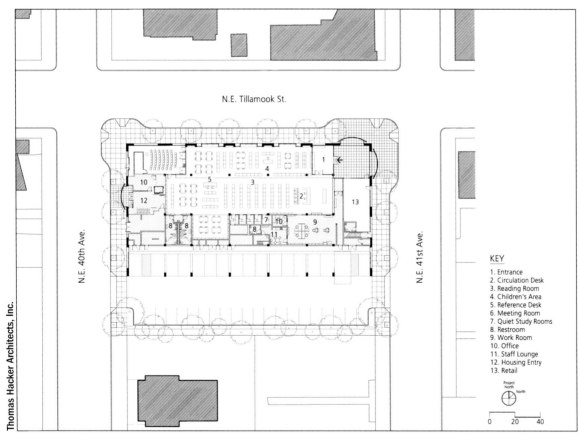

N.E. Tillamook St.

N.E. 40th Ave.

N.E. 41st Ave.

Thomas Hacker Architects, Inc.

KEY

1. Entrance
2. Circulation Desk
3. Reading Room
4. Children's Area
5. Reference Desk
6. Meeting Room
7. Quiet Study Rooms
8. Restroom
9. Work Room
10. Office
11. Staff Lounge
12. Housing Entry
13. Retail

Project North

0   20   40

The Hollywood-Bookmark site is located near Sandy Boulevard, a high-use corridor for buses and bicycles. The Portland Region 2040 Growth Concept calls for greater density near such transit routes. The Hollywood-Bookmark building has responded to that call by providing 47 housing units on a site that previously held only a handful of single-family homes.

The Bookmark Apartments at the Hollywood Library

Primary Contact

Francesca Gambetti
503-242-0084
francesca@sojpdx.com
www.sojpdx.com/hollywood.html

Project Team

Owner/Developer
Douglas L. Obletz, Manager
Sockeye Hollywood, LLC
115 N.W. First Avenue
Suite 200
Portland, Oregon 97209
503-242-0084
dougo@sojpdx.com

Project Manager
Shiels Obletz Johnsen, Inc.
115 N.W. First Avenue
Suite 200
Portland, Oregon 97209
503-242-0084
www.sojpdx.com

Architect of Record
Thomas Hacker Architects, Inc.
733 S.W. Oak Street
Portland, Oregon 97205
503-227-1254
www.thomashacker.com

Design Consultant
GBD Architects, Inc.
1120 N.W. Couch Street
Suite 300
Portland, Oregon 97209
503-224-9656
www.gbdarchitects.com

Landscape Architect
Walker Macy
111 S.W. Oak Street
Suite 200
Portland, Oregon 97204
503-228-3122
www.WalkerMacy.com

Structural Engineer
KPFF Consulting Engineers
111 S.W. Fifth Avenue
Suite 2500
Portland, Oregon 97204
503-227-3251
kpff.com

General Contractor
Walsh Construction Company
3015 S.W. First Avenue
Portland, Oregon 97201
503-222-4375
www.walshconstructionco.com

Development Schedule

Site purchased	November 1998
Planning started	November 1999
Construction started	April 2001
Leasing started	April 2002
Project completed	April 2002

Land Use Information

Total site area   0.69 acres
Number of residential units at buildout   47

Land Use	Square Footage (at Buildout)
Retail (Café Uno)	815
Residential	44,000
Other (county library)	13,000
Total	57,815

Site Coverage

Use	Square Footage
Buildings	20,000
Streets and surface parking	9,000
Landscaping and open space	1,000
Total	30,000

Residential Information

Multifamily Units

Unit Type	Square Footage	Number of Units Leased	Rental Prices
Income restricted			
Studio	530	1	$576
One bedroom	610–635	18	$613
Market rate			
One bedroom	630–660	13	$795–$915
One bedroom plus den	750–870	2	$1,020–$1,030
Two bedroom	915–950	11	$1,000–$1,295
Two-story loft	715–830	2	$1,225–$1,295

Affordable Residential Units

Unit Type	Number of Units	Targeted Income Group	Rental Prices
Studio	1	60% of median family income (MFI)	$576
One bedroom	18	60% of MFI	$613

Retail Information

Gross leasable area   815 square feet (Café Uno)
Percentage of GLA occupied   100%

Gross Leasable Area

Use	Square Footage
Retail	815
Residential	44,000
Other (county library)	13,000
Total	57,815

Development Costs

Site acquisition	$745,000
Site improvement	$350,000
Construction	$7,100,000
Furniture, fixtures, and equipment	$55,000
Soft costs	
Architecture and engineering	$775,000
Project management	290,000
Leasing and marketing	50,000
Legal and accounting	250,000
Taxes and insurance	25,000
Title fees	30,000
Construction interest and fees	150,000
Other	1,030,000
Subtotal, soft costs	$2,600,000
Total	$10,850,000

Casa del Maestro
Santa Clara, California

Project Information

When it comes to providing affordable housing for a municipal workforce, few places in the United States have faced quite the same crisis as California's Silicon Valley. During the late 1990s, median sales prices for existing homes shot past $500,000, and the average rent on a two-bedroom apartment soared to over $2,000 per month. Even following the "tech wreck" of the early 2000s, prices remained exorbitant— and rents, particularly for new apartments, were still out of reach for the region's workforce.

Silicon Valley's technology pioneers are well known for their aggressive approach to problem solving, but they have nothing on the Santa Clara Unified School District. Maintaining a base of highly qualified teachers in an area with skyrocketing housing costs is difficult enough; but in the late 1990s, California mandated smaller class sizes, which forced significant hiring increases at a time when attrition rates for teachers had increased more than 300 percent. On the basis of national research and local experience, both of which indicated that once teachers are housed in a community, they often become lifelong employees, the school district's forward-thinking leaders realized that the cost of attrition was higher than the cost of providing housing.

The result was Casa del Maestro, an apartment development for teachers constructed in a suburban neighborhood of Santa Clara. Built in 2002, the project was conceived and spearheaded by the Santa Clara Unified School District, which (1) contributed surplus land on an existing school campus for the development, and (2) through a competitive bid process, awarded a fee development contract to Thompson|Dorfman, which shepherded the project through the design, entitlement, and construction process.

The property consists of two buildings with 20 units each: 12 one-bedroom units, four one-bedroom-plus-den units, and 24 two-bedroom units. Units are offered to teachers in the district at below-market rent, and the development was fully occupied immediately upon delivery. Casa del Maestro is now professionally managed by a local property management concern.

Workforce Housing Information

The effort undertaken by the Santa Clara Unified School District built on an existing Santa Clara County mortgage-assistance program that is designed to help teachers purchase their own homes. The Teacher Mortgage Assistance Program (TMAP) buys an equity share of a teacher's house for $500 per month for five years (a total of $30,000). At the end of the five years, the teacher must pay back the $30,000, plus a share of the equity that has accrued in the home (roughly 3 percent per year). The school district decided, however, that high-quality rental housing was needed to recruit and retain younger teachers. Affordable rental housing was identified as a key means of bringing the best teachers into the district and giving them an opportunity to save for a downpayment. These two programs— the teacher mortgage-assistance program and the rental-housing program—work together to attract and retain the very best talent.

Thompson|Dorfman/KTGY

The architecture at Casa del Maestro was based on historic buildings in San Francisco's Presidio.

Site, Surroundings, and History

School districts are often blessed with surplus building sites, and such was the case with Santa Clara. The district identified a 2.16-acre (0.87-hectare) site on the western edge of the city, abutting the Curtis School site, as the optimal location for the proposed development. The low-rise, suburban neighborhood had been developed mostly in the 1950s and had a strong character and sense of cohesion. While the local housing stock (predominantly detached, single-story homes) is modest, values are quite high. There are also a number of small, two-story apartment complexes in the neighborhood that influenced the design of Casa del Maestro.

The Curtis School, of similar vintage, was built at a time when land was inexpensive and schools planned for physical growth. The Casa del Maestro site had been used as a dog park for many years; although there was some resistance to the loss of that use, the neighborhood was supportive of the development effort from the time that it was announced.

The project location is within walking distance of neighborhood retail and offers conven-

ient freeway access. The area is served by Caltrain heavy rail, although Caltrain is not within walking distance.

Planning, Development, and Entitlements

A request for proposals (RFP) for a fee developer was issued in 2000. The school district proposed to reimburse all costs by securing bond financing. The assumption was that a not-for-profit developer would pursue the entitlements and oversee design and construction; upon completion, the project would be turned over to a foundation established by the district, which would arrange for property management by a third party. To maintain an arm's-length relationship between employer and employee, the foundation was created to act as landlord and as intermediary between the district and the teachers.

Surprisingly, the successful RFP respondent was Thompson|Dorfman, a for-profit developer. Based in Sausalito, the firm is a leading regional provider of luxury housing and has created some of the most successful upscale rental and condominium communities in the San Francisco Bay Area. The motivation for the firm's involvement was a unique twist on the "double bottom line" approach to development, in which a developer trades a lower return for the satisfaction and public acknowledgement of having provided a community service.

Thompson|Dorfman proposed to act as the project developer in return for reimbursement of costs, including those for in-house project management, but no additional fees or profit. The "return" would be strengthened relations with the Santa Clara Unified School District and the city and county of Santa Clara, an area in which Thompson|Dorfman is already active and in which the firm plans to continue pursuing for-profit development opportunities. In the words of principal Bruce Dorfman, "This project was a way of giving back to a community that had dealt generously and professionally with us in the past, and with whom we hope to be partners in new developments in the future."

Under the agreement, Thompson|Dorfman completed financial, market, and economic due diligence and prepared and presented a conceptual design to the district, which was quickly accepted. Thompson|Dorfman's project manager navigated the entitlement process. According to the developer, the length of time required to secure entitlements and permits, while not extensive or deal-breaking, was the primary obstacle to the development.

Thompson|Dorfman bid out the project to a general contractor, and ground breaking was in April 2001. After construction was complete and a certificate of occupancy had been issued, the developer turned the key over to the district in May 2002. The total project time, from RFP to delivery, was two years. The developer noted that having everyone, including the school district and subcontractors, adhere to a well-managed time schedule was crucial to the firm's willingness to participate in this type of project in the future. The fear of extensive delays and political difficulties did not materialize in this case. The design and build model was particularly effective because it left Thompson|Dorfman to do what the firm is good at—designing and building— and eliminated the need to send out individual scopes of work for public bid.

Financing

The last major hurdle of the Casa del Maestro project was financing, which was coordinated by the school district. The district owned the land and enjoyed the support of both local political leaders and the public. However, the district had

Thompson|Dorfman/KTGY

The two-bedroom units are all "split master" configurations, allowing additional, affordable options for teachers who are willing to share an apartment.

Thompson|Dorfman/KTGY

All units have generous porches or balconies.

Attractive architecture and generous landscaping were key to garnering community acceptance of the project.

Because they were patterned after townhouses, the apartments have individual addresses and direct access from the street.

substantial debt-service obligations, and putting another bond issue on the ballot could further delay the project's completion. For these reasons, the district decided to pursue certificate of participation (COP) financing.

The California School Boards Association (CSBA) Finance Corporation assists school districts throughout California with fiscal matters. The CSBA helps finance renovations, operates lend-lease programs for large items, invests cash reserves, and administers the certificates of participation program. The program allows school districts to finance capital improvements—such as buildings, buses, athletic facilities, or major renovations—with favorable interest rates and little or no downpayment. By the end of 2003, the COP program had financed 135 projects worth over $623 million.

Repayment for capital improvements is structured through a lessor-lessee contract. Because the district, as lessee, is repaying the funds through lease payments, the financing of the project is not viewed as taking on debt. Public referenda are, therefore, not needed, making certificates of participation more advantageous than issuing bonds. However, in order to be eligible for COP financing, the district's funding request had to be placed in the category of infrastructure. The Santa Clara school district argued, successfully, that housing for teachers was as critical an infrastructure need as school buses, athletic fields, or portable classrooms.

Design and Architecture

The school district and the developer take particular pride in the fact that the design, architecture, general execution, and finish are similar to what Thompson|Dorfman would bring to any of its luxury, for-profit developments. The exterior articulation and interior finish work are comparable to those of most luxury rental apartment complexes

Thompson|Dorfman/KTGY

The 1,000-square-foot (93-square-meter) community clubhouse anchors the space between the two apartment buildings and is framed by two large palm trees.

in the area; within the units, standard countertops and cabinets are the only significant exception.

One unique challenge in developing housing for teachers is that the renters or owners have sophisticated tastes and high expectations. Recognizing that the residents of Casa del Maestro were similar in profile to Thompson| Dorfman's target market, only with lower incomes, the firm resisted the temptation to decrease the size of the units in order to cut costs. In fact, the residences at Casa del Maestro are patterned after townhouses rather than conventional apartment units. To reinforce the character of a townhouse development, most of the units are accessed directly from the street and have individual street addresses. All units have generous porches or balconies, large kitchens, and in-unit washers and dryers. An on-site parking ratio of 1.8 spaces for every unit includes one private garage space per unit; 70 percent of the units have direct access to the apartment from the garage parking space.

Land planning is particularly well handled. Because the buildings are small and discrete, every unit looks onto open space. The generous garage allocation results in very limited street parking. Using only two-story buildings, KTGY, an Irvine-based project architect and land planner, and Guzzardo Partnership, a San Francisco–based landscape architecture firm, managed to achieve a density of almost 20 dwelling units per acre (49 per hectare). Although the density is somewhat higher than that of the surrounding, 1960s-era apartment buildings, the project blends in well with the existing community.

The architecture, based on historic buildings in San Francisco's Presidio, features red, asphalt-shingled roofs; a high-quality synthetic composite was used in place of off-white painted wood siding. The design relies on the careful arrangement of asymmetrical building forms, and includes exterior stairways and large hipped roofs. Fine details—including roof lines, porch trellises, and building-number placards—and the

Thompson|Dorfman/KTGY

Casa del Maestro provides 40 rental apartments located in two buildings. Every unit looks onto open space.

graceful handling of the exterior staircases make for a handsome project.

Generous interiors allow for a variety of layouts and a comfortable balance of private and social spaces. Units are designed specifically for singles, unrelated roommates, and families. The one-bedroom units range in size from 722 to 785 square feet (67 to 73 square meters). One-bedroom-plus-den units are 976 square feet (91 square meters). And the two-bedroom, two-bath units, which range from 1,045 to 1,170 square feet (97 to 109 square meters), are all "split master" configurations, which are particularly accommodating to roommates.

Architecture was key to ensuring the development's appeal to potential renters and to gaining neighborhood acceptance. The developer and the school district worked hard to make certain that the community would not be perceived as an "affordable-housing project."

During the design process, Thompson|Dorfman carefully balanced the need for a sophisticated design against the need to remain within budget (since there was no profit motive for the developer, Thompson|Dorfman would have had to cover any budget overruns). The firm also wanted to create buildings that would

be energy efficient and environmentally low impact (which meant, for example, preserving mature trees). Thompson|Dorfman worked closely with local utility providers, who subsidized the installation of upgraded windows, insulation, and mechanical equipment in return for lower levels of future energy use.

Creative land planning and landscape architecture were also used to help create a sophisticated community. Expenditures on landscaping were generous throughout the project. The residential units are arranged around a central green space that is open to the street; two gracious and mature palm trees were planted at each end of the green space. The 1,000-square-foot (93-square-meter) community clubhouse—a handsome, freestanding building that is often used for parties and other gatherings—anchors one end of the space, just behind two of the palm trees.

Marketing and Operations

Needless to say, the response to this housing opportunity was overwhelming, and the school district had to develop a lottery to ensure that future residents were chosen fairly. To qualify, employees had to have worked in the district for less than three years; priority was given to teachers first, administrators second, and certified employees third. The mix of renters is varied and includes families, couples, and singles. Because Casa del Maestro represented a unique opportunity for young teachers newly out of college to avoid having roommates (often a necessity in high-cost locations), the one-bedroom units were the first to be occupied.

Rents were set at the minimum required to cover operating costs and debt service on the underlying financing. This arrangement resulted in rental rates for one-bedroom units of $650 to $730, or $0.93 per square foot ($10.00 per square meter). Two-bedroom units currently rent for $970 to $1,090, also approximately $0.93 per square foot ($10.00 per square meter). All units are individually metered for utilities, with utility costs paid directly by tenants. Rents are estimated at less than 50 percent of market rate.

Perhaps not surprisingly, vacancy during the first year of operation was very low, 0.5 percent (significantly lower than projected). Because of the success of this first phase, the district is considering developing an additional 30 units on an adjacent parcel. More importantly, the district has been inundated with inquiries from other districts throughout northern California that are considering a similar solution to a growing problem.

A local property-management firm oversees the operation of the property, including all maintenance, accounting, and regulatory compliance. The district maintains a waiting list for units as they become available.

Experience Gained
On the basis of its experience with Casa del Maestro, the developer, Thompson|Dorfman, outlined three factors that were key to the project's success:

■ The site needs to be contributed by a public agency. Many municipalities have surplus school or municipal sites, and housing can be a suitable use even for small sites such as this two-acre (0.80-hectare) parcel.
■ The public/private partnership must be aggressive in identifying public funding

Developed by Thompson | Dorfman, a for-profit developer of luxury multifamily housing, Casa del Maestro has interior finishes that are comparable to those of luxury rental apartment complexes in the area; the only exceptions are the kitchen cabinets and countertops.

Thompson | Dorfman/KTGY

mechanisms (such as certificates of participation or tax-exempt bonds). A cutting-edge understanding of municipal financing mechanisms, which can often be identified by a knowledgeable consultant, is key.

■ Workforce housing programs need a visible, well-respected, and stalwart champion in the government.

Given the success of the Santa Clara program, one must ask why other districts haven't been quicker to follow suit. First, for a school district, getting into the housing business creates significant political risk—including the possibility that stakeholders, including parents, will not understand the value of the approach. Second, financing these programs is not easy. The district will need to invest some capital upfront—and, given the strains on school budgets everywhere, arguing for this allocation of funds may be difficult. Workforce housing pro-

grams like Casa del Maestro need a champion, both in the school district and in the local government administration. Putting one's political reputation on the line for any kind of spending program is always risky. Finally, surplus school sites are often located in established communities, where home values are likely to be high and residents affluent. Such jurisdictions may be less than receptive to the notion of high-density or workforce housing, even for the teachers of the community's children.

Thompson|Dorfman and the Santa Clara Unified School District hope that Casa del Maestro will become a prototype that can be replicated on other sites and by other districts. The development's efficiency and aesthetics, the overwhelmingly positive market response, and the successful effort to give valued teachers a place to form roots in the community all suggest that the partnership deserves to be studied and replicated elsewhere.

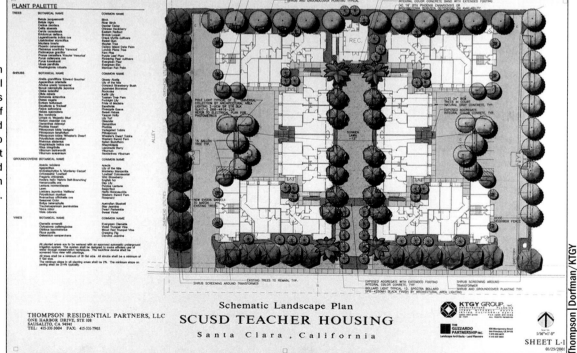

The landscape plan for Casa del Maestro illustrates the creative use of landscaping and common areas to provide each unit with access to and views of open space or plantings.

Casa del Maestro

Primary Contact

Bruce Dorfman
415-331-3004
bd@thompsondorfman.com
www.thompsondorfman.com/

Project Team

Owner/Developer

Roger Barnes
Santa Clara Unified School District
1889 Lawrence Road
Santa Clara, California 95051
408-423-2085
rbarnes@scu.k12.ca.us

Bruce Dorfman
Principal
Thompson | Dorfman
One Harbor DriveSuite 108
Sausalito, California 94965
415-331-3004
bd@thompsondorfman.com

Architect

Stan Braden
President
KTGY Group, Inc.
17992 Mitchell South
Irvine, California 92614
949-851-2133
sbraden@KTGY.com
www.ktgy.com

Landscape Architect

Paul Lettieri
The Guzzardo Partnership
836 Montgomery Street
San Francisco, California 94133
415-433-4672
plettieri@TGP-INC.com

Structural Engineer

Lee Mason
L.S. Mason & Associates
3468 Mt. Diablo Boulevard
Suite B-120
Lafayette, California 94549
925-283-8805
lsmaengr@pacbell.net
http://lsmaengr.com/site/

Mechanical Engineer

Huey Cao
TAD Engineering
4633 East Bond Avenue
Orange, California 92869
714-595-0375
hc@tadengineering.com
www.tadengineering.com

Electrical Engineer

Dale Madler
DGM & Associates
125 East Baker Street
Suite 150
Costa Mesa, California 92626
714-546-3251
dmadler@dgmassociates.com
www.dgmassociates.com

General Contractor

Douglas Ross Construction
909 Alma Street
Palo Alto, California 94301
650-470-4726
dougr@rossconstruction.com
www.rossconstruction.com

Development Schedule

Construction started   May 2001
Phase I completed   May 2002
Project completed   May 2002

Land Use Information

Total site area   2.16 acres
Multifamily residential area   2.1 acres
Number of multifamily units at buildout   40

Site Coverage

Use	Square Footage
Buildings	28,200
Streets and surface parking	28,000
Landscaping and open space	37,600

Residential Information

Multifamily Units

Unit Type	Square Footage	Number of Units Leased	Rental Prices
One bedroom, one bath	720–785	12	$650–$730
One bedroom, one bath, plus den	976	4	$900
Two bedrooms, two baths	1,045–1,170	24	$970–$1,090

Development Costs

Site acquisition (site owned by district)	$0
Site improvement	
Excavation and grading	$120,000
Sewer, water, and drainage	200,000
Paving, curbs, and sidewalks	125,000
Landscaping and irrigation	100,000
Fees and general conditions	660,000
Subtotal, site improvement	$1,205,000
Construction	
Superstructure	$3,000,000
Heating, ventilating, and air conditioning	195,000
Electrical	350,000
Plumbing and sprinklers	450,000
Finish work	100,000
Graphics and specialties	50,000
Subtotal, construction	$4,105,000
Furniture, fixtures, and equipment	$50,000
Soft costs	
Architecture and engineering	$400,000
Project management	230,000
Legal and accounting	50,000
Taxes and insurance	20,000
Construction interest and fees (financed by district)	0
Subtotal, soft costs	$700,000
Total development costs	$6,100,000

Edgemoore at Carrington
McLean, Virginia

Project Information

The Edgemoore at Carrington development, located near Tyson's Corner, Virginia, about 13 miles (21 kilometers) west of Washington, D.C., contains county-mandated affordable-housing units that blend in seamlessly with the surrounding luxury homes, which now sell for over $1 million. This effect is achieved through an architectural illusion known as a "great house"—a structure that appears to be a large, single-family home but that actually contains four townhouse units, each with its own front entrance and garage parking. Until the Carrington development, Fairfax County developers attempting to meet the requirements of Fairfax County's Affordable Dwelling Unit (ADU) Ordinance had built townhouses or low-rise multifamily structures, which tended to stand out—and, often, apart from—the market-rate units elsewhere in the development. The great-house design provides greater uniformity within a development of large, single-family detached homes.

The developer, Edgemoore Homes, had originally planned Carrington as a luxury enclave. In addition to being near the office and shopping destinations of Tyson's Corner, the site has the advantage of proximity to a major state highway (Route 7) and to the Dulles Toll Road, which provides easy access to Dulles International Airport and neighboring business corridors. The project features 105 units: eight affordable units and 97 market-rate units. The market-rate units offer 4,000 to 5,000 square feet (372 to 465 square meters) of space and are located on half-acre (0.2-hectare) lots.

Edgemoore at Carrington was developed on 70 acres (28 hectares) formerly occupied by a dairy farm. The eight affordable townhouses are located at the eastern side of the development, near the entrance.

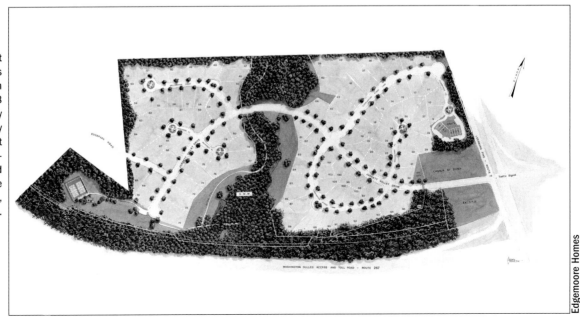

Edgemoore Homes

Workforce Housing Information

The great-house design seems to have appealed to potential purchasers of the affordable units. The first eight families who were eligible to buy the affordable units at Carrington bought them immediately—which, according to the developer, is unusual with Fairfax County ADUs. (More commonly, potential purchasers will dislike either the location or the design of an available unit, and will opt to remain on the county's ADU waiting list.)

The project has given eight families a chance at homeownership in a county where, in 2003, the median price for a single-family home was $379,854, and the median townhouse price was $229,929. There has been little turnover in the units, and the developer describes the families as enjoying their homes.

ADU residents are required to join the Carrington Homeowners' Association, which over-

Edgemoore Homes

sees trash removal and the maintenance of common space. The ADUs are under special covenants to cap appreciation and must remain affordable for 15 years. Fairfax County supervised the homeownership lottery and will oversee turnover sales in the development.

What appears to be a large, single-family home is actually four affordable townhouses. The design of the townhouses enables them to blend in with the community's luxury single-family homes.

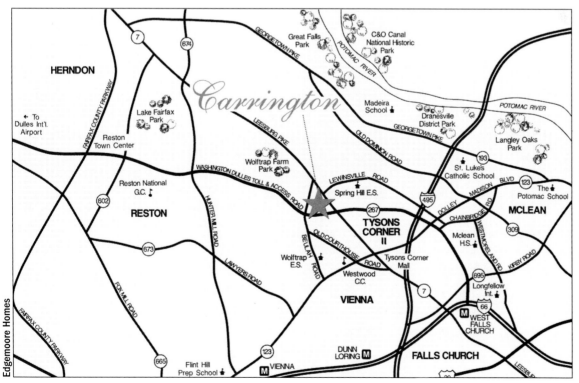

Edgemoore Homes

The Edgemoore at Carrington development is located in Fairfax County, Virginia, an affluent suburb of Washington, D.C., that requires new residential developments to include affordable dwelling units.

The Fairfax County Affordable Dwelling Unit Ordinance

In Fairfax County, Virginia—a suburb of Washington, D.C., and one of the most affluent counties in the United States—the 2003 median family income was $93,000, and the median cost of a single-family home was approximately $380,000. To afford such a house, a family of four would have to earn about $109,000 a year, but 53 percent of the county's families earn less than that amount. Fairfax County, long aware of this discrepancy, has worked to find a suitable solution through its Affordable Dwelling Unit (ADU) Ordinance.

In 1971, Fairfax County passed a mandatory zoning ordinance that required developers of projects that included more than 50 dwelling units to ensure that 15 percent of the units would be affordable to households earning between 60 and 80 percent of the area median income. The Virginia Supreme Court overturned this ordinance in 1973, on the ground that it constituted a "taking" of private property without just compensation.[1] Fifteen years later, a local affordable-housing advocacy group, AHOME (Affordable Housing Opportunity Means Everyone), began lobbying at the state and local levels for a new affordable-housing ordinance. Because Virginia is a Dillon's Rule state, Fairfax County could not devise the ordinance on its own: the state legislature had to grant local planning and zoning authority to the county.[2] Thus, AHOME not only had to persuade local politicians of the value of an affordable-housing ordinance, but also had to work with state lawmakers to obtain enabling legislation that would give jurisdictions the right to pass inclusionary zoning ordinances. In 1989, Virginia amended its state code to allow localities to adopt such ordinances; the Fairfax County ADU Ordinance was enacted the following year. To ensure that the enforcement of the ordinance could not be regarded as a taking, developers are granted a density bonus in return for providing ADUs.

The ordinance applies to developments of 50 units or more for which the developer has proposed densities exceeding those allowed under the R-1 designation. (Developments that either have fewer than 50 units, or for which additional density has not been proposed [or both] are not required to include affordable units; however, the developers of such projects are required to donate 0.5 percent of each unit's estimated sales price to the county's affordable-housing trust fund.) Developments of single-family homes receive a 20 percent density bonus, but 12.5 percent of the units must be affordable (the percentage of ADUs may be lower, depending on proffers or mitigating circumstances). For non-elevator multifamily buildings, or elevator multifamily buildings that have three stories or fewer, a 10 percent density bonus is allowed, and up to 6.25 percent of all units must be affordable. Originally, the ordinance had excluded multifamily buildings of four stories or more that included at least one elevator, but in 2003, the county board of supervisors voted to include mid-rise developments in the ordinance. Developers of mid-rise developments may obtain density bonuses of up to 17 percent, in exchange for up to 6.25 percent ADUs. Developments in which 50 percent of the parking is structured are required to provide no more than 5 percent ADUs.

Site, Surroundings, and History

The parcel—70 acres (28 hectares) of relatively flat land—was a former dairy farm whose owners had resisted selling until the early 1990s, when they sold it to Edgemoore Homes. The site is bordered on the west by the Wolf Trap Woods subdivision, which is made up of medium-sized single-family homes built during the mid-1970s.

Planning, Development, and Entitlements

The site was originally zoned R-1, meaning one dwelling unit per acre (2.50 per hectare), which would have allowed for 70 units. The developer wanted a somewhat higher density and asked the county for a zoning change to R-2, which would have allowed the construction of approximately 100 units—the ideal number for the project. Because of the request for increased density and the fact that the development would yield more than 50 units, the project was automatically required to comply with Fairfax County's ADU Ordinance—which meant providing units that would be affordable to households earning low to moderate incomes. The density and the number of market-rate units determined the total number of units, 8 percent of which were required to be ADUs.

Fairfax County affordable-housing activists continue to lobby for increases in the percentage of affordable-housing units in each development. As of 2003, Fairfax County had 1,436 affordable units, despite the fact that the ordinance had been in place for close to 15 years. The program was not immediately popular with developers, who claimed that they were losing profits and that projects were being slowed down by the NIMBY syndrome. Developers can appeal the ADU requirement, but the county rarely makes exceptions. Circumstances such as infeasibility or proffers may decrease the ADU requirement, but not eliminate it.

Over the past decade, the ordinance has been amended to ease the burden on developers and builders. Developers are now allowed slight increases in sales prices in exchange for using a sympathetic design (such as the great house), or in order to cover the cost of enhancing the appearance of the units. In 1998, the ordinance was amended to allow developers to complete up to 90 percent of the market-rate units upon completion of 90 percent of the required ADUs. Previously, developers could not complete more than 75 percent of the market-rate units before completing 100 percent of the ADUs. To ensure appropriate square footage and amenities, the county provides developers with guidelines for the construction of the units.

For a household to qualify for a unit, its income must be at or below 70 percent of the median income for the Washington, D.C., Standard Metropolitan Statistical Area. Prospective buyers are not permitted to have owned a home in the past three years, and must attend a course on homeownership. The names of buyers who are approved are placed in a lottery. Priority is given to those who live or work in Fairfax County or have children under 18 at home. There are hundreds of names on the waiting list—and, because not many units are produced in a given year, those who do not meet the priority requirements are unlikely to receive a unit.

The units are sold under a restrictive covenant that maintains their affordability for 15 years (a number that was recently lowered, from the original 50 years). In exchange for the opportunity to purchase a below-market-rate unit, and in order to ensure that the unit remains affordable, annual appreciation is linked to the Consumer Price Index. Owners are also given appreciation credit for improvements to the unit. The county oversees the appraisal, pricing, and sale of the units. The county is also responsible for ensuring that the owner does not rent out the unit, and for discouraging owners from taking refinancing offers from predatory lenders. If a unit goes into foreclosure, the affordability covenant is null and void, and the unit must be sold to the highest bidder. Owners may sell at any time, and one-half of the net gain goes into the county's affordable-housing trust fund.

1. Board of Supervisors of Fairfax County et al. v. DeGroff.

2. Dillon's Rule is named after Judge John F. Dillon, a 19th-century authority on municipal law. Under "Dillon's Rule of strict construction," any powers not explicitly granted to local governments are implicitly denied to local governments.

The residents of the neighboring Wolf Trap Woods subdivision resisted the inclusion of affordable housing so close to their homes. As is often the case, neighbors perceived the below-market-rate housing as "public housing," with all the associated implications: increased crime, litter, and noise, and an eventual drop in property values. For many Americans, their home is their biggest investment—and, as William Fischel points out in *The Homevoter Hypothesis,* homeowners will always attempt to protect the value of their homes. Because the density increase required the approval of the Wolf Trap Woods Homeowners' Association, the "not-in-my-backyard" (NIMBY) response significantly slowed the project. Edgemoore Homes made it clear to the residents of Wolf Trap Woods that the firm would be building traditional townhouses, of the sort that Fairfax County had typically approved for affordable dwelling units. However, the homeowners' association argued that the appearance of the townhouses would clash with that of the large, detached, single-family homes in the surrounding area.

In previous Fairfax County developments where affordable housing was required, the townhouses had been designed differently from the detached, single-family homes and were physically segregated from them. Not only was this approach unacceptable to those living near the Carrington

Four-unit floor plan

SECOND FLOOR — Two bedrooms | Two bedrooms | Two bedrooms | Two bedrooms | Bedroom | Bedroom | Bedroom | Bedroom

FIRST FLOOR — Kitchen | Kitchen | Kitchen | Kitchen | Living room | Living room | Living room | Living room | Door

BASEMENT — Garage | Garage | Garage | Garage | Storage space | Storage space | Storage space | Storage space

Single-family floor plan

SECOND FLOOR — Master suite | OPEN TO BELOW | Master bath | Bedroom | Bedroom | Bedroom

FIRST FLOOR — Kitchen | Family room | Dining room | Foyer | Living room | Library | Garage

BASEMENT — Storage space or optional bedrooms

Edgemoore Homes

Each 1,200-square-foot (111-square-meter) townhouse (left) has a parking garage in the rear of the unit. Single-family homes in the development (right) are typically over 4,000 square feet (372 square meters) in size.

The luxury single-family homes at Carrington sell for over $1 million. The affordable townhouses sold for $134,000 each.

The main entrances to the end units are through side doors that are not visible from the front. The entrances to the two center units are in the front, but one door is screened from view, to maintain the appearance of a single-family home.

project, it also discouraged potential buyers: the developers discovered that not many people wanted to buy a $500,000 detached house in a neighborhood that included $120,000 townhouses. In response to this dilemma, architects at Custom Design Concepts Architecture, in McLean, Virginia, developed the great-house design. (Great-house duplexes had been built in previous Fairfax County projects, but Carrington was the first project to use the multiplex model.) According to Carrington's developers, disguising the townhouses as large, single-family houses that were architecturally compatible with the market-rate units eased the concerns of the Wolf Trap Woods Homeowners' Association, and did not discourage potential purchasers of single-family units within the development.

In exchange for using the great-house design, the developers were allowed to sell the units for slightly more than the typical ADU townhouse. When the units went to market in 2002, they were selling for $134,000 each—about $10,000 more than the typical three-bedroom ADU. The $10,000 difference put the units out of reach of about 5 percent of the 329 people on the county's waiting list. To afford a great-house unit, a family of four would have to earn $39,000 or more. According to the county, raising the sales price also helped to quell the surrounding communities' anxieties over the affordable units—for the most part. Newspaper accounts of the controversy quote a Wolf Trap Woods resident as saying that ADUs should be banned from developments that include large, single-family homes, and that the county should not "try to solve sociological problems by breaking the zoning."[1]

Architecture and Design

The developer credited the appeal of the Carrington ADUs to the sophisticated exterior design, the garage space, and the large bedrooms. Residents include public-school teachers, cab drivers, a waiter, and a toll collector.

Although Carrington's great houses were the first of their kind in Fairfax County, construction did not present any problems. The builder was able to put them up quickly, which was especially important because the completion of the ADUs was necessary to obtain permits for the market-rate units. Since great houses typically do not have driveways, additional parking and garbage pickup areas are located behind the houses, at a lower grade. Carrington's developers were also careful to integrate the two great houses into the development, and to avoid isolating them from the 97 market-rate units. In fact, the units were placed near the front of the development and are readily visible from the main roadway, alongside the market-rate units.

Carrington's developers encountered no difficulties in obtaining financing for the project, and noted that although Fairfax County dictated the minimum square footage, room sizes, and amenities, the county was amenable to the developers' design suggestions. The great-house style blends easily with the English country manor design of the market-rate units.

Experience Gained

The great-house design is a unique way of addressing the physical discrepancies between Carrington's 4,000 to 5,000-square-foot (372 to 465-square meter) market-rate homes and the 1,200-square-foot (112-square-meter) ADUs. The approach has also succeeding in preventing outright rejection of affordable housing in one of the most affluent counties in the nation. As of 2003, two more projects in Fairfax County had applied the great-house design to their ADUs.

Note

1. Peter Whorisky, "Find the Affordable Housing in This Picture," *Washington Post,* August 17, 2001, A1.

To conserve space, the townhouses feature eat-in kitchens, whereas the single-family homes have large, separate dining rooms.

Bay windows in the living rooms bring plenty of natural light into the end units.

To keep the units affordable, less expensive finishes were used in the townhouse kitchens and baths.

Edgemoore at Carrington

Primary Contact

Rick Snider
703-691-8475
rds@edgemoorehomes.com
www.Edgemoorehomes.com

Project Team

Owner/Developer

Edgemoore-Jarrett, LLC
3925 Old Lee Highway
Suite 100
Fairfax, Virginia 22030
703-691-8475
www.edgemoorehomes.com

Architect of Record

Custom Design Concepts Architecture, P.C.
6710 Wittier Avenue
McLean, Virginia 22101
703-749-9040

Landscape Architect

Christopher Consultants, Ltd.
9900 Main Street
Fourth Floor
Fairfax, Virginia 22031
703-273-6820
www.christopherconsultants.com/index.html.

Marketing/Sales

Edgemoore Homes
3925 Old Lee Highway
Suite 100
Fairfax, Virginia 22030
703-691-8475
www.edgemoorehomes.com

Development Schedule

Planning started	October 1998
Site purchased	February 1999
Construction started	July 1999
Sales started	February 1999
Phase I completed	January 2000
Project completed	August 2002

Land Use Information

Total site area: 70 acres

Land Use	Acres	Number of Units (at Buildout)
Residential	70	105
Single-family detached	77.25	97
Single-family attached	0.75	8

Site Coverage

Use	Percentage of Site Area
Buildings	42
Streets and surface parking	18
Landscaping and open space	40
Total	100

Residential Information

Unit Type	Square Footage	Number of Units Sold	Sales Prices
Single-family detached			
Andover	4,200	31	$895,000
Briarcliffe	4,750	39	$935,000
Cambridge	5,250	26	$900,000
Single-family attached			
Affordable dwelling unit ("great house")	1,240	8	$134,000

Affordable Residential Units

Number of affordable units	8
Sales price	$134,000

Development Costs

Site acquisition	$11,500,000
Site improvement	$6,300,000
Hard construction costs (affordable units only)	$1,050,000
Soft costs (architecture)	$100,000
Total	$18,950,000

Fall Creek Place
Indianapolis, Indiana

Project Information

An innovative public/private endeavor has transformed Fall Creek Place—a deteriorating, crime-ridden, 26-block site in Indianapolis—into an attractive, mixed-income residential neighborhood. Using a federal grant for land assembly, along with other subsidies and incentives, the city created a solid foundation that (1) enabled private developers to build and market 261 new, single-family homes (208 detached homes and 53 townhouses) and (2) allowed nonprofit partners to stabilize or restore 55 historic houses.

Workforce Housing Information

As part of the grant requirements set by the U.S. Department of Housing and Urban Development (HUD), 51 percent of the homes in Fall Creek Place were reserved for low- or

The architectural guidelines established by the developer addressed scale, proportions, orientation, and elevation. A local architectural firm produced five prototype home designs. Builders were free to use either the prototypes or their own designs, as long as their designs were consistent with the guidelines.

moderate-income households earning 80 percent or less of the area median income (AMI); the remainder were sold at market rate. (Based on the AMI in Indianapolis, the income-restricted homes were reserved for households with yearly incomes no higher than $35,900 for a one-person household, and $51,300 for a four-person household.)

Site, Surroundings, and History

Located on Indianapolis's Near North Side, the Fall Creek Place site is bounded by Park Avenue on the east, Pennsylvania Street on the west, Fall Creek Parkway on the north, and East 22nd Street on the south. Since the 1950s, the 160-acre (65-hectare) neighborhood had suffered decades of poverty and neglect, losing nearly 80 percent of its housing stock between 1956 and 1999. At the time of the redevelopment, only about 90 owner-occupied homes remained.

Planning, Development, and Entitlements

The redevelopment of Fall Creek Place was launched with the help of a $4 million Homeownership Zone (HOZ) grant from HUD, awarded to the city of Indianapolis in 1998. The HOZ program is designed to support housing construction in blighted urban areas. The grant was obtained through a partnership between the city of Indianapolis and the King Park Area Development Corporation.

Upon receiving the federal grant, the city of Indianapolis initiated a yearlong urban design

Mansur Real Estate

and master-planning process. The goal was to reinvent the blighted inner-city neighborhood and create a diverse, mixed-income community providing a range of housing choices. In 2000, the city selected Mansur Real Estate Services, a local company specializing in urban development, as the project developer. Mansur would oversee the implementation of the Fall Creek Place master plan and coordinate the builder-selection process for the construction of the new homes.

The city decided that its role would be to lay the groundwork for the project by providing the necessary infrastructure and offering incentives for redevelopment. The city hoped that by removing some of the many barriers to redevelopment, it could attract builders and homebuyers—and let the private sector assume most of the traditional development responsibilities, including home construction, construction financing, marketing, and home sales.

The city used the HUD grant primarily to acquire the property and to relocate residents who had been living in substandard rental housing. The city allocated Community Development Block Grant and HOME funds to provide qualified homebuyers with down-payment assistance.

The city also committed $10 million to infrastructure improvements, including new streets, curbs, sidewalks, alleys, streetlights, and landscaping. The improvements were funded by a bond approved by the city-county council in 2001. The infrastructure investment also included water and sewer connections for each lot, a pre-construction outlay that helped to keep housing prices affordable. Finally, to provide fully buildable homesites, the city underwrote the costs of removing subsurface debris that was left after the demolition of housing units.

Project management for Fall Creek Place was similar to that for a conventional subdivision,

Mansur Real Estate

with model homes, lot purchases, multiple builders, and many choices for buyers. However, instead of simply selling lots to individual builders, which is the approach used for many subdivisions, Mansur focused its marketing efforts on attracting potential homeowners to the development and allowing them to choose their lot, builder, and home type.

In conjunction with the construction of new homes, the King Park Area Development Corporation and the Historic Landmarks Foundation of Indiana are working to stabilize or renovate 55 historic homes in the neighborhood.

Slightly less than half of the homes in Fall Creek Place were sold at market-rate prices. The affordable units were successfully integrated with the market-rate homes.

Financing

Both builders and buyers have received financial assistance. The project team (the city, Mansur, and the King Park Area Development Corporation) originally brought in eight builders to launch home construction, a number that has since settled at five. To provide equal opportunity for builders of all sizes, the project team provided each builder with funding to construct one model home, and worked with local banks to provide each builder with a line of credit.

The city invested $10 million in infrastructure improvements, including new streets, curbs, sidewalks, alleys, streetlights, and landscaping.

Mansur Real Estate

The project team also established a process to assist buyers with their home purchase. Six local banks are offering mortgages to buyers at an average of 1 percent below market rates. Interested buyers submit a mortgage application to one of these lenders. The lender provides a preapproval letter that indicates (1) the loan amount for which the buyer qualifies and (2) the total amount of downpayment assistance for which the buyer is eligible, depending on household income. A buyer who has been preapproved by one of the participating lenders is permitted to reserve a homesite and choose a builder and home type. All buyers, whether low- or moderate-income or market rate, can choose any house they wish, and are limited only by what they can afford to purchase.

The city also assists buyers with downpayments. Depending on income level and household size,

low- and moderate-income households are eligible for up to $24,000 in downpayment assistance. All such assistance is financed as a soft second mortgage, fully amortized after five to ten years. To stimulate interest during the first six months after the project was launched, market-rate homebuyers were also offered matching downpayment assistance of up to $10,000.

Provided that their building permit was issued before December 31, 2002, all homebuyers were eligible for a five-year, 100 percent property-tax abatement on the first $36,000 of assessed valuation. In 2002, this represented an annual savings of about $1,300.

Through the combination of downpayment assistance, a below-market-rate mortgage, and the property-tax abatement, a household that would ordinarily qualify for a $100,000 home can instead afford a $140,000 home. The incentives have been highly successful in drawing buyers of all income levels to Fall Creek Place.

Design and Architecture

The design goals for the new neighborhood had three priorities: to maintain the historic character of the area (including the original urban street grid); to make the homes for low- and moderate-income households indistinguishable from the market-rate units; and to incorporate affordability into good design.

The architectural guidelines established by Mansur, the city of Indianapolis, and the Historic Landmarks Foundation of Indiana address characteristics such as scale, proportions, orientation, and elevation. As in other new urbanist developments, required features include double-hung windows, deep front porches, and detached, rear-entry garages with alley access. Working with Mansur, a local architectural firm produced five prototype homes consistent with the design guidelines. As long as the guidelines are observed, builders at Fall Creek Place may use these prototypes or provide their own designs. However, before a home plan can receive a city building permit, it must be approved by a design review committee that includes representatives from Mansur, the city, and the project architectural firm.

Marketing and Operations

Mansur is in charge of an umbrella marketing program for the entire project, which was originally capitalized through $250,000 in seed money provided by the city of Indianapolis. Additional funding for the marketing program

Mansur Real Estate

Fall Creek Place has been transformed from a crime-ridden, 26-block area into an attractive, mixed-income residential neighborhood. The renaissance was brought about by new construction and by the renovation of existing homes.

After receiving a $4 million federal grant, the city of Indianapolis launched a year-long design and master-planning process; the result was the Fall Creek Place master plan.

under contract during the first year—far more than the 40 that had been projected by the market study. Over half the buyers had previously resided in or near downtown, and 60 percent were first-time homebuyers. Most buyers are either single professionals or young married couples; many are gay. Nearly 10 percent of the households have dependent children. Fall Creek Place is also somewhat diverse: while 75 percent of the residents are white, the rest are either African American, Hispanic, Asian, or Native American.

Experience Gained

The local government should anticipate the reasons that builders, developers, and lenders may be reluctant to invest in the inner city, and should be aware that the target market may be reluctant to move there. Local government representatives must be prepared to readily answer questions about design, affordability, land assembly, and neighborhood safety.

It is essential to include members of the community in the planning process and to establish public support before implementation. In Indianapolis, strong support from Mayor Peterson's office helped the project gain credibility with the public.

Public sector sponsors should bring in private sector leadership. Mansur helped the city define where it could provide the most help—through subsidies and incentives that advanced the project.

The project team must have a clearly defined structure for the project that specifies the duties of the city, the developer, and the builders. In this case, the city determined that its goal was to provide the necessary incentives to launch the mixed-income development; it then brought in a

comes from a 1.5 percent marketing fee (with a maximum of $2,500) that builders pay on each home sale. This fee is calculated as part of the total closing costs and is not due until a home has sold.

The marketing program has included brochures and flyers, special events, and a Web page highlighting the project. The Fall Creek Place Welcome Center, funded in part by a $50,000 donation from Citizens Gas and Coke Utility, provides general information about the community; describes the purchase incentives and available homesites; lists builders with a description of their model homes; and explains how to purchase a home in the neighborhood.

The target market for an urban mixed-income project is broad and can be difficult to identify. Nevertheless, more than 200 new homes came private developer to oversee the project. The developer worked directly with the builders, who purchased lots and financed construction of the homes.

It should be possible for builders of all sizes—from large to small—to participate. The builders involved in Fall Creek Place include both larger, production builders and smaller, custom home-builders; several woman-owned and minority-owned builders also participated.

It is important to allow sufficient funds for marketing, and to make a good impression upfront. By providing an inviting welcome center and undertaking a strong marketing effort—one that includes literature, special events, model homes, and a Web presence—project sponsors can create an appealing image that breeds further success.

Good design should be incorporated throughout the development. Low- and moderate-income units should not be distinguishable from market-rate units.

A variety of financial incentives will be needed to meet the goal of creating a mixed-income development. Below-market-rate mortgages, downpayment assistance, and a residential tax abatement were highly successful in helping to generate a strong demand from all income levels for units at Fall Creek Place.

Mansur Real Estate

Safety is a key element in the success of urban communities. Local leaders should be prepared for questions about the safety of proposed projects.

Mansur Real Estate

The 53 townhouses constructed as part of the revitalization of Falls Creek Place provide affordability and broaden the options for residents who are seeking less home maintenance.

Fall Creek Place

Primary Contact

Chris Palladino, AICP
317-464-8200
cpalladino@mresi.com
www.fallcreekplace.com

Project Team

Development Team
Chris Palladino
Project Manager
Mansur Real Estate Services, Inc.
700 Market Tower, 10 West Market Street
Indianapolis, Indiana 46204
317-464-8200
cpalladino@mresi.com
www.mansurrealestateservices.com

Jennifer Green
Project Manager
Department of Metropolitan Development
City of Indianapolis
City County Building
Suite 2041
200 East Washington Street
Indianapolis, Indiana 46204
317-327-5861
jcgreen@indygov.org
www.indygov.org/dmd

Robert Frazier
Executive Director
King Park Area Development Corporation
2430 North Delaware Street
Indianapolis, Indiana 46205
317-924-8116
rfrazier@kpadc.org
www.kpadc.org

Architect
Todd Rottmann, AIA
Rottmann Architects
1060 North Capitol Avenue
Suite C-360
Indianapolis, Indiana 46205
317-767-9807
todd@rottmannarchitects.com
www.rottmannarchitects.com

Landscape Architect
Kevin Parsons, ASLA
Kevin K. Parsons and Associates
212 West 10th Street
Suite A-290
Indianapolis, Indiana 46202
317-955-9155
kpa@landarkkt.com
www.landarkkt.com

Master Planners
Don Carter, FAIA, AICP
Urban Design Associates
Gulf Tower
31st Floor
707 Grant Street
Pittsburgh, Pennsylvania 15219
412-263-5200
dcarter@urbandesignassociates.com
www.urbandesignassociates.com

Gina Tirinnanzi, ASLA
The Schneider Corporation
Historic Fort Benjamin Harrison
8901 Otis Avenue
Indianapolis, Indiana 46216
317-826-7319
gtirinnanzi@schneidercorp.com
www.schneidercorp.com

Marketing/Sales
Chris Williams
Hirons and Company
135 South Illinois Street
Indianapolis, Indiana 46225
317-977-2206, ext. 22
cwilliams@hirons.com
www.hirons.com

Rehabilitation
Mark Dollase
Historic Landmarks Foundation of Indiana
1028 North Delaware Street
Indianapolis, Indiana 46202
317-639-4534
central@historiclandmarks.com
www.historiclandmarks.com

Homebuilders
Davis Homes
Minkis Homes
QDB Enterprises, Inc.
RussBow Builders
Vintage Homes

Infrastructure Construction Management
Mansur Construction Services, LLC

Infrastructure General Contractor
Calumet Construction, Inc.

Financial Participation
Bank One
Citizens Gas
City of Indianapolis
Fannie Mae
Fifth Third Bank
Fund for Landmark Indianapolis Properties
Huntington Bank
Indianapolis Bond Bank
Indianapolis Neighborhood Housing Partnership
Key Bank
Local Initiative Support Corporation
National Bank of Indianapolis
National City Bank
U.S. Department of Housing and Urban Development

Development Schedule
Property acquisition started	Fall 1998
Planning started	Fall 1998
Home rehabilitation started	Fall 1999
Master plan and implementation plan completed	Fall 2000
Financing completed	Summer 2001
Infrastructure construction started	Fall 2001
Phase I new home construction started	Fall 2001
Sales and marketing started	Summer 2001
Phase I home sales completed	Spring 2002
Phase II new home construction and sales started	Summer 2002
Phase I and Phase II infrastructure completed	Spring 2003
Phase I new home construction completed	Fall 2003
Phase III infrastructure started	Summer 2003
Phase III new home construction and sales started	Summer/Fall 2003
Phase II new home construction completed	Fall/Winter 2003
Phase III infrastructure completed	Fall 2004
Project completed	Spring 2005

Land Use Information

Total site area: 160 acres (26 city blocks)

Land Use	Acres	Estimated Square Footage (Existing)	Estimated Square Footage (at Buildout)
Retail		10,000	35,000
Office		5,000	5,000
Other (parks)	4.0		

Residential Information

Type and Number of Units

Unit Type	Number of Units at Buildout
New construction	
Single-family detached	315
Single-family attached	47
Rehabilitation	
Single-family detached	44
Single-family attached	14
Total	420

Single-Family Detached Units

Unit Type	Square Footage	Number Sold	Sales Price Range
The Belmont	1,265	18	$108,000–$162,000
The Carrolton	1,620	27	$112,000–$180,000
The Douglass	1,624	7	$110,000–$200,000
The Evanston	1,774	5	$155,000–$230,000
The Fairfield	1,995	18	$135,000–$255,000
The Elizabeth the Third	1,422	3	$140,000–$160,000
The Carson	1,645	2	$155,000–$165,000
The Peterson	2,014	4	$152,000–$188,000
The Georgetown	2,400	10	$156,000–$209,000
The Cottage Grove	1,380	12	$114,000–$151,000
The Street Charles	1,902	2	$209,000–$245,000
The Benjamin I	1,288	9	$109,000–$124,000
The Benjamin II	1,456	15	$119,000–$146,000
The Newport	1,173	12	$94,000–$130,000
The Harrison	1,675	6	$125,000–$149,000
The Savannah	1,320	8	$112,000–$127,000
The Christopher	1,232	5	$113,000–$142,000
The Murray	1,378	4	$124,000–$189,000
The Thurmond	1,384	4	$115,000–$125,000
Other (custom designs)	Various		$165,000–$300,000

Single-Family Attached Units (New Construction Only)

Unit Type	Square Footage	Number Sold	Sales Price Range
Adams Townhomes: Phase I	1,260–1,640	20	$104,900–$134,175
Adams Townhomes: Phase III	1,260–1,640	33	$118,000–$167,000
Park Avenue Townhomes: Phase III	1,650–2,200	7	$157,000–$240,000

Affordable Residential Units (New Construction Only)

Unit Type	Number Sold	Sales Price Range
Adams Townhomes	14	$104,900–$167,000
The Belmont	11	$108,000–$141,000
The Carrolton	12	$112,000–$132,000
The Douglass	3	$110,000–$116,000
The Cottage Grove	9	$114,000–$142,000
The Benjamin I	9	$109,000–$124,000
The Benjamin II	12	$119,000–$145,000
The Newport	10	$94,000–$126,000
The Harrison	3	$125,000–$146,000
The Savannah	8	$112,000–$127,000
The Christopher	4	$113,000–$116,000
The Murray	3	$124,000–$136,000
The Thurmond	4	$115,000–$125,000
Other low- to moderate-income homes	16	$101,000–$136,000

(Information continued on next page)

Development Costs

Site acquisition	$4,000,000
Relocation and demolition	$1,200,000
Downpayment assistance	$3,800,000
Site improvement	
Subsurface debris removal	$3,100,000
General cleanup and lot	
maintenance	150,000
Earthwork	950,000
General conditions[a]	1,300,000
Fall Creek improvements	250,000
Drainage and storm	
improvements	400,000
Sanitary taps	700,000
Water laterals and meter pits	500,000
Paving and milling	
(streets and alleys)	1,750,000
Curbs	900,000
Sidewalks	1,100,000
Street lighting	250,000
Parks	600,000
Street trees	450,000
Decorative pavers	
and monuments	300,000
Traffic-signal upgrades	
and bus shelters	100,000
Subtotal, site improvement	$12,800,000
Construction management	$700,000
Total	$13,500,000

a. Includes change orders added to budget after infrastructure construction was begun.

Construction Costs

Rehabilitation costs, single-family units
$80,000–$165,000

Average Hard Construction Cost[a]

Single-family homes	$55–$65 per square foot[b]
Townhomes	$52–$57 per square foot

a. Excludes lot purchase price, builder's overhead, and profit.
b. Depending on the level of finish, the cost per square foot for some homes was $80 or more.

Soft Costs[a]

Engineering, staking,	
and inspections	$1,200,000
Landscape architect	
(parks, trails, streetscape)	100,000
Master architect	95,000
Master planning and	
infrastructure plan	300,000
Developer fees	1,600,000
Not-for-profit project sponsor fees	330,000
Legal and accounting	150,000
Title fees, survey, and closing costs	400,000
Marketing	500,000
Appraisals	200,000
Environmental and	
geotechnical testing	110,000
Total	$4,985,000

a. Applicable only to overall site development; excludes any soft costs related to specific residential or commercial construction.

Greenleaf Village
West Dallas, Texas

Project Information

For decades, West Dallas, Texas, was best known for its deteriorating federal housing units and for factories belching pollution into the air. Home to the largest low-rise public housing project in the United States and to a lead smelter that operated for 50 years, the area was once referred to as "forgotten Dallas." Today, both the image and reality of West Dallas have changed dramatically. A series of court rulings led to the demolition of most of the public housing units, the smelter was razed, and an environmental cleanup was undertaken in the smelter site and in the adjacent properties.

In the forefront of the revival of West Dallas is Greenleaf Village, a new, mixed-income community of 310 single-family homes. Greenleaf Village is the result of a partnership among public, private, and nonprofit organizations: the Dallas Housing Authority (DHA), KB Home and American CityVista (working jointly), and the Dallas Area Habitat for Humanity.[1] The partnership represents a national model for creating new, large-scale, economically integrated communities designed to expand homeownership opportunities in a redevelopment area.

Workforce Housing Information

The new community is located on a 75-acre (30-hectare) portion of the 460 acres (186 hectares) that formerly contained 3,500 public housing units. KB Home and American City-Vista built 210 homes, and the Dallas Area Habitat for Humanity built 100. All units are single-family detached homes; lots average 5,100 to 5,350 square feet (474 to 497 square meters), and the homes—all of which are air-conditioned—range in size from 1,200 to over 3,300 square feet (111 to 307 square meters). To provide residents with access to the wealth creation and tax shelters not usually available to people in the income groups served by the community, all homes are for-sale units.

The homes constructed by American CityVista and KB Home (one of the largest homebuilders in the country) are considered market-rate workforce housing and are not income restricted. Although American CityVista and KB Home reported that purchasers represented a wide range of income groups, most households reported incomes between $23,000 and $58,000—that is, between 50 and 80 percent of the area median income (AMI) for a family of four in the Dallas region. The Greenleaf Village homes constructed by American CityVista and KB Home sold for between $90,000 and $160,000.

The Dallas Area Habitat for Humanity built all the homes that were not constructed by American CityVista and KB Home. The 100 homes built by Habitat were reserved for households whose incomes were between 25 and 50 percent of AMI. For the Dallas region, this translated to an annual income of between $16,000 and $32,000 for a family of four. To ensure that the neediest households were served, Habitat strictly enforced the upper income limit of 50 percent of AMI; households with incomes above 50 percent of AMI had a chance of qualifying for a market-rate home from American CityVista or KB Home.

In April of 2002, Habitat for Humanity conducted a "blitz build" in which 1,500 volunteers built the first 25 homes in Greenleaf Village.

Site, Surroundings, and History

As noted earlier, the Greenleaf Village site was the former location of one of the largest public housing projects in the country; by the early 1990s, the 460-acre (186-hectare) development had become severely blighted. In 1992, a series of reports in the *Dallas Morning News* painted a grim picture: "Sadly, the worst housing in West Dallas today exists within the federal developments themselves, at least two-thirds of the low-income units are boarded up and deteriorating, row after row of apartments stand vacant behind barbed wire. They are silent, but eloquent testament to the failure of the public housing system in West Dallas." Eventually, the situation became so dire that the courts issued what became known as the Walker Consent Decree, which led to the demolition of the 3,500 public housing units. Included in the decree was a requirement that no more than 900 units be rebuilt on the site.

Along with the demolition of the public housing, the removal of the lead-smelting operation, which had long polluted the neighborhood, was integral to laying the groundwork for reinvestment and revitalization. In 2001, the smelting operation, along with its 300-foot- (91-meter-) high smokestack, was meticulously removed. Also removed were over 46,000 cubic yards (35,170 cubic meters) of contaminated soil from 420 residences and from schools, playgrounds, and parks. In 2003, the smelter owners and two subsidiaries agreed to reimburse the EPA and the state of Texas for more than $25 million in cleanup costs, and to continue to clean up the site.

Once the failed public housing had been removed and the smelting operation had been shut down and cleaned up, the community's assets became more apparent. West Dallas is conveniently located just minutes from downtown Dallas, and the Greenleaf Village site is within a mile (1.6 kilometers) of the Texas Medical

To qualify for a Habitat home, applicants were required to provide two years of tax returns, to have the legal right to work in the United States, and to commit 400 hours of time to work on the house. The qualification process generated a waiting list of three to nine months for the Habitat homes, which sold for $65,000. The homes required no downpayment, and purchasers received 25-year, no-interest loans financed by the Dallas Area Habitat for Humanity.

Center, one of the region's largest employers, and a short distance from Love Field Airport. With a convenient location and a blank canvas, the DHA was able to create the award-winning Lakewest Master Plan. (Lakewest, a community within West Dallas, includes Greenleaf Village.)

The master plan called for the creation of retail establishments, parks, schools, and a variety of housing types, all to be situated in independent urban villages. The new community of Lakewest features upgraded retail, including a grocery store, a gas station, a Subway, a Payless Shoes, and a KFC/Taco Bell. A housing development for seniors (funded by the U.S. Department of Housing and Urban Development {HUD}) is nearby, as is a YMCA named after Alphonso Jackson, secretary of HUD and former head of the DHA. The DHA sold parcels of land to Goodwill Industries, which is now one of the largest employers in the area. New industrial and office development in nearby Pinnacle Park also created new job opportunities, which helped foster the revitalization of West Dallas.

Planning, Development, and Entitlements

Philip Wise, a Dallas-area real estate developer and former chairman of the board of the Dallas Area Habitat for Humanity, first suggested the unique idea of a collaboration between a for-profit developer, a nonprofit developer, and a public agency. Wise hopes that the partnership will become a model for similar programs nation-wide. Beginning in January 2000, Wise began to work with the DHA and the Dallas Area Habitat for Humanity to see whether a potential partnership with the DHA and Habitat could be used to attract a private developer to the West Dallas housing project. Despite the appeal of bringing privately developed housing to the

The community includes two parks, and over 10 percent of the site is reserved as green space.

site, the challenges of marrying public sector and private sector culture made for slow progress. Nevertheless, after six months of effort, Wise was able to bring one of the nation's largest homebuilders into the partnership, and work began on a market study and on the Lakewest Master Plan.

Although the market study showed demand for market-priced homes in the new community, progress remained slow—and, after two years, the private homebuilder dropped out. Wise and the Dallas Area Habitat for Humanity pushed on, and by 2002, American CityVista, a for-profit developer of workforce housing, entered into a joint venture with homebuilder KB Home, and the two private entities agreed to join the project.

Habitat for Humanity is the largest national nonprofit homebuilder, and the Dallas affiliate, formed in 1985, is now the seventh-largest homebuilder in Dallas. With Habitat's commit-

Cienda Partners

Jennifer Backover

In keeping with the low-density development typical of the Dallas suburbs, the 310 homes at Greenleaft Village are all detached, single-family units, and are laid out in a typical suburban pattern.

tional neighborhoods where market-rate housing, without income restrictions, can be made affordable to working families.

An infill development of Greenleaf's size is large enough to create a community with its own civic identity. To attract first-time home-buyers, the market-rate homes were priced at or below the median price. Through outreach efforts undertaken by Habitat for Humanity, the project was linked to the schools, neighborhood institutions, and churches of West Dallas.

The idea for Greenleaf Village was presented to the DHA in January 1999; roughly 32 months of discussion and planning followed, and the project was publicly announced in November 2001. Because of the blighted conditions in the surrounding area, there was no community opposition to the new development proposal. Nor were there any issues regarding zoning, setback requirements, or wetlands. The mayor and the city council were supportive of the project and integral to its success; however, the nonprofit and private partners reported difficulties dealing with the bureaucracy of the DHA. Initially, the DHA wanted to serve as the developer of the project, which was unacceptable to all the other parties.

The DHA owned the land on which Greenleaf Village was to be situated, and was under a court order to dismantle the higher-density low-income housing projects on the site. By 2002, the partnership between DHA, Habitat for Humanity, CityVista, and KB Home had been formed, and most of the public housing on the 460-acre (186-hectare) site had been razed, including all the structures on the Greenleaf Village site. DHA contracted out the infrastructure according to the master plan prepared by the partnership, and sold lots to KB Home and Habitat for $18,500 per lot—the cost of completing the infrastructure. By April of 2002, Habitat for Humanity had purchased 50 lots and begun construction on the first 28 homes.

ment to build and to provide 100 percent financing for the first 100 homes, American CityVista and KB Home agreed to build the remaining 210 homes. American CityVista was founded in 2000 by former HUD secretary Henry Cisneros; its mission is to create "villages within a city" in inner-city neighborhoods. Greenleaf Village fit in with the plans of American CityVista and KB Home, which focus on transi-

To celebrate the beginning of construction, Habitat held events that generated excitement and publicity: in March 2002, Habitat constructed all its model homes during a "24-hour build." The next month, Habitat conducted a "25-home blitz build": in a nine-day period, over 1,500 volunteers built the first 25 homes in Greenleaf Village. It was the largest such effort ever undertaken by the Dallas Area Habitat for Humanity.

Both events proved tremendously successful in generating public interest and support for the new community. The blitz build received extensive press coverage—and, more importantly, significant corporate support from Bank of America, the Dallas Bar Association, Exxon Mobil, and other private sector organizations. In addition to its public relations value, the blitz build provided a terrific jump start for the community. New residents had neighbors immediately, and potential buyers had a sense of the community's ultimate form. The first move-ins were in July 2002, and the first resident of the community was Arvvel Wilson, pastor of the West Dallas Church and School, which was situated on an adjacent site. Wilson had spent the previous 20 years working in the West Dallas community.

The rest of the community was constructed in various phases, and the last homes were complete within 20 months of the start date. The homes sold quickly; in fact, one-third sold before ground breaking.

Financing

As noted earlier, the lots were sold to Habitat and to KB Home for $18,500 each, which was what it cost the DHA to build out the infrastructure. Because of cost overruns, the city of Dallas stepped in with a $450,000 grant to Habitat, which made it possible to write down the cost of a lot to $14,000, and thus make the

All homes in Greenleaf Village were required to have brick on three sides. Accepting the reality of the auto-dependent Dallas lifestyle meant providing all homes with a driveway and a garage.

homes affordable to working families. The homebuilders also used Dallas's Developer Fee Rebate Program, which offers a fee rebate of $2,500 per home, provided that it is located within the city limits and is sold to a low- or moderate-income buyer.

Habitat provided 100 percent financing for each of its homes. For buyers of American CityVista and KB Home units, several options were available to make the homes more affordable, including special financing programs from KB Home Mortgage. In addition, Fannie Mae's zero downpayment/zero closing costs mortgage product was available to police officers, firefighters, teachers, and nurses.

Habitat for Humanity also obtained funding from HUD's Self-help Homeownership Opportunity Program (SHOP), which grants money to eligible national and regional nonprofit organizations for the construction of affordable housing

The market-rate homes range in size from 1,200 to 3,300 square feet (111 to 307 square meters) and have two-car garages; the affordable homes average 1,250 square feet (116 square meters) and have one-car garages.

Jennifer Backover

in cases where the homebuyer puts a significant amount of sweat equity into the home.

Design and Architecture

Dallas is a relatively low-density city: the majority of the population lives in single-family homes in the suburbs. Greenleaf Village was therefore designed according to a traditional suburban plan, with single-family homes located on modest-sized lots. The master plan includes two parks, and over 10 percent of the property was set aside as green space. To give the community a sense of identity, the plan includes 37-foot- (11-meter-) wide streets with cul-de-sacs and elbows, and a masonry screening wall with monumental features at the community entrances.

The Habitat for Humanity lots were clustered together in four locations throughout the community. Since the Habitat homes tended to be smaller than the American CityVista and KB Home units, clustering the lots created more cohesiveness and avoided jarring contrasts between the Habitat homes and the other units.

All homes in Greenleaf Village were required to be faced with brick on three sides. The American CityVista and KB Home units ranged in size from approximately 1,200 to 3,300 square feet (111 to 307 square meters). Several models— one-story and two-story homes, with 12 different

West Dallas, where Greenleaf Village is located, is just minutes from downtown Dallas. Greenleaf Village is convenient to the Texas Medical Center and Love Field Airport.

Cienda Partners

floor plans—were offered. Units featured three to four bedrooms, two to three baths, and a two-car garage. The Habitat for Humanity units averaged 1,250 square feet (116 square meters) and had three bedrooms, one-and-a-half baths, and a one-car garage. All homes were constructed to meet Energy Star guidelines.

Like other cities in the West and Southwest, Dallas is relatively auto-dependent; however, Greenleaf Village is transit accessible, and some residents who cannot afford to own cars rely entirely on mass transit. Other residents use one car for all their transportation needs. Because of access to mass transit and limited car ownership, there has not been a parking problem at Greenleaf Village.

Four principles guided the development of Greenleaf Village: homeownership, safety in scale, mixed income, and mixed use. The developers of Greenleaf Village view homeownership as the foundation for wealth creation and the development of strong communities. Because the project partners prefer to construct larger developments, it was possible for them to create a new community, and therefore to build safety into the project. Mixed-income communities have diverse populations and offer opportunities for low-income families to move up without having to move out. Mixed-use communities provide needed services in close proximity to homes, limiting the time spent driving to take care of everyday needs. Now that there is over $40 million in new homes at Greenleaf Village, the project partners hope that service providers will be encouraged to locate in the community.

Marketing and Operations

As would be expected, the opportunity to purchase a new, single-family home at a price affordable to working families was well received. By

Jennifer Backover

Jennifer Backover

April 2002, before the ground breaking, fully one-third of the American CityVista and KB Home and American CityVista units had been sold. The two construction events conducted by Habitat for Humanity generated both positive news coverage and significant interest in the community.

Almost all the buyers of the Habitat homes were families; although the buyers of the KB Home and American CityVista units were more

A masonry screening wall at the entrance of the community.

mixed, the majority were also families. The fore-closure rate for the homebuyers was quite low: only five of the 310 households have been foreclosed on to date, and the property values in the community have steadily increased.

A homeowners' association was formed to address the maintenance of common areas and the enforcement of deed restrictions. Dues are an affordable $25 per month and increase annually by 15 percent. The association was handed over from the developer to the residents in 2004.

Experience Gained

Building at a large scale can transform a neighborhood and create value. In the case of Greenleaf Village, the sheer size of the new community transformed the surrounding area of West Dallas. A smaller project would not have been able to overcome the negative image that West Dallas had acquired over the years.

Writing down the land costs and providing clean, developable building lots (including infrastructure) were integral to the financial feasibility of the project: these two steps removed a substantial amount of risk for developers and builders, and allowed the units to be sold for a price that was affordable to working families.

A partnership between a for-profit builder, a nonprofit builder, and a government agency can work if the roles and expectations of each party are clearly defined. Clarity about the role of the governmental agency is especially important. Private sector firms that are not normally subject to government protocol and that are accustomed to setting and meeting their own strict deadlines may view some public sector processes as time consuming and redundant. In the case of Greenleaf Village, the private sector partners reported that the project might have been developed more quickly if the role of the DHA had been limited to razing the existing buildings.

A highly publicized "blitz build" can generate both substantial interest in a new community and significant corporate support.

Note
1. American CityVista is now known as CityView.

Greenleaf Village

Primary Contact

Philip Wise
214-269-1623
pwise@cienda.com

Project Team

Owner/Developer
Dallas Area Habitat for Humanity
2800 North Hampton Road
Dallas, Texas 75212
214-678-2300
Info@Dallas-Habitat.org
www.dallas-habitat.org

CityView (formerly American CityVista)
454 Soledad
Suite 300
San Antonio, Texas 78205
210-228-9574
www.city-view.net

Builder/Marketing/Sales Agency
KB Home
10990 Wilshire Boulevard
Los Angeles, California 90024
310-231-4000
www.kbhome.com

Development Schedule

Planning started	January 2000
Site purchased	March 2002
Construction started	March 2002
Sales started	March 2002
Phase I completed	April 2002
Project completed	February 2004

Land Use Information

Total site area	75 acres
Total number of detached, single-family residential units	300

Residential Information

Single-Family Detached Units

Number of units sold	300
Square footage	1,200–3,300
Sales prices	$65,000–$160,000

Affordable Residential Units

Number of affordable units	100
Targeted income group	25–50% of area median income
Sales price	$65,000

Development Costs

Site acquisition	$0
Site improvement	
Excavation	$250,000
Paving	1,400,000
Landscaping and irrigation	150,000
Subtotal, site improvement	$1,800,000
Fees and general conditions	$470,000
Other	$3,230,000
Total	$5,500,000

The Mills of Carthage
Cincinnati, Ohio

Project Information

The Mills of Carthage is a 13-acre (5.3-hectare) single-family housing development built on a former industrial site in Cincinnati, Ohio. One of the largest manufactured-housing developments built in an urbanized area, the project has successfully demonstrated that manufactured housing can be designed for urban environments. Such housing offers an attractive option for municipalities and developers interested in bringing new, affordable, single-family housing to infill sites.

Workforce Housing Information

The Center for Housing Policy estimates that nearly 10 percent (19,970) of working families in the Cincinnati metropolitan statistical area have critical housing needs.[1] "Critical housing need" means either that more than half of total household income is spent on housing, or that a household is living in a severely inadequate unit.

Currently, the city of Cincinnati does not offer any specific incentives to develop workforce housing; nor was the Mills of Carthage developed as workforce housing. Nevertheless, the Mills of Carthage qualifies as a workforce housing project simply because of the low cost of manufactured housing. According to the Manufactured Housing Institute, per-square-foot construction costs for a new manufactured home are, on average, between 10 and 35 percent lower than those for a comparable site-built home, depending on the region of the country.[2] The lower costs realized through the factory construction process offer one way to combat the high development costs associated with infill development—costs that can drive prices out of the range of affordability for working families.

Site, Surroundings, and History

Carthage, a neighborhood of about 2,500 located on the northern side of Cincinnati, has not seen a large-scale housing development in 40 years. The Mills of Carthage is being built on 13 acres (5.3 hectares) formerly occupied by a linoleum factory called Carthage Mills. The site was surrounded by single-family homes that were largely owned and occupied by mill workers. The area is bisected by a major rail line that served the linoleum factory and other nearby industrial uses. In the 1970s, the linoleum factory relo-

Courtesy of Potterhill Homes

Every home at the Mills of Carthage has a two-car detached garage.

The Urban Design Project of the Manufactured Housing Institute

It was the Urban Design Project of the Manufactured Housing Institute (MHI) that inspired Potterhill Homes to take on the challenge of developing manufactured housing in urban areas. In the fall of 1995, MHI, which is the national trade organization for all segments of the factory-built housing industry, created the Urban Design Project to demonstrate that manufactured housing (1) could be built in urban areas and (2) could meet urban needs for affordable, market-rate housing.

The project had four goals: first, to highlight manufactured housing as an option for addressing the barriers to infill housing development; second, to show how to overcome zoning and regulatory barriers that can prohibit manufactured housing from being developed in urban areas; third, to demonstrate that manufactured homes can be made compatible with existing neighborhoods; and fourth, to show that because of the cost savings associated with the production process, manufactured-housing units could be sold at prevailing market prices and still be affordable to many buyers, reducing the need for subsidies.

Through a request-for-proposals process, MHI chose five cities to participate in the program: Birmingham, Alabama; Louisville, Kentucky; Milwaukee, Wisconsin; Washington, D.C.; and Wilkinsburg, Pennsylvania. MHI selected Philadelphia-based Susan Maxman &

Partners Ltd. to oversee the development process for each city's team. At each site, one or two homes were designed (through community input), constructed, and then placed on the market. The results varied: for example, the Washington, D.C., homes sold quickly, but the Milwaukee project failed because the nonprofit developer went bankrupt. Through both successes and failures, MHI identified several lessons, many of which were reinforced by the Mills of Carthage project:

■ It is important to identify new markets for manufactured housing.
■ Focus groups can be used to help change public perceptions of manufactured housing.
■ The entire development team should be familiar with the culture and language of manufactured housing.
■ The entire development team should be familiar with the processes and terminology associated with manufactured housing.
■ Project sponsors need to ensure that local building departments are educated about the characteristics of manufactured housing.
■ Developers should be prepared for a learning curve with manufactured housing.
■ The crews responsible for setting and finishing the housing on site should be experienced with manufactured housing.

cated to expand operations and gain better highway access. The building then became a warehousing facility, which moved goods in and out by truck. But neither the surrounding street network nor the building itself were suited to 18-wheel truck traffic. A series of different owners did little to improve the site.

By the 1980s, in response to constant truck traffic and the deterioration of the former factory building, residents—led by the Carthage Civic League, a neighborhood organization—lobbied the city to fix the situation. The problem caught the mayor's attention, and the city eventually brokered a deal with the property owners, who moved to a more suitable site within the city. Between 1998 and 2001, the city council appro-

priated $8.5 million in general funds to acquire and clean up the site, demolish the existing buildings, and make infrastructure and streetscape improvements.

Planning and Development

The first step in the development processes was to clean up the site. Fortunately, contamination was minimal: the fairly typical list of brownfield issues included buried storage tanks, paint waste, asbestos, and a few areas of petroleum contamination along the rail spur.

While the buildings were being demolished and the site was being cleaned up, the city planning department developed six potential uses for the site, of which housing was the most

The rear of the detached garage can be accessed from the rear of the house.

expensive option. The surrounding residents initially wanted the site to be made into a park, but both the residents and the city ultimately agreed that single-family housing was the most appropriate use, given the surrounding single-family neighborhood.

The Carthage Civic League hired the Pittsburgh urban design firm Urban Design Associates (UDA) to develop a site proposal for single-family housing that would be based on the architecture and spatial characteristics of the surrounding neighborhood. Armed with the UDA site proposal, the city invited proposals from developers and received plans for large, single-family homes with price tags of $200,000 or more. Although these proposals were not compatible with the surrounding neighborhood, either in price or in size, they were the only way that traditional housing developers could envision turning a profit on a relatively small infill site.

The city and Carthage faced a dilemma that is all too common in urban areas: how to develop housing that is both affordable for middle-class buyers and profitable for developers. At this point, Potterhill Homes—a producer of high-quality manufactured homes—became involved with the project.

Potterhill is a division of Holiday Homes, a large developer of manufactured homes in the Ohio, Indiana, and Kentucky tristate area. Holiday had historically built in rural or exurban areas, where manufactured housing has typically been built. But after seeing the Manufactured Housing Institute's Urban Design Project, Holiday decided to diversify its line of manufactured homes, and founded Potterhill to provide affordable, traditionally designed, single-family homes in urban areas.

Potterhill had been building manufactured homes on scattered sites throughout Cincinnati and was looking for a larger infill project. Herman Bowling, the city's project manager at the Carthage site, was familiar with the work that Potterhill had done; he contacted Carolyn Rolfes, Potterhill's president, to let her know about the project and its goal of developing affordable single-family homes. Bowling also shared UDA's concept work with Rolfes.

Carolyn Rolfes jumped at the chance to work on a larger infill site and submitted a proposal to Bowling that called for the development of 60 manufactured single-family homes and for the creation of a public architectural review board to approve home designs. She also promised that Potterhill would put on a home show to market the project in conjunction with the Manufactured Home Builders Symposium, which was scheduled to take place in Cincinnati in the fall of 2002. Both the Manufactured Housing Institute and the Automated Builders' Consortium were planning to hold their annual seminars and conferences in conjunction with the symposium.

Since the city had already rezoned the property as single-family residential after the UDA study, no rezoning, special exceptions, or waivers were necessary. The city resurfaced the streets around the site and was prepared to pay for utility upgrades and new streets, pending the development of the final master plan. Construction of Phase I started in June 2002.

Because both the city and the surrounding community supported the project, Potterhill had few problems during the planning, development, or construction phases. One problem that did crop up was the city building inspectors' lack of familiarity with manufactured housing. Carolyn Rolfes and Herman Bowling worked closely with the inspectors to educate them about the large differences between inspecting manufactured housing and inspecting traditional, frame-built housing.[3]

Financing

As noted earlier, the costs of acquiring the site, demolishing the existing buildings, cleaning up the property, and making infrastructure and streetscape improvements were covered by about $8 million from the city's general fund. The city's expenses included the following:

Site acquisition	*$2,100,000*
Resident relocation and job retention	*2,000,000*
Demolition and remediation	*2,100,000*
Testing, taxes, maintenance, and permits	*250,000*
Engineering services	*250,000*
Staff charges	*250,000*
Infrastructure, Phase I	*250,000*
Infrastructure, Phase II	*750,000*
Total	*$7,950,000*

Carolyn Rolfes observed that the project would not have happened without the city's significant financial commitment. After Potterhill purchased the site, the company financed the rest of the project through a private line of credit. While governmental funds were used in predevelopment, no government programs played a role once predevelopment was complete.

The project consists of two phases. Phase I offers units on the perimeter of the site. Because they rely largely on the existing street network

Homes range in size from 1,400 square feet (130 square meters) to 2,296 square feet (213 square meters).

Courtesy of Potterhill Homes

Homes were designed to be compatible with the existing neighborhood architecture.

Courtesy of Potterhill Homes

and utilities, these units were quicker and cheaper to build, and were therefore put up first. Time was particularly important during Phase I because the home show for the project was being held in conjunction with the Manufactured Home Builders Symposium. This schedule allowed less than five months to build, landscape, furnish, and market the project. The 15 homes that were displayed at the home show were built in just over 90 days.

All homes have front porches and a minimum 5/12 roof pitch.

Courtesy of Potterhill Homes

Phase II, in the interior of the site, completed the development. Because of the lack of infrastructure within the site, this phase was more time-consuming and costly.

Financing Incentives for Homeowners

The efficiencies of the manufacturing process are the main reason that manufactured housing is affordable. A controlled environment and assembly-line production techniques eliminate many of the problems associated with site-built housing, such as poor weather, theft, vandalism, and damage to materials stored on site. And, instead of using the subcontracting system employed in the construction of traditional, frame-built housing, manufactured housing relies on factory employees who are trained and managed by one employer—an approach that reduces labor costs. These cost savings are transferred to the buyer. The homes at the Mills of Carthage range from $127,000 to $210,000, an affordable price range in region where the median home value is $116,500.

Neither the state of Ohio, nor Hamilton County, nor the city of Cincinnati offers any specific incentives, such as downpayment assistance, to support workforce housing. Public sector financing assistance is limited to tax abatements: to stimulate the construction of new homes within the city of Cincinnati, Hamilton County allowed owners of any new construction within the city limits to pay taxes only on the value of their land for 15 years (the program expired in 2006). The Mills of Carthage received an additional abatement package through the Ohio Environmental Protection Agency, under which owners are allowed to pay one-half of the land-only property tax for ten years.

There was also some informal assistance from the private sector: according to Carolyn Rolfes, several employers provided mortgage and down-payment assistance for homes at the site.

Design and Architecture

When members of the general public think of manufactured housing, what comes to mind is the typical mobile-home park. For that reason, Potterhill, the city of Cincinnati, and the Carthage Civic League wanted to ensure that the Mills at Carthage homes would showcase the best of what the manufactured-home industry had to offer.

Thanks to a number of technological innovations, the design of manufactured homes has become much more flexible, making it possible to meet the needs of a wide range of rural, suburban, and urban buyers of single-family homes. The combination of design and construction innovations has made it increasingly difficult to tell the difference between a manufactured home and a traditional, frame-built house.

As noted earlier, Potterhill proposed the creation of a design review board to approve or reject proposals for housing designs. The board consisted of the head of the Cincinnati planning department; a senior city architect; a member of the Carthage Civic League; Diane Cordy, a planner with expertise in manufactured-housing design and development; and Dan Rolfes, the chairman of the Manufactured Housing Institute and the president of Holiday Homes.

Potterhill pitched the project at the 2002 regional show of the Midwest Manufactured Housing Association. Proposals had to be single-family homes that would fit on narrow urban lots, be oriented to the street, and mesh with existing housing in the area. Other minimum criteria included a minimum 5/12 roof pitch; front porches on all models; craftsman, Victorian,

Courtesy of Potterhill Homes

American foursquare, bungalow, or farmhouse style; and at least eight-foot (2.4-meter) flat ceilings on the first floor.

Initially, builders had difficulty coming up with proposals that would fit into an urban context. As Carolyn Rolfes notes, Potterhill 'Homes "had to tug most of the builders a long way." The design review board ultimately chose six different builders to develop 15 different house models: the Commodore Corporation, Redman Homes, Schult Homes, Patriot, and Genesis Homes, all based in Indiana, and New Era Building Systems, which is based in Pennsylvania.

The Homes

The 15 models, many of which are named after homebuilding companies from the first quarter of the 20th century, provide a variety of sizes and styles that are compatible with the existing neighborhood architecture and offer options that would appeal to a diverse target market. The

Architectural styles in the Mills of Carthage include a number of styles popular in America in the early 20th century: Victorian, American Foursquare, bungalow, and farmhouse.

All the homes at the Mills of Carthage are market rate. The homes are affordable because of cost savings created through the efficiencies of the manufacturing process.

homes average 1,650 square feet (153 square meters), and all models have at least three bedrooms and two baths. The largest model, the Eames, has 2,296 square feet (213 square meters), three bedrooms (including a master suite with a whirlpool tub), two-and-a-half bathrooms, and an optional fourth bedroom or sitting room. The smallest models, the Ford and the Rookwood, each have 1,400 square feet (130 square meters). All but one of the models offers a master bedroom suite.

Marketing and Operations

Because of the common misconceptions about manufactured housing, marketing was particularly important. In fact, Dan Rolfes identified marketing as crucial to the success of the project. Potterhill hired Dan Pinger Public Relations to handle marketing, and hired the Powers Agency to handle advertising.

The marketing plan for the Mills of Carthage did not shy away from the fact that the homes were manufactured: instead, the plan addressed the manufactured-housing issues upfront, by explaining why manufactured housing was better for the Carthage project site. From the urban-

design demonstration project that had been undertaken by the Manufactured Housing Institute, Dan Rolfes knew that the biggest fear about manufactured housing is the way it looks. But he felt that the home designs chosen by the design review board would speak for themselves—and he was right. Rolfes notes that once people saw that the manufactured housing looked like traditional, frame-built housing, their concerns about manufactured housing largely disappeared.

The marketing campaign used direct mailings, other print media, television, radio, and the Internet to inform the public about the project. Much of the marketing promoted the Mills of Carthage home show. Planned in conjunction with the National Manufactured Home Builders Symposium, the home show became the centerpiece of the symposium. The city, the Home Ownership Center of Greater Cincinnati, Fannie Mae, and Bank One provided funding for and helped market the event. The show was a success: an estimated 5,000 attendees viewed the site and the model homes. Ten new homes were sold in the first two days of the home show.

Experience Gained

The public sector needs to play an active role in preparing infill sites for redevelopment. There are far too many barriers to infill development for municipalities to assume that development will "just happen" on vacant or underused land. The city of Cincinnati deserves credit for taking control of the site, demolishing existing structures, and undertaking site improvements and environmental remediation. Perhaps even more important, however, was the fact that the city worked with the community to articulate multiple visions for the site. Subsequently, both the city's financial support and a community-supported vision combined to reduce uncertainty for the developer.

A developer with experience in manufactured housing, and more specifically, experience in manufactured housing on infill sites, is central to success. Potterhill's knowledge of manufactured housing development allowed the firm to identify issues and provide solutions before they became problems.

Strong partnerships are also essential to success. Coordination and cooperation between the city, Potterhill Homes, and the Carthage Civic League were hallmarks of the development process. From initial planning through construction, Potterhill developed mechanisms, most notably the design review board, that encouraged both public sector and community input.

Potential developers of manufactured housing need to be aware that the urban development process is geared toward traditional, frame-built housing. Potterhill had to work closely with the city's building inspectors to educate them about how manufactured homes are inspected.

Property tax abatements can be a valuable tool. Tax-abatement programs for housing built on infill parcels offer a simple way to promote infill housing to potential homebuyers.

Manufactured housing can succeed in urban areas. The Mills of Carthage illustrates several reasons why manufactured housing can be a competitive option for developing affordable, single-family homes on infill sites. First, it is a viable option for returning marginal land to tax-producing use. Second, since most of the production takes place off site, manufactured housing can be constructed quickly on site, reducing the risk of vandalism and the theft of construction supplies and equipment.

The lower costs of producing manufactured housing allow the developer to turn a profit while still maintaining affordability for homebuyers. Manufactured housing can bring new housing, with modern amenities, into central

Courtesy of Potterhill Homes

cities and first-ring suburbs, many of which have seen very little new-housing construction, let alone affordable housing for middle-income buyers, for many years.

Fifteen different house models were built by six different builders.

Manufactured housing built in an existing urban context must blend in with its surroundings, and should not look like "typical" manufactured housing. By ensuring that the home designs and overall urban design were compatible with those of the surrounding neighborhood, the design review board achieved both of these goals.

Marketing is crucial for manufactured-housing developments. Because of popular misconceptions, marketing manufactured-housing projects is as much about education as it is about selling the product. Potterhill's marketing plan did not try to hide the fact that the housing was manufactured; instead, the plan let the project and the home designs speak for themselves. The coordination between the project opening and the manufactured-housing symposium helped to draw local media interest and also helped the project gain the attention of industry professionals nationwide.

Notes

1. Michael Stegman, Roberto Quercia, and George McCarthy, "Housing America's Working Families," *New Century Housing* 1, no. 1 (2000).

2. Manufactured Housing Institute, "Quick Facts: Trends and Information about the Manufactured Housing Industry," www.manufacturedhousing.org/media_center/quick_facts2003/index.html (accessed October 27, 2003).

3. The inspection of manufactured housing is governed by the Federal Manufactured Home Construction and Safety Standards of the U.S. Department of Housing and Urban Development (known throughout the manufactured-housing industry as the HUD Code). Under the HUD Code, inspection occurs in the factory, while the housing is being constructed; finished homes arrive on site with certification that they have passed inspection.

The Mills of Carthage

Primary Contact

Potterhill Homes
513-575-1491
CRolfes@potterhillhomes.com
www.potterhillhomes.com

Project Team

Owner/Developer

Dan Rolfes and Carolyn Rolfes
Potterhill Homes
100 TechneCenter Drive
Milford, Ohio 45150
513-575-1491
CRolfes@potterhillhomes.com
www.Potterhillhomes.com

Planner

CDS Associates, Inc.
7000 Dixie Highway
Florence, Kentucky 41042
859-525-0544
www.cds-assoc.com

Landscaping

Bard Nurseries
351 West Ohio Pike
Amelia, Ohio 45102
513-732-9355
Potterhill Homes
513-575-1491

Public Relations

Dan Pinger
Dan Pinger Public Relations, Inc.
708 Walnut Street
Cincinnati, Ohio 45202
513-564-0700
www.danpinger.com

Advertising

Powers Agency
1 West Fourth Street
19th Floor
Cincinnati, Ohio 45202
513-721-5353
www.powersagency.com

Sales

Potterhill Homes
513-575-1491

Development Schedule

Site purchased	April 2002
Planning started	October 2001
Phase I started	June 2002
Sales started	September 2002
Phase I completed	Summer 2003
Project completed	Winter 2006/2007

Land Use Information

Total site area	13 acres
Total number of units at buildout	62
Total acreage, single-family detached residential	13 acres

Site Coverage

Use	Square Footage (Existing)	Square Footage (Proposed)
Buildings	54,120	157,440
Streets, surface parking, and sidewalks	27,000	107,600
Yards, landscaping, and open space	281,800	213,400
Total	362,920	478,440

Residential Information

Unit Type	Square Footage	Number of Units Sold	Sales Price Range
Ranch-style floor plan, HUD Code manufactured housing	1,400–1,700	12	$127,000–$175,000
Ranch-style floor plan, modular home	1,600–1,700	1	$155,000–$190,000
Two-story home, HUD Code	1,400–2,000	1	$160,000–$180,000
Two-story home, modular home	1,400–2,300	3	$145,000–$210,000

Development Costs

Site acquisition	$1
Site improvement	
Excavation	$158,560
Sewer, water, and drainage	129,280
Paving	57,008
Curbs and sidewalks	0[a]
Landscaping and irrigation	37,000
Subtotal, site improvement	$381,848
Construction costs	$1,000,000[b]
Soft costs	
Architecture and engineering	$8,600[c]
Leasing and marketing	150,000
Legal and accounting	10,000
Taxes and insurance	5,000
Title fees	1,500
Subtotal, soft costs	$175,100
Total	$1,556,949

a. The city of Cincinnati paid for the curbs and sidewalks.

b. Homes arrived from the factories complete. Potterhill Homes had $1,000,000 worth of housing inventory financed under a construction loan.

c. The city of Cincinnati paid for most of engineering during the brownfield reclamation process; this represents the portion that the city did not pay.

Portland Place
Minneapolis, Minnesota

Project Information

Located in Phillips, a neighborhood just south of downtown Minneapolis, Portland Place is a seven-acre (three-hectare), $11.8-million, 46-unit, mixed-income workforce housing development. Part of a larger effort to revitalize the Phillips neighborhood, the project demonstrates how joint effort on the part of local employers, community development corporations (CDCs), and the public sector can provide mixed-income housing, spur neighborhood revitalization, and prevent the gentrification that so often accompanies redevelopment.

Workforce Housing Information

During the 1990s, Minneapolis–St. Paul was one of many regions in the country that experienced an economic upturn. This economic growth brought both new jobs and a housing crunch: because many of the jobs created in the region were lower-paying service sector jobs, much of the new housing that was being built was out of reach for workers. During the late 1990s, when Portland Place was being planned and developed, the cost of the average home increased at twice the rate of inflation, rental vacancy rates hovered around 1 percent, and rental rates were steadily outpacing renter incomes. Because of the imbalance between the cost of housing and service sector wages, 10 percent (46,496) of the region's working families had critical housing needs.[1]

Statistically, Phillips is one of the most economically depressed neighborhoods in Minne-apolis. It has the classic symptoms of urban decay: deteriorating housing stock, a low-income population, disinvestment, and high crime rates. At the same time, Phillips is home to three large corporate institutions: the Honeywell Corporation, Abbot-Northwestern Hospital, and Children's Hospital and Clinics.

For many years, these firms provided funding for local nonprofit housing developers. Most of these funds were for scattered new construction, rehabilitation, or home-purchase assistance. But this strategy failed to create the critical mass needed to halt the continuing deterioration occurring throughout the neighborhood. Realizing that this scattershot method was not working, Honeywell decided to try a more targeted approach.[2]

For a number of years, Honeywell had been acquiring parcels situated in a two-block area directly to the east of its property. Predominantly composed of debilitated single-family housing, the two blocks were both an eyesore and a locus of criminal activity. In the spring of 1996, Honeywell executives approached Minneapolis city council member Brian Herron and Mayor Sharon Sayles Belton to talk about how the company could make a stronger impact in the neighborhood. As a result of these conversations, it was decided that Honeywell should build on its community development experience by replacing the existing substandard housing with a new housing project on the two blocks to the east of the company's headquarters.

Honeywell's first step was to create a citizens' advisory group consisting of residents from the neighborhoods surrounding the site. Honeywell

Courtesy of LHB and Brian Droege Photography

The design of the townhouses supports the concept of defensible space. Elevated front porches, strategically placed windows, and landscaping all help to create space that is under the control of those who live there.

then teamed up with Project for Pride in Living (PPL), a citywide nonprofit organization dedicated to helping low- and moderate-income people become self-sufficient. PPL brought in three other nonprofit organizations: Habitat for Humanity, Southside Neighborhood Housing Services, and Powderhorn Residents Group. PPL became the lead developer of the project.

Realizing that many different types of organizations were working toward the same end, Honeywell, Abbot-Northwestern Hospital, Children's Hospital and Clinics, several nonprofit CDCs, the city of Minneapolis, Hennepin County, and a number of investors (notably Fannie Mae, U.S. Bank, and the Minneapolis Foundation) formed the Phillips Partnership. The organization's primary goal is to guide, coordinate, and leverage institutional investment to improve the Phillips neighborhood. The partnership focuses on three interconnected concerns: safety, jobs, and housing. Since its inception in 1997, the Phillips Partnership has made considerable progress in making the Phillips neighborhood a better place to live. In particular, the Phillips Partnership was crucial

to helping make Portland Place a success. By becoming the partnership's first success story, Portland Place has helped bolster other projects that the partnership has undertaken—which, in turn, have helped guarantee the long-term success of Portland Place.

One of Honeywell's original goals for Portland Place was to create a mixed-income housing development. In this regard, the project has been a success. Of the 46 units, six were built by Habitat for Humanity for families earning less than 30 percent of the median household income (MHI) for the Metropolitan Statistical Area.[3] The remaining 40 units were marketed to the general public. Of those, 13 were required to be sold to households earning less than 80 percent of MHI. Ultimately, all the units were sold to households earning less than 115 percent of MHI (see table 1).

Affordability was achieved through reductions in the purchase prices of the homes, which were made possible through private and public sector subsidies. Only about 35 percent of the project's total cost was covered by home sales: although the actual cost per unit was just over $252,000, the units in Phase I sold for an average of $99,320.[4] The success of Phase I and a vibrant real estate market pushed the average sales prices for Phase II to $130,700, which is still a considerable reduction from actual costs. Although PPL used many cost-saving design and construction techniques in an effort to keep costs down, building prices in the region escalated during project construction, erasing much of the savings.

There are no mechanisms at Portland Place to guarantee long-term affordability. All the units except those built by Habitat for Humanity are now considered market rate. Chris Wilson, PPL's project manager for Portland Place, acknowledges that this is a drawback to

Table 1: Income Ranges for Portland Place Homebuyers

Percentage of Units	Income Range	Percentage of Median Household Income[a]
13	<$20,000	<30
20	$20,000–$39,999	30–62
21	$40,000–$49,999	63–78
24	$50,000–$59,999	79–94
22	$60,000>	95–115

a. The median household income for the Minneapolis-St. Paul Metropolitan Statistical Area is $63,600.

the project, but it is something that Honeywell insisted on. PPL tried to address long-term affordability for the initial owners through low-maintenance design, the use of long-lasting materials (such as brick for the exteriors), and various energy-saving strategies.

Site and Surroundings

Honeywell and Portland Place are located on the western edge of Phillips, which is bordered by Interstate 35W (part of the Minneapolis–St. Paul beltway system). As noted earlier, Portland Place is a seven-acre (three-hectare) project that covers two square blocks. It is surrounded on the north, east, and south sides by housing that was built largely between 1900 and 1930. The housing is predominantly single family, though in keeping with the pattern of residential development in the first quarter of the 20th century, it includes a smattering of multifamily dwellings. To the west, Portland Place borders the headquarters of the Honeywell Corporation.

Planning and Development

PPL organized meetings in the surrounding neighborhood to discuss Honeywell's parameters for the project:

- All units would be owner occupied;
- There would be no rehabilitations;
- Project density would be about ten dwelling units per acre (25 per hectare);
- Fifth Avenue would be closed to traffic;
- The project would include shared green space;
- A housing association would be formed;
- Design guidelines would be created;
- The majority of units would front Portland Avenue.

For the most part, Honeywell's parameters were well received, although it was decided that Fifth Avenue would remain open and that one home on the site would be rehabilitated.

Synthesizing Honeywell's parameters and the community input, PPL developed four main goals for the project:

- Make a major contribution to the community around Honeywell;
- Provide opportunities for homeownership in order to fight crime and improve the health of the community;

The single-family homes and "twin-homes" were designed to maximize the height of the structures, which helps the development fit in with the larger-scale structures across the street.

Courtesy of LHB and Brian Droege Photography

- Create mixed-income housing;
- Generate interest in the idea and encourage others to partner with neighborhoods to renovate the housing stock and support neighborhood investment.

In the spring of 1997, PPL brought in the LHB Corporation, a full-service architecture and engineering firm, to conduct a series of community design charrettes. The resulting design vision for the two-block area was based on a new urbanist approach, and called for the development of 52 housing units: a mix of single-family homes, duplexes, and townhouses. The homes' architectural styles would maintain the character of the surrounding neighborhood. In keeping with Honeywell's original parameters, the plan called for common space on the interior of each of the two blocks. PPL hired LHB to finalize the master plan and create the plans for the individual units.

Prior to undertaking the Portland Place project, Honeywell already owned about half of the

properties; in the summer of 1997, the firm began to purchase the rest. Meanwhile, LHB finalized the design, and PPL began to move the project through the approval process. Minneapolis has a planned unit development ordinance, which was used on the project in place of the general code. PPL also worked with the city to develop a tax-increment financing (TIF) district for the project. One pressing issue was the relocation of the remaining residents of the two-block development area. PPL worked with its nonprofit partners to successfully relocate the residents.

As Honeywell was working on acquiring the remaining properties, two landowners decided that they were not willing to sell. One property, located on the periphery of the site, was not a significant issue; it will eventually be acquired by PPL. The other property, however, had a prominent location along Portland Avenue, in the middle of the development. The city considered using eminent domain, but PPL and the city ultimately opted instead to incorporate the house into the site plan. Chris Wilson believes that the property detracts from the overall quality of the development, and that eminent domain should have been used.

In late 1997, in partnership with the Green Institute, PPL began demolition of the existing homes. The Green Institute is a Phillips-neighborhood nonprofit that focuses on sustainable community development—that is, development that fosters economic, environmental, and social gains. The institute offers "deconstruction" services, in which buildings are dismantled by hand and the materials are saved for reuse, instead of being sent to the landfill. The practice yields jobs for area residents, reusable materials for sale at the organization's reuse center, and tax deductions to the developers who donate the building materials.

After an intensive bidding process, PPL chose Flannery Construction, of St. Paul, as the pri-

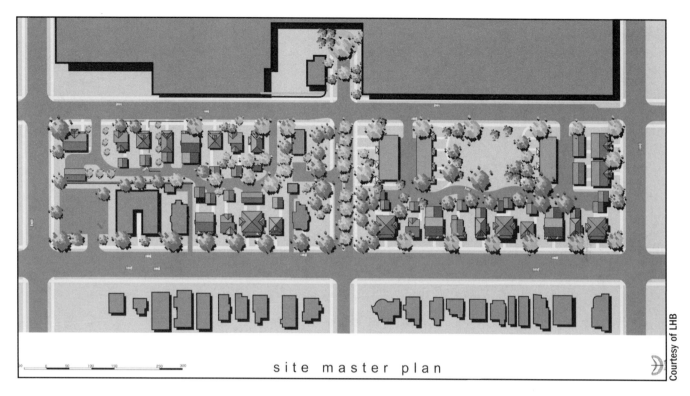

site master plan

Courtesy of LHB

Design and Architecture

mary building contractor. Flannery was chosen, in part, because of its commitment to working with minority contractors. Minneapolis requires that 8 percent of the total skilled labor and 15 percent of the unskilled labor be minority workers. Habitat for Humanity was the other major builder on the site.

The project was completed in two phases to allow for a response to potentially slow sales. Construction on Phase I began in September 1998; by the end of 1999, 30 units had been built and sold to a demographically diverse group of buyers. The unexpectedly early sellout of Phase I made it possible for PPL to use the closing proceeds to pay the construction costs for Phase II, which meant that PPL did not have to draw down a $1 million construction loan that had been approved by U.S. Bank. The success of Phase I also increased the average sales price of the Phase II units by 32 percent, to $130,700.

In developing the site plan, one of the challenges the designers faced was how to create defensible space without isolating the development from the surrounding neighborhood. The environment bordering the development site helped narrow their options. One side of Portland Place faces Portland Avenue, a major street in Phillips. Across Portland Avenue from Portland Place is more housing. The other side of the development faces Fifth Avenue and part of Honeywell's corporate headquarters. Most of the Honeywell property that is adjacent to Portland Place is taken up by a large parking ramp. To integrate the development into the surrounding community and give it a strong, positive presence, the designers oriented the single-family and duplex housing to face Portland Avenue. The site plan opened up the interior of the development for open space and service alleys, and allowed the townhouses to be oriented away from Fifth

Portland Place was designed as a mixed-income, medium-density community in the Phillips neighborhood in Minneapolis.

Table 2: Portland Place Project Financing

	Amount	Terms
Equity		
Honeywell grant	$1,983,440	Equity grant
Honeywell tax-increment financing grant	$1,100,000	Equity grant
Minnesota Housing Finance Agency Community Revitalization Fund grant	$400,000	Equity grant
Fannie Mae Foundation grant	$75,000	Equity grant
Minneapolis Community Development Agency grant	$2,280,000	Equity grant
U.S. Department of Housing and Urban Development (HUD) Section 108 bridge loan	$460,000	Equity grant
HUD Economic Development Initiative grant	$300,000	Equity grant
Family Housing Fund grant	$400,000	Equity grant
Metropolitan Council grant	$250,000	Equity grant
Home sales	$3,899,500	
Debt		
Minneapolis Foundation recoverable predevelopment loan	$200,000	0 percent loan, deferred to closing
Greater Minneapolis Housing Corporation predevelopment loan	$171,000	0 percent loan, deferred to closing
40 mortgages with conventional lenders	$4,057,500	30-year loans at 8.5 percent

Avenue and the parking ramp; instead, they front the open space—an arrangement that allows townhouse residents to control the open areas in front of their homes, a key characteristic of defensible space.

The designers also achieved continuity between Portland Place and the surrounding neighborhood by incorporating existing architectural and urban design patterns into the development. Single-family lots in Portland Place are relatively small, with narrow side yards. For the houses fronting Portland Avenue, the designers matched the setbacks of the homes in the surrounding neighborhoods. Service alleys behind the homes eliminate driveways and garages from the street. The inclusion of front porches and the use of traditional forms and materials reinforced the architectural patterns of the surrounding area.

Financing

Like every other aspect of the project, the financing of Portland Place was a cooperative effort between the private, public, and nonprofit sectors. (See table 2.) Honeywell was the most significant private contributor to the project: its most substantial contribution was the land, which was transferred to PPL for no cost. Honeywell also provided a $1,983,440 grant and financed the tax-increment proceeds ($1,100,000). Honeywell also provided funds for the purchase of playground equipment, donated $146,000 to reduce homeowners' association dues for residents of the Habitat for Humanity units, and outfitted all the housing units with security systems. Other financing from the nonprofit sector included a $400,000 grant from the Minneapolis-based Family

The Minnesota Housing Finance Agency Community Revitalization Fund

Founded in 1971, the Minnesota Housing Finance Agency (MHFA) has established a reputation for successfully addressing the state's basic housing needs and helping to build stronger communities.[1] Since its inception, the MHFA has assisted over 400,000 homeowners by providing funding for a variety of housing needs. The MHFA's mission includes helping first-time homebuyers and assisting in the construction and rehabilitation of affordable apartments, single-family homes, and supportive housing. The agency works in cooperation with other groups, such as Project for Pride in Living, to revitalize older neighborhoods and communities and build new housing for the state's growing workforce.

MHFA accomplishes its mission primarily by providing grants and low-interest loans to builders and buyers of affordable housing. One of the programs administered by the MHFA, the Community Revitalization Fund (CRV), helped to make Portland Place a reality. The goal of the CRV is to maintain and increase the supply of affordable, owner-occupied, single-family housing throughout Minnesota. Funds are provided in the form of a grant, an interest-free or 2 percent interim construction/rehabilitation loan, a deferred loan, or a combination of the three. In the case of Portland Place, the funds came in the form of a grant. Funds can be used for the following:

- Acquisition of land or existing structures;
- Construction or rehabilitation of housing;
- Conversion to housing from another use;
- Demolition or removal of existing structures;
- Interim construction financing;
- Refinancing of existing loans;
- Financing to fill a funding gap (between value and affordability);
- Innovative approaches to housing construction or rehabilitation.

The CRV serves as an umbrella for a variety of limited funding sources. Funding for Portland Place, for example, was obtained through the Economic Development and Housing Challenge Fund Program. Created in 1999 by the Minnesota legislature, the Challenge Program provides state resources that communities can leverage to meet affordable-housing needs. The Challenge Program legislation requires that at least 50 percent of the funds be used in projects that include (1) a financial or in-kind contribution from an area employer, and (2) a contribution from at least one of the following: a local government, a private philanthropic organization, a religious organization, or a charitable organization. Priority is given to proposals that obtain contributions from an area employer. Portland Place was a perfect match for the program.

---

1. For more information on the Community Revitalization Fund, see Minnesota Housing Finance Agency, *Community Revitalization Fund Procedure Guide* (St. Paul: Minnesota Housing Finance Agency), 2003; available at www.mhfa.state.mn.us/homes/CRV%20Manual%20.pdf.

Housing Fund, a $200,000 predevelopment loan from the Minneapolis Foundation, and a $75,000 Fannie Mae Foundation grant.

Public sector financing included a $2,280,000 grant from the Minneapolis Community Development Agency; a $400,000 grant from the Minnesota Housing Finance Agency Community Revitalization Fund, which Wilson noted was particularly helpful; and a $250,000 grant from the Metropolitan Council. The city used a $300,000 HUD Economic Development Initiative grant as well as a $460,000 HUD Section 108 Loan. TIF is popular in Minnesota, and was used on this project for infrastructure improvements. The city's public works department spent $730,000 to reconfigure Fifth Avenue and 27th Street, which separate the two blocks.

PPL did not offer homeowner financing for Portland Place, but qualified buyers had several financing options. Two mortgage lenders increased the affordability of the Portland Place units by reducing application fees, by allowing purchasers to lock in rates for extended periods during construction without incurring additional fees, and by maintaining competitive rates. Some purchasers took advantage of the Neighborhood Advantage Credit Flex home loan, a mortgage

Courtesy of LHB and Don Wong Photo, Inc.

The development of Portland Place involved streetscaping and large-scale rehabilitation, and has stimulated new development and rehabilitation in the surrounding community.

CEO Habitat Blitz Build, in which 1,000 volunteers built four of the six Habitat for Humanity homes.

The marketing concept focused on selling to local residents and to employees of local businesses. A final analysis of sales suggests that the project was attractive to a wider segment of the population than the original target market. Sales from Phase I indicate that the marketing effort reached a diverse demographic: 80 percent of buyers came from Minneapolis neighborhoods, including Phillips; 4 percent from St. Paul; and a surprising 16 percent from suburban locations. One-third of buyers in both Phase I and Phase II were white, one-third were African American, and the remaining one-third were of Hispanic, Native American, Asian, East African, or Middle Eastern origin. The project also attracted a diversity of household types: 22 percent of the homes are owned by single parents, 29 percent by two-parent families, 15 percent by married couples or partners without children, and 34 percent by singles.

program sponsored by BankAmerica Mortgage in the Phillips neighborhood. Unlike traditional mortgage products, this home loan does not require an established credit history; in addition, there are no origination fees, and certain bank fees of up to $1,000 are waived.

Marketing

At the close of the 1990s, Minneapolis was experiencing a building boom and heightened real estate activity. Chris Wilson, project manager for Portland Place, points out that these two factors undeniably helped the overall success of Portland Place and made marketing an easy task. The fact that four separate brokers marketed the project also increased its visibility.

PPL and its nonprofit partners brought years of experience in marketing homeownership to families and individuals who believe that owning a home is not an option for them. Honeywell's involvement brought additional attention to the project. In addition to hosting 200 guests at a public ground breaking in the summer of 1998, Honeywell sponsored the Honeywell

Experience Gained

Choose an appropriate scale. Chris Wilson believes that one of the most critical factors in the success of Portland Place was its scale. The project was neither so small that it would fail to create an impact on the surrounding community, nor so large as to overwhelm the area. The scale also made the project manageable, yet large enough to generate financial support and marketing visibility.

Select a leader. Portland Place is an excellent example of how public/private partnerships can create positive change. But large, multiorganizational partnerships are sometimes plagued by too much leadership (that is, by partners jockeying for the lead role) or by too little leadership. Because all the partners agreed that PPL would be the lead developer, PPL was able to move the

Courtesy of LHB

The architect's rendering shows a mix of detached, single-family homes and two-family twinhomes.

project ahead on schedule and keep objectives in sight. PPL also guided the work of the architect and builders while coordinating the sales effort with the marketing consultant and brokers.

Make the most of corporate involvement. Portland Place would not exist without the support of Honeywell. Besides contributing financial support, Honeywell provided publicity, which the firm was rightfully proud of. Honeywell's involvement in the project was not entirely altruistic. Portland Place replaced two square blocks of dilapidated houses, many of which were known crack houses. The area created a negative image for Honeywell's corporate headquarters; more significantly, it had been the source of attacks on Honeywell employees over the years.

Create mechanisms to build on a project's success. The partnership that was established in order to develop Portland Place led to the formation of the Phillips Partnership. Since its founding, the Phillips Partnership has funded, organized, or helped to support $35 million in improvements, many of which are located in the immediate vicinity of Portland Place. These projects include

■ Phillips Park Initiative (1997–1998; 2003–present). To date, $15 million has been invested to create 29 new homeownership opportunities in townhouses, condominiums, and carriage houses, and to improve the properties adjacent to the new homes. Twenty-four new rental units are now being constructed as part of Phase II, and additional new owner-occupied units are planned. Led by Phillips Eye Institute and Lutheran Social Services.

■ Joseph Selvaggio Initiative (1998–2001). A $6.8 million investment that stabilized a section of West Phillips through home improvement grants, the rehabilitation of multi-unit housing, and streetscape improvements. Housing values have led the metro area three years in a row. Led by Allina Health System.

■ East Phillips Infill Campaign (1999–present). More than $1 million invested in 20 new, single-family homes built on vacant lots in East Phillips. Led by the Fannie Mae Foundation.

■ Joseph Selvaggio Initiative II (2002–present). A $5 million continuation of the winning precedent set by the original Joseph Selvaggio

Courtesy of LHB and Don Wong Photo, Inc.

The open green space on the north block of Portland Place allows residents' children to reach the playground without crossing streets or alleys.

sector developers would otherwise be unwilling or unable to venture.

Ensure long-term affordability. One drawback of Portland Place is the absence of mechanisms for maintaining housing affordability. At least for current owners, PPL did try to built in long-term affordability through designing low-maintenance buildings and grounds, using long-lasting construction materials, and choosing mechanical systems and windows that were durable and energy-efficient.

Notes

1. Michael Stegman, Roberto Quercia, and George McCarthy, "Housing America's Working Families," *New Century Housing* vol. 1, issue 1 (2000).

2. Honeywell has been closely tied to the Phillips neighborhood since the founding of the firm, in the late 19th century. Shortly after the completion of Portland Place, Honeywell relocated its corporate headquarters to Morristown, New Jersey. Wells Fargo Bank purchased the site from Honeywell, and is expanding it to make room for more employees.

3. The median household income of the Minneapolis–St. Paul Metropolitan Statistical Area is $63,600.

4. All of the Habitat for Humanity Homes were built during the first phase, which is one reason that the average home prices were low.

5. Phillips Partnership, "Housing," phillipspartnership.org/housing.html.

Initiative. The new effort has combined an influential anticrime and anti-litter initiative at the Chicago-Lake intersection with a grant program for residents of an eight-block area below 28th Street who are seeking to improve their homes. A workforce housing initiative to add 30 new units in Phillips is being planned.[5]

Preserve continuity when designing defensible space. One of the hurdles in the initial development of Portland Place was the need for a site plan that would provide continuity with the surrounding neighborhood while creating defensible space, where homeowners could feel safe. The solution was to have most of the single-family and duplex units face Portland Avenue, a major neighborhood thoroughfare, and to have the townhouses face the open space within the development; this arrangement allowed the townhouse residents to control the areas in front of their homes.

Take advantage of TIF. TIF can create opportunities for redevelopment in areas where private

Portland Place

Primary Contact

Christopher Wilson
Project for Pride in Living, Inc.
612-455-5100
chris.wilson@ppl-inc.org

Project Team

Owner/Developer
Project for Pride in Living
612-455-5100
chris.wilson@ppl-inc.org
www.ppl-inc.org

Architect and Landscape Architect
Rick Carter
LHB
250 3rd Avenue North
Suite 450
Minneapolis, Minnesota 55401
612-338-2029
rick.carter@LHBcorp.com
www.lhbcorp.com

General Contractor
Gerry Flannery
Flannery Construction
1375 St. Anthony Avenue
St. Paul, Minnesota 55104
651-225-1105
gflannery@flanneryconstruction.com
www.flanneryconstruction.com

Marketing/Sales
Lynn Kadlubowski
Independent Diversified Real Estate Services
612-861-2345
Lynsazsold@AOL.com

Development Schedule

Site purchased	Honeywell owned 51% of the land by 1996
Planning started	Spring 1996
Phase I construction started	September 1998
Sales started	Fall 1999
Phase I completed	Winter 1999
Project completed	Spring 2001

Land Use Information

Total site area	6.9 acres
Total square footage devoted to office uses	6,800

Land Use	Acres	Estimated Square Footage (Existing)	Estimated Square Footage (at Buildout)
Residential	6.9	102	46
Multifamily	0	93	
Single-family detached	1.7	9	12
Single-family attached	5.2		34

Site Coverage

Use	Square Footage (Existing)	Square Footage (Proposed)
Buildings	56,000	58,000
Streets, surface parking, and sidewalks	184,000	70,000
Yards, landscaping, and open space	60,000	172,000
Total	300,000	300,000

Residential Information

Single-Family Detached: Phase II

Unit Type	Square Footage	Number of Units Sold	Sales Price Range
Single-family A	1,850	5	$92,000–$133,500
Single-family B	1,700	3	$90,900–$135,000
Single-family C	1,800	3	$90,900–$135,000
Single-family D	1,800	1	$92,000

Single-Family Attached: Phase II

Unit Type	Square Footage	Number of Units Sold	Sales Price Range
Twinhome E	1,600	8	$87,500–$125,500
Twinhome F	1,650	8	$89,000–$130,000
Twinhome G	1,600	6	$70,000
Twinhome I	1,500	4	$80,000
Twinhome J	1,850	8	$85,000–$87,500

Development Costs

Site acquisition	$1,486,000
Site improvement	
Excavation	$132,981
Grading	75,989
Sewer, water, and drainage	37,995
Paving	69,657
Curbs and sidewalks	44,327
Landscaping and irrigation	177,308
Fees and general conditions	72,850
Lighting and fencing	94,985
Subtotal, site improvement	$706,092
Construction	
Superstructure	$4,575,912
Heating, ventilating, and air conditioning	265,270
Electrical	331,588
Plumbing and sprinklers	397,905
Fees and general conditions	655,648
Finish work	1,061,082
Subtotal, construction	$7,287,405
Soft costs	
Architecture and engineering	$326,650
Project management	405,580
Leasing and marketing	266,471
Legal and accounting	113,600
Taxes and insurance	96,596
Title fees	75,596
Construction interest and fees	507,449
Relocation	400,000
Subtotal, soft costs	$2,191,942
Total	$11,671,439

Rollins Square
Boston, Massachusetts

Project Information

A classic Bostonian streetscape and creative financing are the hallmarks of Rollins Square, an innovative, mixed-income community that has successfully provided workforce housing within a rapidly gentrifying urban neighborhood. The project, which offers 147 condominiums, 37 rental apartments, and 6,000 square feet (557 square meters) of ground-floor retail space, was developed by the Planning Office for Urban Affairs (POUA), Inc., a 501(c)(3) nonprofit housing developer affiliated with the Archdiocese of

Courtesy of CBT Architects/Mark C. Flannery

The newly created Rollins Street runs through the center of the site. Boston. Established in 1969, the POUA has developed approximately 1,686 units of affordable and mixed-income housing throughout the greater Boston area; an additional 650 units are currently under development.

Workforce Housing Information

Rollins Square has successfully met the objective of providing housing for moderate-income, first-time homebuyers from the area's growing workforce. The 73 affordable condominium units integral to the project targeted South End residents—such as teachers, firefighters, and municipal employees—who provide critical services to the community but cannot afford to live there.

The development is unique in that it provides housing opportunities to residents with a broad range of income levels. About 20 percent of the project's 184 units (37) are targeted to low-income residents (those whose income is between 30 and 60 percent of the area median income (AMI). About 40 percent of the units (73) are for-sale condominiums targeted to moderate-income homebuyers (those with incomes between 80 and 120 percent of AMI). This workforce housing component of the project has provided significant homeownership opportunities to first-time homebuyers, a segment of the population that is grossly underserved in Boston's South End. The remaining 40 percent of the units (74) were designed and marketed as high-end, market-rate units selling for up to $750,000.

Site, Surroundings, and History

Rollins Square is located in Boston's South End, a diverse and vibrant urban neighborhood adjacent to Beacon Hill and Boston's Back Bay. Once an old wharf district, the South End features a combination of low-income housing; newly constructed high-end condominiums; and commercial office space, which is occupied primarily by educational and health care institutions. As the South End gentrified, the supply of housing opportunities for the neighborhood's growing moderate-income workforce declined dramatically.

Originally controlled by the Boston Redevelopment Agency (BRA), the Rollins Square site was awarded to the POUA in the mid-1970s. The POUA initially intended to use the 2.2-acre (0.8-hectare) site to expand the adjacent Catholic high school. As time passed, and the demand for low- and moderate-income housing escalated, the POUA changed its plans.

The BRA, which retained ownership of the property until construction was completed, gave the developer a "use it or lose it" ultimatum, which accelerated predevelopment efforts. In the early planning stages, the POUA worked closely with the office of Mayor Thomas M. Menino to craft a creative and attractive mixed-income development program for the site.

Like most urban infill sites, Rollins Square presented numerous challenges, including lead and petroleum contamination and the need to build around three historic rowhouses. Because the site was classified as a brownfield, the Commonwealth of Massachusetts Brownfields Fund provided $1 million in funding for environmental remediation.

Planning, Development, and Entitlements

Given the rapidity of gentrification in the South End and the limited availability of workforce housing, serving a middle-income population was a major objective of the housing office of the archdiocese; there was also considerable

Courtesy of CBT Architects/Mark C. Flannery

neighborhood and citywide support for the idea of developing Rollins Square as a mixed-income community.

Early in the approval process, the POUA met with local citizens' groups, identified by the city, to discuss the community's thoughts and concerns. This process was facilitated by the Washington Gateway Main Streets Association, a newly created neighborhood group formed to preserve the historic urban settlement patterns of the Washington Street Corridor, a section of the South End. This association made several requests of the developer: the use of traditional rather than contemporary architecture; the inclusion of open space to ensure pedestrian safety; retail uses on ground floors; and streetscapes and building massing that would be consistent with the character of the historic neighborhood. Because the developer shared the vision of the city and the local community, the result was a remarkably efficient and effective approval process.

The local neighborhood group that formed to preserve the historic urban patterns of the community requested traditional architecture that would be consistent with the area's historic character.

Courtesy of CBT Architects/Mark C. Flannery

Rollins Square—shown at bottom right in this photo—is located in Boston's rapidly gentrifying South End, adjacent to Beacon Hill and Back Bay.

Financing

The developer's desire to create a mixed-income community that included both rental apartments and for-sale condominiums dramatically increased the complexity of the project financing. A focused, highly committed, and professional financing team was essential for the ambitious development program, which was previously unparalleled in the city's history. The key participants in that team were the city of Boston, the Commonwealth of Massachusetts, FleetBoston, and the AFL-CIO. This somewhat unusual combination of entities used creative and flexible financing approaches to achieve an important policy outcome.

Among the challenges were (1) the need to apply for funds twice (because of the mix of for-sale and rental units), which significantly increased the project's predevelopment period; (2) issues associated with collateral; and (3) the complexity of the legal structures that were required to address the concerns of all parties. In the end, the POUA assembled a complicated mosaic of debt, equity, and grants that included 13 financing sources in all.

The BRA played an invaluable role in site assemblage and financing by writing down the land value to $1.5 million and deferring payment until construction was complete. (This purchase price represented the market value of the land for the 74 units of market-rate housing; zero land value was attributed to the project's affordable units.)

The POUA secured several scarce financing resources available to developers of for-sale low- and moderate-income housing within the Boston marketplace, including

- $1.17 million in state-administered HOME funds;
- $2 million in Massachusetts Affordable Housing Trust Funds;
- $2.9 million in permanent financing from MassHousing;
- $1.17 million in Leading the Way Funds (a discretionary affordable-housing fund controlled by the office of the mayor);
- Over $2.5 million in funding from Boston's Neighborhood Housing Trust, which is directly funded by Boston's housing linkage program (see feature box).

These funding sources financed only a portion of the development costs attributable to the for-sale housing units. Because of its unique mission and nonprofit status, however, the POUA was able to use the net revenue generated by the sale of the market-rate condominiums to subsidize these units. The POUA used roughly $11 million in revenue to subsidize the units, in lieu of taking the revenue as a development fee.

Perhaps one of the most unique aspects of the financing was the prominent role played by a private sector commercial bank, FleetBoston, in a project focused heavily on public purposes. FleetBoston (which merged with the Bank of America in 2004) was the lead lender on the

Boston's Linkage Program

In 1983, to connect nonresidential development with the housing demand that it creates, the city of Boston amended its zoning regulations: under the "linkage ordinance," developers of major commercial, retail, hotel, and institutional projects must either (1) pay a specified impact fee or (2) develop on-site affordable housing that is equivalent in value to the fee. (For the purposes of this program, the city defines "affordable" as housing that serves residents whose income is at or below 80 percent of Boston's median income.) The linkage program recognizes and addresses one of the basic facts of urban development: within the urban core, opportunities for residential development tend to be costly and challenging; nonresidential development, by comparison, enjoys an economic advantage.

The city of Boston established the Neighborhood Housing Trust to manage the linkage funds and to administer linkage grant money to qualified housing developments. Where commercial development directly affects the housing market for a particular neighborhood, between 10 and 20 percent of the linkage payments are reserved for the affected area.

Developers pay linkage fees on either a seven-year (for downtown development) or a 12-year (for neighborhood development) schedule, and usually begin payment when a building permit is issued. Because developers can pay linkage fees out of operating revenues from the project, rather than as soft costs associated with development, the linkage program does not increase the level of financing required to begin construction. The payment schedule thus provides an element of flexibility that may be valuable to developments facing financial challenges.

Boston's Linkage Program has provided a predictable and long-term funding stream for affordable and workforce housing development while reducing the imbalance between jobs and housing within the central city.

$52 million construction loan (with Mass-Housing as a 50 percent participating lender), and also provided more than $3.8 million in equity through low-income housing tax credits.

The unusual financing approach and the mix of income levels among targeted households created underwriting challenges for the construction loan, which were addressed by a creative approach to collateral proposed by FleetBoston. In the early stages of buildout, the bank required the developer to inventory and "hold in escrow" (that is, not sell) a significant percentage of the workforce condominiums. These "escrowed" units offered additional security that compensated for the limited financial guarantees that the nonprofit developer was able to provide. Under this arrangement, workforce units were released for sale over time, as market-rate units sold. If the sales prices of the market-rate units did not meet projections, some of the workforce housing units (whose sales prices had been significantly written down) would have been sold

Courtesy of CBT Architects/Robert Benson Photography

The open spaces within Rollins Square were extensively landscaped.

at market rates. This approach recognized, and relied upon, the unrealized economic value of the subsidized workforce housing units.

Courtesy of CBT Architects/Robert Benson Photography

Courtesy of CBT Architects/Robert Benson Photography

Ground-level retail enlivens the streetscape.

The decision to construct many smaller buildings instead of one large complex allowed for 24 different floor plans.

One of the central components of the POUA's mission was to integrate housing for all income levels, so that low-income families would not be isolated or restricted to only one area of the new community. Thus, instead of being consolidated within one building or floor, the affordable rental units at Rollins Square were dispersed throughout the project. Although the low-income rental units were physically integrated into the condominium building, they had to be funded separately. A limited partnership was formed to buy the 37 rental units; the partnership served as the landlord for the units, which were then leased to lower-income residents. To finance the project's rental component, the POUA successfully secured both low-income housing tax credits (9 percent competitive tax credit) as well as Section 8 vouchers.

To assist with project financing, the POUA thoughtfully used its status as a 501(c)(3) nonprofit organization and received a sales tax exemption on all building materials, which saved $1.5 million. However, to maintain its nonprofit status, the POUA had to control all partnership entities during the construction period; this meant that the project's limited partners had to place their investments as debt, which was converted into equity upon the completion of construction.

The financing for Rollins Square became increasingly complicated after the events of September 11, 2001. Because of uncertain market conditions and the loss of a significant number of presale commitments, the developer was unable to obtain the construction loan and was forced to seek bridge financing. The POUA

The six-story structures are linked by four-story townhouses—an arrangement that provides a variety of building heights and a diversity of exterior materials.

The view down Rollins Street.

approached the AFL-CIO Housing Investment Trust, a national leader in pension real estate investment for housing development. Fortunately, the trust was able to design a customized $28 million bridge loan that provided the essential capital necessary to maintain construction progress during the post-9/11 remarketing of the development. The arrangement required union labor and resulted in the creation of 644 union jobs during construction.

Design and Architecture

The Rollins Square project occupies two square city blocks and is bordered by Washington Street and Harrison Avenue on the north and south, and by Savoy and Waltham streets on the east and west. The newly created Rollins Street runs through the center of the site. A six-story building stands at each of the four principal street corners; rows of four-story townhouses link the six-story structures. The center of the site is occupied by a small, well-landscaped park. The project includes a two-level underground parking garage with 277 spaces.

There are 20 townhouses, 16 of which front directly on the park. Adjacent pairs of townhouses share private front and rear entrances and have direct access to the garage. The remaining 164 residential units are located in the project's four six-story buildings. Each of these buildings has a private entrance lobby at ground level and an elevator serving the residences and the garage. The ground-floor residences that face the park feature private raised patios, and many upper-floor residences include roof terraces or French

A landscaped courtyard located between four-story townhouse units.

Special design treatments were used to address the corners of the buildings.

balconies. To maintain street-level activity along the busy Washington Street commercial corridor, Rollins Square includes approximately 6,000 square feet (557 square meters) of ground-floor retail space.

The buildings in Rollins Square are faced with a variety of materials, including brick, natural and synthetic stone, and precast concrete, and feature synthetic slate mansard roofs and metal-clad window bays. The result is an attractive streetscape that complements the project's historic surroundings. With its varying building heights and diverse exterior materials, Rollins Square appears to have been constructed over time.

A primary design goal for the developer was to create a family- and neighborhood-friendly residential community within an urban context.

Instead of a central lobby and elevator core, the project offers 16 separate building entries. And instead of long, double-loaded corridors, the project features smaller buildings constructed around a tighter core.

The developers felt that smaller buildings, which contain fewer units on each floor, would create a greater sense of community among the residents. This design concept resulted in the creation of seven building types and 24 different floor plans. Although this neighborhood-friendly design approach was successful from the perspective of urban planning and design, the lack of standardization reduced many of the efficiencies that are often gained through a production approach, thus increasing the overall cost of the project.

The structural system for each building consists of load-bearing walls of reinforced concrete block and precast concrete plank. The developers chose "block-and-plank" construction instead of steel and concrete because it provides better soundproofing and allows greater floor-to-ceiling heights—both of which create significant marketing advantages. Block-and-plank construction, however, reduced design flexibility within residential units and made it more difficult to combine units if it turned out that the market preferred larger units to smaller ones.

Marketing and Operations

Because of the high demand for workforce housing, the POUA established a lottery system to market the subsidized units. The initial marketing efforts—advertisements in neighborhood and minority newspapers—yielded over 1,500 requests for applications. Five hundred prospects completed the application and submitted pre-qualification letters from lenders in time to participate in the lottery; applications continued to come in long afterward, evidencing the strong need for this type of housing. The city of Boston and the Commonwealth of Massachusetts oversaw the lottery, which assigned random numbers to each of the 500 applicants; applicants with the lowest numbers were given first priority.

Deed restrictions, enforced by the city of Boston, were used to ensure the long-term affordability of the workforce housing units. Under these restrictions, residents are permitted to exceed affordability restrictions over time; however, the incomes of future residents may not exceed 120 percent of AMI. If current residents wish to resell their units, the city will help them find and qualify income-eligible buyers.

To avert the tension that could arise between income groups if operating expenses and association fees were not allocated equally across all

Courtesy of CBT Architects/Robert Benson Photography

units, residents of subsidized units pay condominium fees on the same basis as residents of market-rate units do. To achieve this objective, the POUA first had an appraisal conducted to determine the market value of each unit; each home's share of the operating expenses and the association budget was then calculated according to two factors: the square footage of the unit and the appraised, rather than the subsidized, value. To calculate the monthly rent level and condominium sales prices for the low-income and workforce housing units, the developer used the projected association dues, keeping in mind that a resident's housing expenses, including association dues, should not exceed 30 percent of gross income.

Under the bylaws for the Rollins Square homeowners' association, the limited part-

Bay windows and variations in the roofline break up the massing on the street facade.

Courtesy of CBT Architects/Robert Benson Photography

A six-story building stands at each of the four principal street corners.

Experience Gained

As is the case with many urban housing projects, parking was critical. The project included the development of 277 parking spaces, many of which were intended for sale to neighborhood residents to ease the pressure for parking in the area. In fact, the sale of parking spaces represented approximately 20 percent of the project's gross sales proceeds. Although 98 percent of the residential units have been sold and occupied, and the developer anticipates meeting both its social and financial goals for the development, in the end the project's financial success was perhaps too dependent on the income derived from the sale of parking spaces to nonresidents of the development.

Determining income qualification for workforce housing can be a time-consuming process. To avoid delays in closings, it is critical to allocate a reasonable amount of time for proper income qualification and documentation early in the process.

The mission of a nonprofit development entity can conflict with market dynamics. For example, the developers of Rollins Square could have accelerated absorption by meeting the market's strong demand for one-bedroom units. The development mission of the POUA, however, is to create housing for families rather than for single-person households. As a result, the developers chose to reduce the number of one-bedroom units and to increase the number of three-bedroom units.

The project's seven building types and 24 different floor plans created additional complexity for the development, construction, and marketing teams. Limiting the number of unit types would have increased efficiency, decreased cost, and enhanced marketability.

The sales of market-rate units were initially spearheaded by a high-end, "boutique-style"

nership that owns the rental apartments has the same rights in the management and operation of the property as the condominium owners. This arrangement addressed the concerns of the investors, who financed the apartments through low-income housing tax credits, about the predictability and cost of future capital improvements and the resulting impact on investment returns. In exchange, the limited partnership agreed to allow apartment residents limited rights to represent their interests with regard to the operations of the association, including the right to vote for the officers and trustees of the homeowners' association.

Courtesy of CBT Architects/Robert Benson Photography

A small landscaped park was created in the center of the development; 16 of the 20 townhouses front directly on the park.

Courtesy of CBT Architects/Robert Benson Photography

Rollins Square successfully integrates units for low-income residents with high-end, market-rate units.

real estate sales and marketing group. The developer eventually changed marketing approaches and hired a marketing agency with significantly more experience in the merchandising and sale of newly constructed housing, dramatically increasing preconstruction absorption. Approximately 50 percent of the market-rate units were presold early in the construction process.

The complexity associated with mixing uses (condominiums, apartments, and retail) and incomes within a single condominium association has significant implications for both marketing and transactional expenses. In this instance, the high-quality design and amenities associated with the development, and the developer's ability to forgo traditional development profits, made this arrangement work for all parties.

Rollins Square

Primary Contact

Lisa Alberghini
Executive Vice President
Planning Office for Urban Affairs, Inc.
617-350-8885
lba@poua.org
www.rollinssquare.com

Project Team

Owner/Developer
Planning Office for Urban Affairs, Inc.
185 Devonshire Street
Suite 600
Boston, Massachusetts 02110
617-350-8885
lba@poua.org

Architect
Childs Bertram Tseckares
110 Canal Street
Boston, Massachusetts 02114
617-262-4354
hill@cbtarchitects.com
www.cbtarchitects.com

Landscape Architect
CBA Landscape Architects
212 Elm Street
Third Floor
Somerville, Massachusetts 02144
617-566-0834
www.cbaland.com

Structural Engineer
Weidlinger Associates
One Broadway
11th Floor
Cambridge, Massachusetts 02142
617-374-000
drisch@ma.wei.com
www.wei.com

Mechanical Engineer
Fitzemeyer & Tocci, Associates, Inc.
206 West Cummings Park
Woburn, Massachusetts 01801
781-376-9600
ee@f-t.com
www.f-t.com

General Contractor
Suffolk Construction
65 Allerton Street
Boston, Massachusetts 02119
617-445-3500
jfish@suffolk-construction.com
www.suffolk-construction.com

Marketing/Sales
Peabody Properties, Inc.
159 Burgin Parkway
Quincy, Massachusetts 02169
617-328-1313
ppimail@peabodyproperties.com
www.peabodyproperties.com

Development Consultant
Peter J. Roche
Real Estate & Community Development
79 Quincy Avenue
Winthrop, Massachusetts 02152
617-846-5326
pjroche1@attbi.com

Development Schedule

Planning started	November 1999
Site purchased	February 2001
Construction started	March 2001
Sales started	October 2000
Phase I completed	January 2003
Project completed	June 2003

Land Use Information

Total site area	2.2 acres
Site area devoted to residential use	2.2 acres
Total number of units at buildout	184
Total retail square footage at buildout	6,000 square feet

Site Coverage

Use	Square Footage
Buildings (excluding garage)	249,337
Garage	99,488
Total	348,825

Residential Information

Multifamily Units

Unit Type	Square Footage	Number Sold/Leased	Range of Sales Prices/Monthly Rents
Moderate-income condo	600–1,900	73	$140,000–$260,000
Market-rate condo	600–1,900	74	$280,000–$750,000
Low-income apartment	600–1,900	37	$354–$1,022

Affordable Residential Units

Unit Type	Number of Units	Targeted Income Group	Range of Sales Prices/Monthly Rents
Condominium	25	80% of median area income (MAI)	$140,000–$160,000
Condominium	48	120% of MAI	$210,000–$260,000
Apartment	37	30–60% of MAI	$354–$1,022

Retail Information

Percentage of gross leasable area	100%
Approximate annual rents	$32–$35
Average length of lease	Ten years

Tenant Name	Gross Leasable Area (Square Feet)
Mercantile Bank & Trust	3,000
7-11	3,000
Total	6,000

Gross Leasable Area (at Buildout)

Use	Square Footage
Retail	6,000
Residential	44,400
Total	50,400

Development Costs

Site acquisition	$1,500,000
Site improvement; construction; furniture, fittings, and equipment	$53,000,000
Soft costs	$11,151,000
Total	$65,651,000

Stapleton
Denver, Colorado

Project Information

The Stapleton project is a mixed-use, master-planned community currently under construction on the former site of the Stapleton International Airport. The site, ten minutes from downtown Denver and 20 minutes from Denver International Airport, consists of 4,700 acres (1,902 hectares) and will eventually accommodate over 30,000 residents and 35,000 workers. Stapleton was conceived as a sustainable community and seeks to integrate jobs, housing, and the environment. In 1995, to create a vision for such a large undertaking, the principal stakeholders—the city and county of Denver, the Stapleton Redevelopment Foundation, the Citizens' Advisory Board, and the Stapleton Tomorrow Committee—devised the Stapleton Redevelopment Plan, which is known as the Green Book.

The Green Book outlines a clear dedication to affordable housing, traditional neighborhood design, environmental conservation, minority participation, and high-quality educational opportunities. In 1998, the Stapleton Development Corporation chose Forest City Enterprises as the master developer, and began the largest infill redevelopment project in the country. The $4 billion development will take 20 years to complete, and will have a population

The 4,700-acre (1,902-hectare) site of the former Stapleton Airport is the largest infill redevelopment project in the country.

Forest City Stapleton

Special Features

- As of 2003, Stapleton was the largest infill project in the United States.
- To mitigate the risk associated with a project of this size, the Stapleton Development Corporation and Forest City Enterprises, the master developer, created a unique agreement.
- To build the high-quality school system and strong curricula necessary to attract families, the master plan includes educational opportunities from early childhood through grade 12, and provides for collaboration with the Denver public schools.
- All housing will meet or exceed the Built Green Colorado standards of the Home Builders Association of Metro Denver. Infrastructure planning and design stress water reuse, energy conservation, and innovative stormwater management.
- Approximately 800 for-sale homes and 800 rental apartments will be built under a workforce housing program.

more than one-third the size of Boulder's. At buildout, there will be 8,000 for-sale homes, 4,000 rental units, 10 million square feet (929,030 square meters) of office space, and 3 million square feet (278,709 square meters) of retail space.

Stapleton is currently the largest infill redevelopment project in the United States—and, consequently, one of the most complex. In the late 1980s, the city of Denver decided to close Stapleton International Airport in favor of a newer, higher-capacity facility about 20 minutes away. Soon afterward, the city of Denver and local citizens' groups began planning for Stapleton's reuse.

Denver is home to numerous nonprofit housing groups, many of which sought involvement with the redevelopment process. The city, citizens' groups, and the nonprofits agreed that the Stapleton redevelopment must be founded on three principles: economic opportunity, environmental responsibility, and social equity. As of December 2003, a regional retail center; a town center, with offices and residences situated above main-street retail and overlooking a town

green; and 850 for-sale and rental homes had been constructed.

Stapleton is based on the principles of traditional neighborhood design and provides physical and economic connections to the surrounding neighborhood. The development's abundant trails and open space encourage walking and biking. In reflection of the commitment to environmental responsibility, builders must meet or exceed the Built Green Colorado standards of the Home Builders Association of Metro Denver, which encourage energy efficiency, healthy indoor air, reduced water use, and the preservation of natural resources.

Forest City, which will develop much of the commercial and rental portions of the development, agreed to buy the land from the city and county of Denver over time, to eliminate costs and risks associated with having to hold the land. Over a 15-year period, Forest City will pay $79.4 million for the land, and a $15,000-per-acre ($37,066-per-hectare) fee to develop parks and open spaces.

It is estimated that the project will not be complete until 2020.

Affordable Housing Information

Housing affordability is a problem in Denver: to afford a median-priced home (assuming good credit and the funds for downpayment and closing costs), a family needs to earn approximately $65,000. As of 2000, about 56 percent of Denver families earned less than $50,000. Ten percent, or approximately 800, of the single-family homes sold at Stapleton will be built under the HomeBuyer Resource Program, which was designed to put housing within reach of teachers, nurses, police officers, firefighters, and other members of the community's workforce.

Forest City has dedicated itself to establishing a comprehensive affordable-housing program. To assist local nonprofit housing agencies and small development firms that want to build affordable housing within Stapleton, Forest City established the Associate Developer Program, which provides technical expertise and guidance to developers, many of whom do not have experience with the scale or deed limitations associated with the project.

The Stapleton affordable-housing program specifies that the affordable units must be constructed within mixed-income areas, and that they must adhere to minimum-square-footage guidelines: for example, a studio apartment cannot be smaller than 400 square feet (37 square meters), and a three-bedroom unit cannot be smaller than 1,100 square feet (102 square meters). In addition, at least 15 percent of the affordable units must have three or more bedrooms. The developers and Forest City are required to report their progress in fulfilling the affordable-housing requirements to both the city and the Stapleton Development Corporation (SDC), a nonprofit organization charged with the disposal of property at Stapleton.

To be eligible to purchase one of the affordable homes, a buyer's gross household income must be below specific levels published annually by the U.S. Department of Housing and Urban Development (HUD). Thirty-year restrictions on resale prices ensure long-term affordability for future homebuyers. At the end of 30 years, a nonprofit entity—created to control and monitor the for-sale units, and supported by a 3 percent sales commission—has the option of buying back the homes at the restricted price and re-restricting the units, or allowing them to be sold on the open market and collecting the difference. The homeowners' share of the appreciation depends on how long they have lived in the residence.

The resale price for a deed-restricted unit is based on a share of the appreciation, plus fees. For example, if the original sales price of the unit is $140,000 (for a home valued at $150,000), and the market value at the time of resale is $200,000, then the total appreciation is $50,000 ($200,000 - $150,000), and the resale price would be calculated as follows:

Original sales price	*$140,000*
Share of appreciation to nonprofit	*12,500*
Community investment fee	*150*
Closing costs and title fees	*2,000*
Subtotal	*$154,650*
Sales commission (3 percent of subtotal)	*4,640*
Resale price	*$159,290*

Here is a calculation of the seller's return:

Resale price	*$159,290*
Loan repayment	*-121,560*
Closing costs	*-2,000*
Community investment fee	*-150*
Sales commission (3 percent)	*-4,640*
Total return	*$30,940*

Forest City Stapleton

The 80-unit Roslyn Court community offers one-, two-, and three-bedroom homes for families with incomes below 80 percent of the area median income.

Although the seller does not realize the $50,000 appreciation that would have been realized on a market-rate sale, the unit was purchased at a below-market price, and the seller enjoyed minimal associated costs, energy-efficient appliances, and a location within walking distance of retail, office, and open-space uses. Nor does the seller walk away empty-handed: in this scenario, the seller keeps 25 percent of the appreciation.[1] The unit remains affordable, at a price that is 20 percent lower than market rate.

Response to the affordable-housing program has been positive, although some potential buyers are skeptical at first. The appreciation restrictions are a major psychological hurdle, but they are balanced by a number of advantages, including the opportunity to purchase a new house at a price below market rate, and to gain immediate access to a wide variety of amenities.

The 80-unit Roslyn Court development, the first affordable-housing development built at Stapleton, is currently selling one-, two-, and

three-bedrooms homes priced from the $120,000s to $175,000. One-bedroom units are about 600 square feet (56 square meters), and three-bedroom units are about 1,100 square feet (102 square meters). The total development cost for Roslyn Court was $10 million.

To be eligible for housing in Roslyn Court, a household's gross annual income must not exceed 80 percent of area median income (AMI), according to the following limits:

Number of People in Household	Annual Income Limit
One	$40,150
Two	$45,900
Three	$51,600
Four	$57,350

As with all affordable-housing ownership units, buyers are expected to contribute between 3 and 5 percent of the purchase price (depending on the loan they select); work at least 30 hours a week (unless they are disabled or over 62); agree to occupy the home; and agree to the restrictions recorded against the home. Buyers must also attend an orientation and homebuyer education classes.

Syracuse Village, the latest affordable-housing project, consists of condominiums and townhouses ranging in size from 788 to 1,155 square feet (73 to 107 square meters). Prices start at about $150,000.

Twenty percent of Stapleton's rental units, or approximately 800, will be built under Stapleton's affordable-housing program and must serve those who are earning 60 percent or less of AMI. Clyburn at Stapleton, one of the first rental projects constructed in the development, is a 100-unit affordable apartment community for residents over 62 years of age. It is located across the street from the 30-acre (12-hectare) Fred Thomas Park and is adjacent to the 29th Avenue Town Center. Amenities include laundry rooms on each floor, a computer and community room, a second-floor lounge/library, and a large garden courtyard.

For a household to qualify to rent at Clyburn, its annual household income cannot exceed the following levels:

Number of People in Household	Annual Income Limit
One	$29,340
Two	$33,540
Three	$37,740

Monthly rents range from $650 for a one-bedroom to $750 for a two-bedroom. The income limits and monthly rents are based on HUD requirements.

Recently, Mercy Housing Southwest completed the Parkside Apartments, a complex of 68 low-income rental apartments on a two-acre (0.8-hectare) site donated by Forest City.

Site, Surroundings, and History

Stapleton is an urban infill site, but of enormous size: approximately 7.5 square miles (19 square kilometers)—bigger than New York's Central Park. Its 4,700 acres (1,902 hectares) of relatively flat prairie are located ten minutes from downtown Denver and 20 minutes from the Denver International Airport. The decision to redevelop the Stapleton site was based on the desire to unleash the potential of one of the largest parcels of underdeveloped land located in a major American city.

Stapleton International Airport served as Denver's municipal airport from 1929 to 1995. It was Mayor Benjamin Franklin Stapleton who rallied local support for the construction of the airfield, although residents were doubtful of the benefits of aviation and thought it was the province of the elite. The original 640-acre (259-hectare) site, known as Rattlesnake Hollow, was used for dairy farming and cattle grazing, and appealed to airport boosters because of its remote location and relatively cheap price. Once completed, the airport—then known as Denver Municipal Airport—was an instant financial success. During the 1930s, it was heralded as the most modern airport in the United States.

Air traffic grew exponentially, and by the 1950s, Denver's airport (which was renamed Stapleton International in 1964) needed to expand. The city bought additional land from the nearby Rocky Mountain Arsenal, but the facility was soon hemmed in by surrounding residential neighborhoods. By the 1970s, Stapleton had almost completely outgrown its site, and its runway layout was considered inadequate and potentially hazardous. Neighboring residents became frustrated by the constant jet noise and filed suit. Even nearby Adams County sought to block any additional expansion onto the Rocky

Mountain Arsenal lands. The combination of obsolescence and crowding forced the city of Denver to consider a new site, northeast of Stapleton, for what would become the Denver International Airport. Denver was limited in its annexation powers, and anticipated that the redevelopment of the Stapleton site could accommodate residential and commercial uses. The closing of Stapleton International Airport coincided with the conversion of two local military bases: the Rocky Mountain Arsenal became a National Wildlife Refuge, and the 1,800-acre (728-hectare) Lowry Air Training Center was shut down and redeveloped.

The Stapleton site is surrounded by several racially diverse, middle- and lower-middle-class neighborhoods; the former Lowry Air Training Center; the 27-square-mile (70-square-kilometer) Rocky Mountain Arsenal National Wildlife Refuge; a variety of retail, light manufacturing, and commercial uses; and the Fitzsimons Army Medical Center, which is located to the south-

east and is currently being redeveloped. Interstate 70 runs east-west through the middle of the site, and additional highway and rail access are nearby. Being located directly between the Denver International Airport and downtown Denver brings additional advantages to the Stapleton site.

Many areas within the site enjoy views of downtown Denver and the Rocky Mountains. An existing lake, two streams, and a bluff complement the extensive open space that is planned for the semi-arid prairie environment. Developers will restore natural corridors to increase the available wildlife habitat.

As a former industrial site, Stapleton did sustain some environmental damage. Initially, tests indicated groundwater contamination from petroleum products and chemical solvents in about 10 to 15 percent of the site. The city agreed to remediate the contamination to residential levels before any sales were made to developers.

Forest City Stapleton

The scale of the Stapleton redevelopment will eventually create demand for 3 million square feet (278,709 square meters) of retail space. Shown here is Quebec Square, a 740,000-square-foot (68,748-square-meter) regional retail center.

Planning and Development

When the decision to close Stapleton airport was announced in 1988, many citizens in the surrounding neighborhoods asked to be involved in the redevelopment process. Already alert to the problems associated with living next to an undesirable land use, a group of citizens formed Stapleton Tomorrow to ensure that the redeveloped Stapleton would be more harmonious with its surroundings. In 1991, the Denver City Council adopted the concept plan that had been developed by Stapleton Tomorrow, which included input from a broad range of citizens. The concept plan identified goals that Stapleton Tomorrow wanted the new development to reflect, including social equity, job creation, and environmental preservation; the plan also encouraged technical and social innovation.

After the development of the Stapleton Tomorrow concept plan, the city and county of Denver entered into a partnership agreement with the Stapleton Redevelopment Foundation (SRF), a nonprofit 501(c)(3) corporation established by community leaders to assist the city and county in maximizing the opportunities offered by Stapleton. Together, the city, the county, and SRF raised over $4 million to create the Stapleton Redevelopment Plan, also known as the Green Book. SRF also agreed to assist the city and county in defining a long-term management structure for the Stapleton redevelopment program.

A citizens' advisory board worked in conjunction with SRF, and more than 100 community presentations were held during the formulation of the redevelopment plan. In 1993, a team of technical consultants—planners, architects,

Stapleton will not be completely built out until 2020.

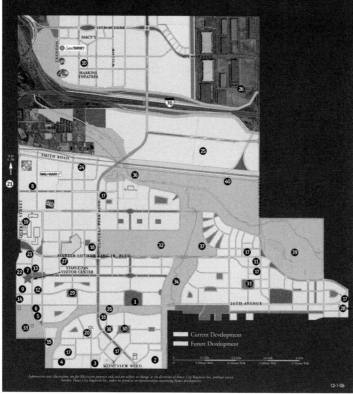

Development Plan 2001-2007

★ Stapleton Visitor Center

Schools
1. Westerly Creek Campus (Westerly Creek Primary & Odyssey Charter School)
2. William R. Roberts School
3. Denver School of Science and Technology High School
4. Johnson and Wales University (Future Use)
5. Primrose School – Early Childhood Learning
6. Anchor Center for Blind Children

Retail
7. East 29th Avenue Town Center
8. Quebec Square Regional Retail Center
9. King Soopers Grocery Store
10. Northfield Stapleton
11. Havana Town Center (opens 2008)

Homes/Apartments
12. Botanica on the Green Apartments
13. Crescent Flats Apartments
14. Clyburn at Stapleton, Rental Senior Community
15. Parkside Apartments
16. Central Park Apartments (coming soon)
17. Future Income Qualified Residential Homes/Apartments

Commercial
18. Stapleton Control Tower
19. United Airlines Training Center
20. Colorado Studios
21. 3,000 Existing Hotel Rooms
22. East 29th Avenue Offices
23. 3055 Roslyn Executive Building
24. Future Light Rail Station
25. Stapleton Business Center South
26. Stapleton Business Center
27. Denver Fire Station, No.26
28. University of Colorado Health Sciences Center at Fitzsimons

Parks/Open Space
29. Aviator Park and Neighborhood Pool
30. Puddle Jumper Pool
31. Third Pool (coming soon)
32. Central Park
33. Fred Thomas Park
34. Westerly Creek Regional Greenway
35. Greenway Park
36. Sand Creek Greenway
37. Future Recreation Center
38. Bladium Sports Club
39. Bluff Lake Nature Center
40. Urban Farm at Stapleton

urban designers, civil engineers, transportation planners, environmental scientists, market and financial analysts, and project managers—also worked on the plan, which was completed in 1994. The plan was approved by the Denver Planning Board and the Denver City Council, and was published in 1995. It won numerous local, state, and national awards, including the 1996 Outstanding Planning Award from the American Planning Association and the 1996 President's Award for Planning from the American Society of Landscape Architects.

The plan assigns 65 percent of the site to urban development and 35 percent to a mix of open-space uses. Development is organized into eight districts, of varying densities and use mixes. Each district features an identifiable center and emphasizes a pedestrian scale, and the integration of employment and housing. The plan reinforces Stapleton's role as a regional employment center while creating strong ties between the Stapleton site and the surrounding neighborhoods. The open-space system ties together the eight districts, and is helping to restore the ecological health of the site.

The plan also called for the creation of a nonprofit organization that would be a vehicle for the disposal of property at Stapleton. In November 1995, the Denver Urban Redevelopment Authority (DURA) signed a cooperative agreement with the city to form the Stapleton Development Corporation (SDC). The SDC is governed by an 11-member board made up of business leaders and community activists; DURA appoints two members, and the mayor of Denver appoints nine.

In 1997, the SDC funded a study to determine whether the Stapleton property should be considered blighted, and therefore designated as an urban renewal area. This was the first step to determine Stapleton's eligibility for tax-increment financing (TIF), a mechanism by which the increase in property or sales tax revenues generated by redevelopment can be used to help finance infrastructure construction.

In July 1998, the SDC entered into a master lease and disposition agreement (MLD) with the city of Denver. The MLD assigns the SDC responsibility for maintaining and leasing Stapleton for 15 years, gives the SDC an option to purchase the property, and allows the SDC the authority to sell parcels for uses consistent with the Stapleton Redevelopment Plan. Once the MLD was signed, the SDC began initiating transactions and seeking to attract employers and developers. Two years before, United Airlines had agreed to build a $140 million expansion of its computer-simulated flight-training facility at Stapleton. Other early clients were the King Soopers grocery chain, which opened a regional distribution warehouse, and the Catellus Development Corporation, which built a 3.6-million-square-foot (334,450-square-meter) business park.

Later in 1998, the SDC initiated a competitive process to choose a master developer to oversee the entire parcel, eventually selecting Forest City Enterprises, Inc., a family-owned and publicly traded national real estate company with experience in mixed-use urban infill projects. In addition to expertise in all aspects of development, Forest City offered access to capital, marketing savvy, and a commitment to affordable housing, sustainable development, minority participation, and other principles of the Stapleton Redevelopment Plan.

Forest City obtained the exclusive right to negotiate with the SDC for the purchase of Stapleton. In February 2000, the SDC and Forest City finalized a purchase agreement that obligated Forest City to buy all developable land at Stapleton. As a condition of selling the balance of the Stapleton property to a master developer,

The heart of Stapleton's first residential neighborhood is Founders' Green, a 2.5-acre (one-hectare) park with a 2,000-seat amphitheater and a dramatic fountain.

tems development fee" of $15,000 for each acre purchased ($37,066 per hectare), resulting in a total payment of $123.4 million. An appraisal process approved by the Federal Aviation Administration and conducted by Peter Bowes and Company set the purchase price. Forest City is responsible for all in-tract infrastructure and for the creation of additional neighborhood parks. The developer advanced the front-end financing for the regional infrastructure, with repayment through a $30 million TIF arrangement. Forest City bought its first land in 2001 and agreed to buy 1,000 acres (404 hectares) every five years until 2015; the baseline per-acre price was established in 2001, and will increase annually according to the Consumer Price Index.

Both Forest City and the SDC had to go through lengthy due-diligence processes before any sale to Forest City could take place. Besides Forest City and the SDC, other parties involved included the city of Denver, citizens' groups from the surrounding neighborhoods, the Federal Aviation Administration, and the airlines that were former Stapleton tenants.

Because of the sheer size of the site, the land surveys, environmental assessments, and title transfers took longer than expected. Forest City, however, was ready for the challenge and the long wait. Unlike many development firms, Forest City is vertically integrated, meaning that it controls all stages of the project. The firm not only builds commercial space—office buildings, shopping centers, and entertainment venues— but also has expertise in land development, financing, and residential construction. Forest City even has its own lumber wholesaling business. In short, Forest City's large, diverse portfolio (with assets exceeding $5 billion) allowed it to sustain the extended due-diligence process.

the Denver Department of Aviation agreed to undertake environmental remediation, substantially demolish unwanted buildings, and obtain rezoning for redevelopment.

Over a period of 15 years, Forest City will pay $79.4 million for 2,935 acres (1,188 hectares), which is the amount of remaining land that had not already been sold or set aside for the 1,116 acres (452 hectares) of open space, plus a "sys-

Financing

Stapleton is very much a public/private partnership. The TIF arrangement was essential to funding the $600 million in local and regional infrastructure costs. Since DURA is the only entity in Denver with the statutory power to fund redevelopment through the use of TIF, its involvement in Stapleton was crucial.

DURA was created in 1958 by the city, pursuant to state law, and is charged with responsibility for urban renewal—including the prevention and elimination of blight—throughout the city and county of Denver. DURA is governed by an 11-member board of commissioners appointed by the mayor of Denver and confirmed by the city council.

TIF, simply defined, captures the net increase in property or sales taxes in a redeveloped area and directs the funds toward the costs of specific public projects. When a redevelopment project is being planned, DURA estimates how much additional tax revenue will be generated once it is completed. DURA can then use that "tax increment" either to finance the issuance of bonds or to reimburse developers for a portion of their project financing. In either case, the new tax revenue must be used for improvements that have a public benefit and that support the redevelopment effort; examples include site acquisition and clearance; the construction or improvement of streets, utilities, parks, or schools; and the removal of hazardous materials or conditions.

TIF is used only when an area or property cannot be redeveloped without public investment and when redevelopment meets a public objective—and then only to fill the gap between the total project cost and the level of private financing the project can support. In the case of developer reimbursement, the level of reimbursement depends on the success of the project: the developer gets the money only if the project creates the extra value for the city. All the additional taxes created by the redevelopment revert to the normal taxing entities once DURA has fulfilled the financial obligations related to a project. Thus, the neighborhood benefits from the creation of revitalized, productive properties, and the taxing entities get new, permanent revenue sources that would not have existed if DURA had not made it possible for the project to be undertaken.

Special districts, including TIF districts, provide a means of imposing additional taxes and fees to support capital improvements and operations. And because Denver's property tax rates are low when compared with those of adjacent jurisdictions, the use of special districts seems less burdensome in the Denver area than it might elsewhere. Under Colorado statutes, TIF districts may be in place for 25 years. For Stapleton, the 2001 assessed value was $28,189,478; the estimated increment is $16,982,682; and the estimated incremental revenue is $835,000. It is anticipated that over the 25-year construction period, as new residential and commercial real estate projects are added to the tax base, the annual property tax increment will grow to $93 million.

During the first five years of TIF revenues, 100 percent of the property tax increment will be devoted to Stapleton redevelopment projects. Thereafter, the city will retain an increasing percentage of the total tax increment (both sales and property). By year 20, the retained percentage will reach 47 percent; these funds will go largely toward paying for the increased demands from new residents for city services, such as police, fire, roads, and utilities.

One of the main and earliest revenue generators in Stapleton is Quebec Square, whose big-box tenants will create plenty of sales volume—which will, in turn, yield large amounts of sales

The 100 Clyburn at Stapleton apartments are reserved for income-qualified seniors.

Forest City Stapleton

tax revenues. Forest City estimates that Quebec Square will generate $8 million in tax revenues annually; 1,000 homes, in contrast, would generate $1.2 million in tax revenues.

To underwrite the initial infrastructure required for the redevelopment, Forest City purchased $145 million in bonds from the Park Creek Metropolitan District, a transaction that was financed by Lehman Brothers. For the initial purchase from the SDC, Forest City secured a $25 million loan from National City Bank.

The fact that Forest City is a large, integrated firm that emphasizes long-term investments allowed it to bear much of the upfront costs. By assuming this risk, the firm will also reap most of the project's rewards. Forest City intends to deliver between 550 and 600 single-family residential units per year, at varying price points. Delivering the units in phases will allow the firm to tailor plans to market needs.

The affordable housing at Stapleton has, so far, been financed in part by the Fannie Mae Foundation's American Communities Fund, tax-exempt bonds, and Low-Income Housing Tax Credits; it has also been assisted by discounted land costs from Forest City.

Design and Architecture

Stapleton's master plan calls for the development to fit seamlessly into the patterns of the surrounding neighborhoods. The nearby housing stock consists mostly of single-family homes with front porches. Lots are modest, the neighborhoods include pocket parks, and the streets are lined with sidewalks and mature trees. The homes in Stapleton will mirror these patterns, and will also reflect other characteristics of historic downtown Denver, such as shade trees and facade ornamentation. The neighborhood streets will be relatively narrow, to lessen the speed of automobiles.

The residential properties in the early phases will fall into 12 categories: six single-family, detached-home products; two types of row-houses; apartments; rental units, some of which will be live/work; and four- and six-unit buildings designed to look like vernacular mansions. To ensure diversity in design, household income, and family profile, the housing types will be mixed in each of the districts. Consistent with the new urbanist approach, the garages will be placed in the alleyways.

Forest City worked with homebuilders to design homes that, although mass-produced at least in part, are aesthetically pleasing and reflective of Denver's history. The Stapleton Design Book, created under the direction of Forest City Stapleton by EDAW, Inc., Wolff Lyon Architects, and Calthorpe Associates, and published in 2000, recommends four primary styles: Victorian, craftsman, colonial revival, and Denver foursquare; and two secondary styles: English revival and Mediterranean revival.

As noted earlier, all the homes at Stapleton are required to meet, and preferably exceed, the minimum standards of the Built Green Colorado program. Built Green Colorado is administered by the Home Builders Association of Metro Denver and supported by the Governor's Office of Energy Management and Conservation. It is a voluntary program that uses buyer demand, market education, and builder training to encourage builders to construct homes that emit less pollution, are energy-efficient, have healthier indoor air, reduce water usage, preserve natural resources, and have greater durability and lower maintenance.

Within Stapleton's eight districts are seven planning zones, and plans for five mixed-use town centers. Each planning zone covers roughly 500 acres (202 hectares), which will be further divided into 100-acre (40-hectare) neighborhoods. The master plan calls for a 1,116-acre (452-hectare) open-space system, which will be maintained by the city and county of Denver and will traverse the site from north to south. Office and retail uses will be within walking distance of residential neighborhoods.

The mixed-use town centers will feature prominently in the development; each center will be focused on a main street lined with two- and three-story buildings. Retail and office uses will occupy ground-floor spaces, and offices and residential lofts will be built on upper levels. The first town center, East 29th Avenue Town Center, and a regional retail center, Quebec Square, have been developed in the first district.

One of the goals of the Stapleton project was the efficient reuse of some of the unique aspects of the old airport. The 264-foot (80-meter) control tower has been preserved and will be used as a visitors' center. Old hangars and outbuildings have been adapted to house Colorado Studios, a local news channel, the Denver Police Training Academy, the Bladium Sports Club of Denver, and R.K. Mechanical Contractors.

When the remaining terminal buildings were demolished, 50 percent of the concrete, rebar, and sheet metal was recycled. The 1,100 acres (445 hectares) of asphalt on parking lots and former runways was crushed up, for use as road base and concrete aggregate for Stapleton's roads, trails, and sidewalks, as well as for use in other projects around Denver. The first new bridge on the Stapleton site was constructed out of Staple-Stone (otherwise known as old runway material), and more than 200,000 tons (181,437 metric tons) of asphalt were transported to the Rocky Mountain Arsenal National Wildlife Refuge, where they were used to create road base. The terminal's 5,000-car garage has become the

Stapleton Transit Center, now one of the busiest transportation hubs in the metropolitan area. Even some of the old carpeting from the former terminal complex was recycled into carpet backing that is durable, cheap, and free of the outgassing that can cause indoor air pollution.

More than one-third of the site has been preserved for open space and parks. A new golf course will eventually be built on the northern half of the site. The 123-acre (50-hectare) Bluff Lake Natural Area serves as an outdoor classroom for thousands of children who study the wetlands and observe wildlife, including bald eagles, great horned owls, foxes, and a variety of aquatic fowl. When the network of recreation trails is complete, it will be the first loop of trails ever to surround a major U.S. city. Stapleton's bike paths will connect to Denver's regional bikeway and flow into the 27,000-acre (10,927-hectare) Rocky Mountain Wildlife Preserve.

Forest City, the SDC, and the Denver Regional Transportation District are jointly involved in planning for a future multimodal transit center that will be incorporated into the regional retail center and office development to be built between Quebec and Yosemite streets. Currently, bus service runs along the edges of the site, and stops will eventually be located within Stapleton.

Marketing

With the addition of ballparks, bike paths, microbreweries, and upscale boutiques, Denver is promoting itself as a hip and culturally vibrant city. This is an image on which Stapleton, with its range of retail offerings and housing types, hopes to capitalize. As of 2003, prices and sales rates for new homes in the city remained strong, despite a recent economic slump. Blueprint Denver, the city's 20-year growth management plan, estimates that the city will add 130,000 people and 109,000 jobs between 2000 and 2020.

The first purchasers of Stapleton properties were large clients, such as corporations and builders of industrial parks; eventually, however, smaller clients with specialized projects became interested—and homebuilders, in particular, were eager to become part of Stapleton. Forest City is trying to attract homeowners who are looking for a "third choice"—the first two choices being the old home in the city and the new house in the suburbs. Stapleton provides an urban feel, but is filled with greenery, open space, and parks.

The Forest City Stapleton Visitor Center welcomes visitors, buyers, renters, business owners, and the press to its storefront presence in the East 29th Avenue Town Center. The center features a video wall that integrates actual aerial footage of the property with "virtual reality" images of the first neighborhoods built. Another highlight of the visitor center is a network of pavilions, each with its own display, that offers glimpses into the residential, office, retail, and open-space elements in the new, mixed-use neighborhoods. The pavilions also provide information about Stapleton initiatives, including sustainable development, an educational environment that fosters lifelong learning, modern telecommunications linkages, and other features that will create a diverse, walkable urban community.

One of the most important strategies for making Stapleton appealing to families, and for competing with suburban developments, was to ensure that the schools were of high quality. At the time the master plan was being developed, the Denver public school system was struggling to maintain standards, and it was thought that potential Stapleton homebuyers would not want to send their children to the Denver public schools. Forest City worked with the Denver public schools to negotiate the establishment of public schools on the grounds of Stapleton (but

The higher-density residential development at Stapleton allowed for the preservation of significant amounts of open space.

Forest City Stapleton

within the Denver system), because Stapleton students would otherwise have been bussed to city schools. Charter, private, vocational, and online-learning schools will also be built. Current plans call for at least four elementary schools and two high schools, as well as a number of early-childhood-education facilities.

Stapleton's Westerly Creek Campus, which opened August 18, 2003, is an 80,000-square-foot (7,432-square-meter) building in which a charter school and a traditional elementary school share common facilities. The Denver School of Science and Technology, a $14 million charter high school dedicated to increasing the proficiency of high school students in mathematics, science, and technology, opened in Stapleton in 2004. Forest City donated 10 acres (four hec-

tares) of land and $500,000 toward the construction of the school. Additional support came from the Bill and Melinda Gates Foundation, Hewlett-Packard, and numerous other national and local organizations. Forest City has also committed funds to schools in the surrounding area, to increase Stapleton's positive impact and to avoid creating the sense of a gated community.

Developers estimate that houses will be coming on line at a rate of 50 to 75 every month for the next 12 years. Stapleton's residential offerings range from workforce housing to "urban estates"—homes priced between $600,000 and $1 million. The designs of the larger homes reflect traditional Denver architectural styles and offer carriage units, broad front porches, and high-end finishes.

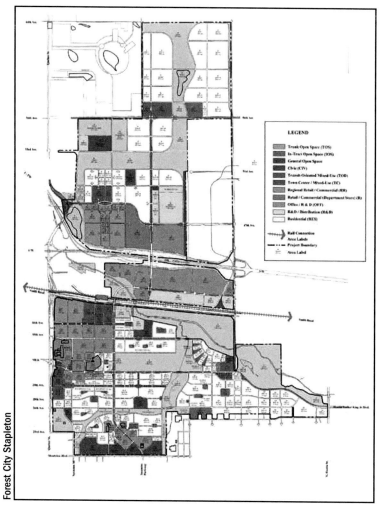

Forest City Stapleton

The Stapleton Redevelopment Plan, also known as the Green Book, guides development of the site. The plan outlines a clear dedication to traditional neighborhood design, environmental conservation, minority participation, and high-quality educational opportunities.

Because of its proximity to Interstate 70, Stapleton has tremendous appeal to retailers. Stapleton can accommodate a range of retailers in its big-box centers, town squares, and main streets. Quebec Square, the first retail center to open in Stapleton, sits on 80 acres (32 hectares) and contains 800,000 square feet (74,322 square meters) of big-box retail stores. A 1.2 million-square-foot (111,484-square-meter) outdoor mall opened in 2005. Both centers are located on Interstate 70 and have good freeway visibility.

The 57,000-square-foot (5,295-square-meter) East 29th Street Town Center provides a more pedestrian-oriented scale than Quebec Square. It features a variety of neighborhood restaurants

and specialty stores, a King Soopers grocery store, and services such as banking and dry cleaning. The town center also includes Crescent Flats: 66 one- and two-bedroom rental flats above ground-floor retail. The Main Street Office Suites offers 34,000 square feet (3,158 square meters) of executive offices overlooking 29th Avenue, Stapleton's first main street. Two projects complete the town center: the Botanica on the Green Apartments, 232 one-, two-, and three-bedroom rental flats, townhouses, and live/work lofts, with attached garages available on select floor plans, and Clyburn at Stapleton, 100 units of affordable rental apartments for seniors.

The Stapleton Technology Master Plan was developed to equip Stapleton's homes with high-speed communications wiring and, in turn, increase their appeal to future residents. The technology master plan has three integrated components: home wiring, service providers, and a community network. To ensure adequate capacity, Stapleton allied with Qwest Communications and AT&T broadband to develop the Stapleton Residential Wiring Guidelines. Stapleton also has its own intranet, where residents can browse through forums and newsgroups and learn about new stores, services, and events.

Stapleton recently incorporated wireless technology, which resulted in lower construction costs. When installing and subsequently moving data cables for the construction trailers became problematic and expensive, Forest City decided to link the trailers to a wireless system, which involved a one-time expenditure of about $50,000. Companies on the wireless network discovered that the former air-traffic control tower could be used as a generation and transfer point for the signals. Stapleton's transfer to wireless technology will eliminate the time required to install fiber-optic cable, yielding approximately $2.2 million in savings over a 15-year period.

Stapleton is marketed as a walking and biking community, but it also offers access to Honda Civic Hybrids (gasoline-electric engines) that can be rented by the hour or by the month. A single fee covers gas, insurance, maintenance, and emergency service. The program is an attractive option for those who choose not to own a vehicle, or who need a second vehicle for short trips.

Stapleton is located in Denver's Urban Enterprise Zone, a state program under which businesses that move to or expand in the zone are eligible to receive credits against their liability for business income taxes.

Experience Gained

Because of the sheer scale of the Stapleton redevelopment, one of the greatest challenges facing Forest City has been the coordination and implementation of a range of development activities that are nearly unprecedented in their scope. To construct the single-family homes, for example, Forest City had to coordinate the work of 18 different builders who had been selected for their ability to create housing that meets high standards for urban design and energy efficiency, and is also affordable to a wide range of incomes. Obtaining the permits, plat approvals, and zoning changes for such a large property was another major hurdle.

Forest City points to its positive working relationship with city officials, local nonprofits, and the surrounding community as a major source of the project's momentum. The firm respected the plans that the city and the citizens' groups made, and included minority- and women-owned business as contractors.

Another challenge was to economically jump-start the project so that homes, retail shops, and office space could be constructed simultaneously. Often, a large portion of the homes in a project must be built out to create the base needed to justify retail space. In the case of Stapleton, the economic generator that started the project was Quebec Square, a regional, automobile-oriented shopping center. Citizens' groups were taken aback, however, by the scale of the proposed big-box center, and pointed out that it was not in the spirit of the neotraditional planning patterns applied elsewhere in the development. The designers approached this problem through education, and by reminding all the parties involved what the overall goals of Stapleton were. To be built successfully, the pedestrian-oriented neighborhoods and business districts needed an economic generator. Regional retail, while not ordinarily consistent with pedestrian-oriented development, would provide the necessary economic security. The designers also planned the regional retail site so that it could eventually accommodate denser uses. Specifically, the surrounding street grid was extended into Quebec Square, bringing with it pedestrian access and public transit, and ensuring connections from adjacent uses.

Although Stapleton has almost 20 years to go until buildout, its presence is already having a positive effect on surrounding neighborhoods. The demolition of some of the large, unsightly utility buildings, the restoration of open space, the reduction of noise pollution, and the infusion of new retail businesses have brought increased property values, tax revenues, and neighborhood pride.

Note

1. Although the seller walks away from the table with $30,940 (62 percent of $50,000), $7,000 of that amount was the seller's 5 percent downpayment, and $11,440 was paid down through the seller's mortgage payments; thus, the remaining $12,500 is the seller's share of the appreciation—which is 25 percent of the estimated $50,000 in appreciation.

Stapleton

Project Team

Owner/Developer
Forest City Stapleton, Inc.
    (a wholly owned subsidiary of
    Forest City Enterprises, Inc.)
7351 East 29th Avenue
Denver, Colorado 80238
303-382-1800
www.Stapletondenver.com

Master Planner
Calthorpe Associates
739 Allston Way
Berkeley, California 94710
510-548-6800
www.calthorpe.com

Architects: Design Book
Calthorpe Associates
EDAW, Inc.
Forest City Stapleton, Inc.
Wolff Lyon Architects

Architects: Building Architecture
Alan Eban Brown
EDAW, Inc.
Harold Massop
KA Architects
Nuszer Kopatz
Semple Brown
The Mulhern Group, LTD
The Urban Design Group
Thomas Cox Architects
Wolff Lyon Architects

Engineers
JF Sato
HCL Engineering
Matrix Engineers
ME Engineering
Milestone Engineering
SA Miro
URS

Development Schedule

Site purchased	February 2000
Construction started	May 2001
Projected completion	2020

Land Use Information

Total site area	4,700 acres
Number of single-family detached units	249
Number of single-family attached units	780

Land Use	Square Footage (Existing)	Square Footage (at Buildout)
Retail	900,000	3,000,000
Office	34,000	10,000,000

Retail Information

Tenant Type	Number of Stores
General merchandise	2
Food service	17
Clothing and accessories	2
Shoes	3
Home furnishings	3
Gift and specialty	5
Pharmacy	2
Personal services	19
Recreation and community uses	1
Financial	8
Other	10
Total	72

Development Costs

Category of Cost	Spent to Date (in Millions)	Project Total (in Millions)
Site acquisition	$40	$125
Site improvements	$80	$620
Construction	$410	$3,470
Soft costs	$220	$1,840
Total	$750	$6,055

Tierra Contenta
Santa Fe, New Mexico

Project Information

Located in Santa Fe, New Mexico, Tierra Contenta is a 1,007-acre (408-hectare) mixed-income housing development with a strong workforce housing component. The project features both single-family homes and multifamily housing, and at least 40 percent of the housing will be affordable to families whose incomes are at or below 80 percent of area median income (AMI). Plans for the site also include commercial areas, the Santa Fe Business Incubator, public schools, a public library, a youth facility, and over 300 acres (121 hectares) of open space and parks connected by a trail system.

The impetus for the development came in 1992, when the City of Santa Fe purchased 862 acres (349 hectares) of the 1,007 acres (408 hectares) that would become Tierra Contenta from a recently bankrupt land developer. Upon completion, the development is expected to

The property on which Tierra Contenta is being built is bisected by an arroyo (a streambed with many dry tributaries), which forms the structure for a system of bicycle and pedestrian trails.

house 3,800 households, or 9,500 people. Tierra Contenta represents an aggressive effort by the City of Santa Fe and other key stakeholders to address local and regional dynamics that limit the construction of homes that are affordable for the workforce.

Workforce Housing Information

New Mexico has a median household income of $31,981, one of the lowest in the country. In stark contrast to the rest of the state, the median household income in Santa Fe County is $66,000, which places it among the wealthier counties in the country. The disparity comes from two changes that have occurred during the past 25 years: first, Santa Fe has become increasingly attractive to wealthy homebuyers and retirees; second, the area has become a tourist destination, which has increased the need for workers in the low-wage tourism industry. Thus, the wealthy population has increased the region's median income and driven up housing prices, while the demand for cheap labor has increased the need for affordable housing. By the 1990s, 80 percent of the county's population could no longer afford a median-priced home, and 40 percent of the population was expending an excessive amount of income for housing. By 1994, local housing prices were 50 percent higher than the national average, and wages were 20 percent lower. This was the environment that created the need and the impetus for Tierra Contenta.

The workforce housing component of Tierra Contenta is straightforward: in return for the generous terms provided to the Tierra Contenta

Norton Francis

(continued on page 134)

The Santa Fe Affordable Housing Roundtable

The Santa Fe Affordable Housing Roundtable is a public/nonprofit partnership established in the early 1990s to implement the city's strategic plan for housing. It is a policy-making and coordinating committee made up of representatives from the city and the nonprofit sector, and many of its members were involved in the original strategic planning process. The roundtable was key to building support for Tierra Contenta and has played an important role in its development—demonstrating that, given the right stakeholders, such a partnership can create positive policy changes and coordinate their implementation.

Organization and Objectives

The roundtable has a formal set of bylaws and established policies and procedures, but it is not incorporated and has no paid staff or operating budget. Staff from the Enterprise Foundation and the City of Santa Fe Community Development Division serve as administrative staff for the roundtable. The roundtable was originally made up of representatives from ten organizations, seven of which were local nonprofits working in some capacity with housing in Santa Fe: Neighborhood Housing Services of Santa Fe; the Santa Fe Community Housing Trust; the Santa Fe County Housing Authority; the Santa Fe Civic Housing Authority; Santa Fe Habitat for Humanity; the Santa Fe Land Trust; the City of Santa Fe Community Development Division; the Enterprise Foundation; United Way of Santa Fe County; and the Transitional Housing Coalition. The current makeup of the organization is largely the same.

The Strategic Housing Plan for Santa Fe had four goals:

■ To build the capacity of nonprofit providers;
■ To obtain new sources of low-cost capital;
■ To bring more affordable land to market;
■ To assist 700 households over three years.

To ensure that these goals were met, the following objectives were developed for the roundtable:

■ Coordinate and monitor the implementation of the Strategic Housing Plan;
■ Serve as a vehicle for communication and collaboration among housing organizations;
■ Leverage new resources for affordable housing;
■ Allocate certain resources (primarily funds from a newly created housing trust fund);
■ Assist participating organizations in advocating for changes in public policy;
■ Educate the public about affordable-housing issues.

Results

The roundtable has been very successful at meeting the goals of the strategic plan. In 1996, in recognition of its achievements, the organization received an Innovations in American Government award, sponsored by the Ford Foundation and the John F. Kennedy School of Government at Harvard University.

The large increase in the capacity of nonprofit housing organizations in Santa Fe is perhaps the most important achievement of the roundtable. Three organizations that the roundtable helped develop—the Tierra Contenta Corporation, the Santa Fe Community Housing Trust, and Neighborhood Housing Services of Santa Fe—have been particularly successful. The collaboration fostered by the roundtable has greatly increased the pool of money available for affordable-housing projects—and has, in turn, leveraged millions of dollars from private foundations, provided match money for federal grants, and helped projects achieve the level where they would be most competitive for state funding. The roundtable was a key advocate in persuading the city to purchase the land that would eventually become Tierra Contenta, a decision that expanded the amount of affordable land available in the Santa Fe market. Finally, collaborations fostered by the roundtable greatly expanded the number of new housing programs and projects, thereby increasing assistance to low- and moderate-income households.

Among the programs and policies for which the roundtable is responsible are the following:

■ The Affordable Housing Trust Fund is a funding mechanism for the development of affordable housing. The fund is largely made up of donations from Santa Fe developers and is administered by the Santa Fe Community Housing Trust; however, the members of the roundtable collectively determine how the dollars are to be allocated. The money, matched with other federal and conventional funding, is used exclusively for affordable-housing projects in Santa Fe. Had the city accepted the donations directly, use of the funds would be restricted by state law; but because a separate fund has been created, the dollars can be used by nonprofits to cover the costs of their affordable-housing projects and to leverage other funding.
■ For nonprofit developers of affordable housing, Santa Fe waives upfront construction fees and building-permit fees.
■ New developments in which at least 25 percent of the homes will be affordable receive fast-track approval (these projects are given priority in the development review and permitting processes).

■ Three nonprofit housing agencies offer homebuyer education programs. Two programs—sponsored by the Santa Fe Community Housing Trust and Neighborhood Housing Services of Santa Fe—feature evening and weekend classes taught by representatives from banks, real estate agencies, county government, and the construction industry. The offerings include classes on personal budgeting and the homebuying process; topics include how to apply for a loan, the tax benefits of owning a home, preventing foreclosure, and home maintenance.

■ The Housing Opportunity Program, an initiative undertaken by the Santa Fe Community Development Division, is designed to create affordable housing and to help increase economic integration in Santa Fe. Administered through the city's inclusionary zoning ordinance, the program requires that developers of projects in which all the homes will be priced above $202,000 set aside a certain number of the new homes for low- to moderate-income households. In exchange for building the more affordable homes, developers are allowed to increase the number of high-end homes by the same percentage. (Tierra Contenta does not fall under this policy.)

■ Under the Land Trust/Land Lease Program, administered by the Santa Fe Community Housing Trust, land is donated to the trust, which then develops and sells homes on the land; however, only the homes themselves are sold. The land remains in a trust that is managed by a membership organization made up of the individual homeowners. Taking the cost of the land out of the home's price reduces the overall cost of housing production. In addition, the homebuyers sign limited-appreciation contracts to ensure long-term affordability.

Corporation (TCC) for the transfer of land, at least 40 percent of the housing units are required to be priced affordably for residents who earn up to 80 percent of AMI.[1] These housing units are defined as the "most affordable" homes. In the short term, the affordability of these units comes from the fact that the below-market cost of the land that TCC acquired from the city has been passed through to the homeowners. This arrangement allows the "most affordable" units to be sold for approximately $160,000, while most of the market-rate units sell for $200,000 to $250,000. Through a program managed by TCC, families that need the extra money to make a home purchase possible receive a $6,000 soft second mortgage. The loan is gradually forgiven between years seven and ten. If a home is sold before year ten, the owner must use sales proceeds to repay whatever balance remains on the subsidy.

Longer-term affordability is ensured in two ways. Some of the single-family homes were built through land trusts, which ensures that the land is held in perpetuity for the benefit of the community and takes the cost of land out of the total housing price, reducing the price of the final product. For several of the multifamily apartment complexes within the development, the use of the Low-Income Housing Tax Credit ensures that rents will be restricted for 40 years.

Site, Surroundings, and History

Tierra Contenta sits to the southwest of Santa Fe's central business district. The property was originally unincorporated land in Santa Fe County and was owned by multiple landowners. Because the property was bisected by an arroyo (a streambed) with many dry tributaries and featured challenging topography, large-scale development was perceived as risky. Developers began to take notice of the property in the 1980s: arroyos or not, the property was in the direct path of growth moving out from central Santa Fe. In the early 1980s, Bellamah Community Development purchased 862 acres (349 hectares) from a number of separate landowners and developed a master plan for a bedroom community on the site. Bellamah was one of the many development firms caught up in the savings-and-loan scandal of the 1980s. The firm's property portfolio was taken over by the Resolution Trust Corporation, which was established by Congress to deal with troubled savings and loans.

In the early 1990s, housing affordability emerged as a major issue for the city. In May 1991, the Enterprise Foundation, a nationwide community development organization, was asked to assess housing issues in Santa Fe and to propose solutions. The foundation's two key recommendations were to develop a strategic housing plan, and to create a public/private partnership to implement the plan. The strategic plan called for the city to spur affordable-housing creation through financial assistance. The plan also led to the creation of the Santa Fe Affordable Housing Roundtable, an affordable-housing trust fund, and a land trust. All three elements have added to the success of Tierra Contenta.

Ouida MacGregor, a former city councilwoman, and others within the affordable-housing community urged the city to take an active role in affordable-housing creation, but only if the resulting developments would be mixed income and mixed use. MacGregor's arguments in favor of mixed-income, mixed-used development won the city over. In early 1992, the city of Santa Fe purchased the 862 acres (349 hectares) from the Resolution Trust Corporation for $6.28 million, with the intention of developing it as a mixed-income and mixed-use community. It was annexed to the city in 1994.

In 1992, the city funded a master plan; the team that developed the plan included Peter Calthorpe and a local firm, Mazria and Associates. The plan is based both on new urbanist principles and on planning and design concepts native to the Santa Fe region.

In 1993, the city created TCC to oversee the development of the project, and sold its acreage to TCC. TCC is repaying the city the $6.28 million note that came with the purchase of the land. A condition of this arrangement is that at least 40 percent of the housing units are required

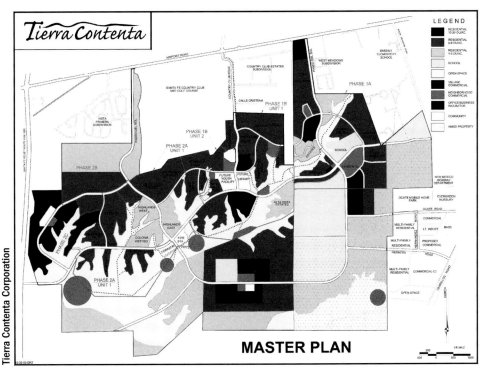

The master plan for Tierra Contenta, developed by Peter Calthorpe and a local firm, Mazria and Associates, is based on new urbanist principles and planning and design concepts native to the Santa Fe region.

The Tierra Contenta Corporation (TCC) does all the preliminary development work and sells lots to a variety of builders. In return for providing affordable lot prices, TCC requires that 40 percent of the units be affordable.

The master plan emphasizes several fundamental characteristics of new urbanist planning and design, including the following:

- Orientation to the pedestrian, instead of to the automobile;
- Dispersed community and commercial centers;
- A mix of affordable and market-rate housing;
- Preservation of open space;
- Mixed use;
- Street connectivity;
- Alternative transportation choices.

to be priced affordably for households earning 80 percent of Santa Fe's median income, as defined by the U.S. Department of Housing and Urban Development (HUD).

Planning and Development

The planning and development of Tierra Contenta are guided by two key documents: Santa Fe's Planned Residential Community (PRC) ordinance, and Tierra Contenta's master plan. The PRC details the requirements for large-scale developments; it also allows deviations from the city's planning and development regulations—an important factor, since new urbanist developments do not meet the requirements of traditional planning regulations.

Tierra Contenta's master plan established the development's overall configuration. The master-planning team used the arroyo that bisects the development to create an open-space channel through Tierra Contenta; the arroyo's numerous dry tributaries act as open-space "fingers," creating a unique framework for development. The arroyo system forms the structure for a bike and pedestrian trail system that is linked to the regional Arroyo Chamiso trail system.

Goals for Tierra Contenta that have been defined by TCC, the city, and other stakeholders also help guide the development. These goals are categorized by type, and address economic, ecological, visual and aesthetic, social, and health and safety issues. They reinforce and provide specific guidance for (1) the city's original objective, which was to provide affordable housing in a mixed-income setting; (2) the master plan; and (3) TCC's development program and day-to-day management of the project.

Operations

TCC manages the overall development of the site with a lean staff of three. In 1993, the TCC board of directors created a development program for the Tierra Contenta master plan. The development program outlines the type, density, and arrangement of land uses and establishes pricing strategies for both land and housing products. Since at least 40 percent of the housing within Tierra Contenta must be affordable to households earning no more than 80 percent of AMI, the pricing structure is designed to ensure that Tierra Contenta meets the 40 percent affordability goal while remaining competitive in the Santa Fe market. Using the proceeds from land sales alone, TCC was able to construct the spine of infrastructure necessary for the development, pay back its debt to the city, and manage without subsequent financial subsidy from the public sector.

TCC secures development entitlements for tracts of land on a phase-by-phase basis; phasing is consistent with the master plan. The entitlement process includes preparing design standards and subdivision plats, readying tracts for sale to developers, and preparing the development plan for each phase. TCC also manages the building of the spine infrastructure, and dedicates land for parks, open space, and other public uses. TCC has completed the master platting for three phases: Phase IA, Phase IB, and Phase IIA. This represents about 54 percent of the total residential development owned by Tierra Contenta. A fourth phase, Phase IIB, was recently platted.

For each phase of the project, TCC recruits builders to develop the residential and nonresidential land uses. Given the high demand for its development tracts, TCC can be selective in its choice of builders. For-profit builders include BT Housing; Centex Homes; Colonia Prisma/ Allied Homes; Las Fuerzas, LLC; and Philip Gudwin. Habitat for Humanity has also been active in the development.

TCC develops the infrastructure in phases of ten to 15 tracts at a time. Prior to construction, projects must receive the approval of the city's Permit and Development Review Division, the Santa Fe Planning Commission, and the Tierra Contenta Architectural Review Committee. Builders are required to provide interior streets and to distribute the required affordable-housing units throughout their subdivisions.

Norton Francis

Financing

The economic goals for Tierra Contenta and TCC are focused on ensuring (1) that the development will be self-supporting, (2) that it will succeed within the free-market framework of the Santa Fe economy, and (3) that it will not strain the city's budget. Financing arrangements for Tierra Contenta held relatively true to these goals. James Hicks, executive director of TCC, explained that without the city's initial financial backing, Tierra Contenta would not have been possible; there was just too much risk associated with the project for traditional private lending institutions to bear.

Paying in cash to avoid bonds and interest payments, the city purchased the bulk of Tierra Contenta from the Resolution Trust Corporation for $6.28 million. As noted earlier, this cost was transferred to TCC when TCC was established. To complete the development, additional property was purchased from a private landowner who happened to be a member of the family of Sam Pick, who was mayor of Santa Fe at the time. This $1.6 million purchase was funded through a $3 million, three-year municipal

The combination of low land costs and low-income housing tax credits helps builders meet the goal of making 40 percent of the units affordable.

Although the village centers at Tierra Contenta have not attracted retailers (because of an inward-facing road network and the perception that the population has yet to reach critical mass), a few parcels on the periphery have succeeded in drawing commercial uses. A 30,000-square-foot (2,787-square-meter) business incubator was developed on one such parcel.

Norton Francis

bond, and was the city's major financial contribution to the project. A $1.6 million special-purpose HUD grant provided needed cash for the initial construction of infrastructure.

In the early stages of development, TCC ran into some cash flow problems. Under TCC's financial plan, the sale of tracts for commercial and community uses was intended to help fund infrastructure costs. But for various reasons, the commercial parcels did not sell. The problem was rectified when residential sales in Phase I injected the needed capital. TCC continues to have problems with commercial parcels, however, many of which remain undeveloped. The organization is considering selling off several of the parcels along the edge of the development, which would remove them from the master plan.

Revenue from TCC's sale of land to developers funds the expansion of Tierra Contenta's spine infrastructure, TCC's administrative and marketing costs, interest expenses, and repayment of principal for the land transferred from the city.

TCC currently repays the city about $12,000 per lot—which, given the escalating value of land in Santa Fe, translates into a subsidy from the city. The lower land costs make it possible to sell homes in the development for below-market value.

Builders have HUD's HOME program and federal Low-Income Housing Tax Credits as key sources of low-cost capital to leverage more traditional investments for the construction of the affordable housing. Builders also get financial breaks through citywide policies that grant affordable-housing developers waivers of building permit fees and impact fees, reduced utility expansion charges for water meter services, and fast-track approvals. The city's Affordable Housing Trust Fund, administered by the Santa Fe Community Housing Trust, channels donations from market-rate housing developers to nonprofit developers for affordable housing, and has assisted with the financing of affordable homes within Tierra Contenta.

Design and Architecture

Since the inception of the project, the quality of Tierra Contenta's design has been a primary concern for stakeholders. The project got off to a good start with a master plan co-created by Peter Calthorpe, one of the country's most sought-after new urbanist designers. The plan used the natural features of the land to create a framework for development, and combined new urbanist concepts and traditional Santa Fe development patterns. The goals of the Tierra Contenta development program, as established in the master plan, were as follows:

- Set a ceiling for development intensity on a phase-by-phase basis;
- Create a neotraditional urban form by locating a mix of uses in a pattern that promotes access for pedestrians and nonmotorized vehicles, as well as for automobiles;
- Create three village centers to provide goods and services to the resident population;
- Reflect some of Santa Fe's traditional development patterns by clustering residential units around a common point or area of interest;
- Establish the spine transportation and utility system for the planning area.

Many new urbanist concepts have been tested in Tierra Contenta, with varying results. The village centers have been the biggest failure because of the difficulty of attracting retailers. Hicks explained that retailers were not comfortable moving into a development that wasn't built out; they were also concerned that even when the project was completed, it would not provide a large enough market to support successful retail. Retailers were also concerned about the street network, which discouraged through-traffic. Although it may be ideal for households, such a network is not attractive to retailers.

Norton Francis

The architecture for new development must receive the approval of several groups, including the Tierra Contenta Architectural Review Committee.

Because of the reluctance of retailers to move into the village centers, TCC has modified the concept, opting instead to focus the village centers around community amenities such as libraries and youth facilities.

This is not to say that the notion of mixed use has been entirely abandoned. TCC has two parcels of land zoned for office or business-incubator use, and two parcels zoned for neighborhood commercial use. All these parcels sit on the periphery of the development, with easy access to major arterials. One of the office/business-incubator parcels is home to a 30,000-square-foot (2,787-square-meter) business incubator; the other half of the space is devoted to light manufacturing uses. Plaza Contenta, the development's first neighborhood commercial

Norton Francis

While the city reviewing bodies focus on design issues such as lot size, setbacks, and parking, the Tierra Contenta Architectural Review Committee looks at the configuration of groups of homes, building facades, roof form, landscaping, and solar access.

center, will include small shops and second-story residential condominiums. An elementary school, middle school, and high school are also located within the development.

Parking has been another source of disappointment. Phase I called for two spaces plus a garage per dwelling unit, but it soon became apparent that this standard would not provide enough parking. TCC found that lower-income households tend to have more cars, often because an older car is kept as a spare, in case another car breaks down. Moreover, since the Tierra Contenta units do not have basements, the garages are used as storage areas instead of as parking space. TCC solved the problem in subsequent phases by providing 2.5 parking spaces, plus a garage, for each dwelling unit. Because emergency vehicles had difficulty navigating the street network in Phase I, TCC is also gradually moving to slightly wider streets.

Tierra Contenta has also tested new urbanist approaches to residential density. The master plan calls for three densities in residential zones: ten to 20 dwelling units per acre (25 to 49 per hectare), six to nine dwelling units per acre (15 to 22 per hectare), and one to five dwelling units per acre (2.5 to 12 per hectare). Because of concerns about marketability, however, developers have tended to build at only about 80 percent of the allowed density, which has raised housing prices.

The new urbanist concept that has been most successful is the diverse mix of income levels. There are several reasons for this success, chief of which is the design quality of the housing. The design review process ensures design quality at Tierra Contenta. As noted earlier, each project must receive approval from the Santa Fe Permit and Development Review Division, the Santa Fe Planning Commission, and the Tierra Contenta Architectural Review Committee (ARC). The city and the ARC have separate approval processes, which means that there is some overlap between the two applications. TCC works with developers to prepare the applications for both the city and the ARC.

The design review process is guided by several important documents, including the city's PRC ordinance, the master plan, and detailed design standards. The design standards created for each phase of development provide the nuts-and-bolts guidance for the implementation of the design concepts that are articulated broadly in the master plan. It was intended that the design standards would be modified from phase to phase. This tactic has worked well; it allows TCC to adjust the standards according to lessons learned in past phases, and to adapt to changes in the perception of the development and to fluctuations in the real estate market.

The design standards articulate the requirements of the city and of the ARC under seven different categories: neighborhood commercial centers, single-family residential, residential compounds, neighborhood townhouses, neighborhood apartments, landscape requirements, and general standards, which cover street-related

The Master Plan calls for three densities in residential zones, ranging from a low of one dwelling unit per acre (2.5 per hectare) to a maximum of 20 units per acre (49 per hectare). The developer and builders report that for marketability, densities of about 80 percent of the maximum are being built. The townhouses shown here represent a medium-density residential development.

requirements and open-space protection. The city requirements focus on general, code-related items such as lot size and coverage, setbacks, garage specifications, and parking. The ARC requirements focus on the configuration of groups of homes, building facades, roof form, landscaping, and solar access. Neither set of requirements delineates different standards for the affordable and the market-rate units; in fact, much of the ARC review process is focused on ensuring that there are few differences between the two types of units. This effort has paid off: it is very difficult, particularly in the more recent phases, to distinguish the affordable units from the market-rate units.

Marketing

The sheer size and scope of Tierra Contenta are its most valuable marketing tools. Its large scale, and the lack of comparatively sized developments in the region, have ensured that builders and homebuyers are aware of the project. Individual developer/builders are responsible for marketing their developments. TCC has relied on Home-wise and the Santa Fe Community Housing Trust to market workforce housing options to potentially qualified homebuyers. Both organ-

izations also help to qualify families for the "most affordable" homes by certifying income eligibility, conducting homebuyer training, and providing downpayment assistance and other financial services.

Experience Gained

Use strategic planning. The city's strategic plan for addressing its housing affordability issues set the stage for Tierra Contenta. The Enterprise Foundation played a key role by facilitating the

The majority of the homes in Tierra Contenta are built and sold as market-rate units.

Norton Francis

The large scale of the community has created the need for additional community services, including libraries and a new fire station.

Create a flexible master plan. Tierra Contenta has the benefit of a well-developed master plan that clearly defines the scope, goals, and overall design of the development. At the same time, the plan is flexible enough to adjust to new realities.

Take advantage of natural features to design the development. The large arroyo that bisects Tierra Contenta is a visually stunning natural feature, and the land planners were wise to use it as a unifying theme throughout the development. The arroyo supplies open space, provides pedestrian connectivity, and naturally separates some individual development tracts.

Adjust your design concepts to market realities. Market realities required TCC to widen streets, increase parking, and modify the retail component of the master plan. The phasing process allows TCC to learn from past mistakes and make the necessary adjustments to future phases.

Maintain design control. Design control is crucial in ensuring the successful coexistence of housing targeted for workforce and market-rate buyers. The design review process has been a key factor in the development of innovative designs that do not distinguish affordable from market-rate homes. All stakeholders interviewed agreed that the review process has not only created design parity between the affordable and the market-rate units, but has also yielded better overall home design, site planning, and house orientation.

Use a mix of housing affordability strategies. Many different strategies were used to achieve housing affordability in Tierra Contenta, including direct subsidies, reduced land costs, soft second mortgages, and land trusts. Because these strategies are employed at all layers of the development process—from land purchase to permitting, construction, homeowner financing, and long-term affordability—their impact on any one party is reduced.

development of the strategic plan, assessing local housing needs, and providing capacity-building technical assistance to the city.

The plan called for the city to provide financial assistance to spur affordable-housing development and created the Santa Fe Affordable Housing Roundtable, which enhanced the capacity of nonprofit housing organizations and builders. The first factor made Tierra Contenta financially feasible; the second helped make it successful.

Provide homebuyer education. Homebuyer education was identified as an important component of Tierra Contenta's success. Santa Fe's various affordable-housing organizations have played a critical role in educating potential homebuyers and guiding them through the purchasing process.

Avoid concentrating the affordable units in one portion of the development. Pent-up demand for affordable housing made it politically necessary to provide a proportionally larger number of affordable units in Phase I of the development, resulting in concentrations of affordable units and separation between affordable and market-rate homes—potentially hurting the future sales of both. The solution for subsequent phases was to cap the percentage of affordable units at 40 percent, and to distribute them more evenly across the development.

Maintain political support. TCC found that maintaining political support is difficult for long-term, phased development, and that if the political climate changes, weaknesses in agreements executed during politically friendly times can threaten later phases. The city council has lost its most vocal affordable-housing advocates, and "no-growth" advocates do not fully support full buildout of Tierra Contenta. One concern is a potential building moratorium; if a moratorium were to pass, the city would not be able to honor its commitment to TCC, and TCC might be forced to sue. This would damage TCC's working relationship with the city and tarnish TCC's good public image. TCC has responded to the possibility of a moratorium by keeping a low profile—something that is hard to do when Tierra Contenta received 40 percent of the city's building permits in 2003. Political advocacy for Tierra Contenta will be needed to fund increases in city services—including the new library and youth center, for which the city has bought land from TCC. Tierra Contenta's

4,000 residents have an opportunity to affect the outcome of future city council elections, but they will need to mobilize.

Engage in community building. Representatives from TCC, the Enterprise Foundation, and the city of Santa Fe lamented the slow pace of community building within Tierra Contenta. One possible cause might be the failure to incorporate strategies for community building into the early planning for the development. Many of Tierra Contenta's residents have close ties to existing neighborhoods within and around Santa Fe, and have therefore been slow to become involved in their new community. In addition, many residents were originally from Mexico, and a significant number were originally from Tibet; integrating these distinct cultures has been challenging. In response to the problem, the Enterprise Foundation, in collaboration with TCC, the city, and the Santa Fe Affordable Housing Roundtable, is seeking funding for a community-building program at Tierra Contenta.

Note

1. A four-person household at 80 percent of the county median income earns $58,800 per year.

Tierra Contenta

Primary Contact

James Hicks
505-471-4551
www.tierracontenta.org

Project Team

Owner/Developer
James Hicks
Executive Director
Tierra Contenta Corporation
3900 Paseo Del Sol
Santa Fe, New Mexico 87505

Master Planners
Calthorpe Associates
2095 Rose Street
Berkeley, California 94709
510-548-6800
www.calthorpe.com

Mazria, Inc.
607 Cerrillos Road
Suite G
Santa Fe, New Mexico 87501
505-988-5309
www.mazria.com

Homebuilders
BT Homes
Centex Homes
Colonia Prisma/Allied Homes
Habitat for Humanity
Homewise
Las Fuerzas, LLC
Philip Gudwin
Santa Fe Community Housing Trust

Development Schedule

Site purchased	1992
Planning started	1992
Tierra Contenta Corporation created	1993
Construction started	1994
First homes completed	1995
Estimated project completion	2016

Land Use Information

Total site area   1,007 acres
Number of residential units at buildout   3,800

Land Use	Number of Units[a]	Acreage
Residential		
One to five dwelling units per acre	1,198	266
Six to nine dwelling units per acre	2,146	285
Ten to 20 dwelling units per acre	1,092	63
Neighborhood commercial		6
Community		12
Office/business incubator		16
Village commercial		15
Schools		34
Parks and open space		262
Major roads		48
Total	4,436	1,007

a. The actual number of units built may diverge from these figures because of development below permitted densities.

Affordable Residential Units

Number of affordable units at buildout (for-sale and rental)   1,520
Average sales price, for-sale unit[a] $166,00
Rental rates, affordable apartments[b]   Determined by Low-Income Housing
                                             Tax Credit requirements

a. Reserved for households with incomes below 80 percent of area median income (AMI).
b. Reserved for families with incomes below 60 percent of AMI.

Development Costs

Site acquisition: $7,880,000

University Glen
Camarillo, California

Project Information

In California, skyrocketing housing values have made recruitment and retention of faculty and staff difficult at many state universities. The median home price is fast approaching $500,000, and less than 20 percent of households can afford such a home. California State University Channel Islands (CSUCI), in Camarillo, California, is the 23rd campus of California State University and will eventually serve 15,000 full-time students. As the newest campus in the state university system, CSUCI had to undertake extensive recruiting for faculty and staff. Despite competitive salaries and the natural beauty of the area, university planners found that even the highest-paid professors were deterred by California's expensive housing market.

Recognizing that it had a recruitment problem, the university responded with an innovative approach: using surplus university land and leasing the land to homeowners, CSUCI, in partnership with UniDev LLC, created affordable for-sale housing for faculty and staff. Retail, market-rate apartments, and other programs help subsidize the affordable units, making the development self-funding. The resulting community, known as University Glen, offers other universities a model for addressing the growing housing affordability problem for faculty and staff.

Of the 764 housing units in University Glen, 290 are affordable for-sale homes: 218 single-family attached homes and 72 single-family detached homes. The project also features 474 market-rate rental units (88 townhouses and 386 rental apartments), 58 of which have been constructed over commercial space.

Workforce Housing Information

Although the for-sale housing is offered to the general public, priority is given to university faculty and staff. (Making the units available to the public ensures that the sales are in keeping with the Fair Housing Act of 1968.) In fact, demand was so strong that all the units were sold to CSUCI faculty and staff; a waiting list is maintained.

Houses are sold for roughly 65 percent of market value. Annual appreciation is capped at the Consumer Price Index (CPI), and the land is leased from the CSUCI Site Authority. At resale, values can be adjusted for improvements made to the house. The first phase of the for-sale residences sold out quickly: prices ranged from $231,000 to $307,000. Because of appreciation, homes in later phases sold for as much as $400,000.

Although the market-rate apartments are also offered to the general public, most have been leased to CSUCI staff and students because of their proximity to the university. At the time of publication, rents ranged from $1,100 to $2,066 —about 10 percent below current market rate. The apartments have been almost fully leased since opening.

Land-lease payments and rent from the market-rate apartments are expected to generate $800 million for the site authority over a 45-year period. The revenue will go toward bond repayment ($300 million) and will fund university programs and additional campus construction and renovation.

Site, Surroundings, and History

Nestled in a valley between rolling hills, the university is in Ventura County, roughly 50 miles (80 kilometers) northwest of Los Angeles and 40 miles (64 kilometers) southeast of Santa Barbara; it is about 15 minutes from the Pacific Ocean. The university is located on the site of the former Camarillo State Mental Hospital, which opened in 1936 and closed in 1997. At its peak, the hospital housed close to 15,000 patients and staff. Because of its proximity to Los Angeles, it had several high-profile patients, including jazz great Charlie Parker, whose "Relaxin' at Camarillo" was written about the time he spent at the hospital. The university has renovated and converted some of the historic hospital buildings and is constructing new buildings with an eye toward compatibility with the style of the hospital. Long-range plans call for complete campus buildout by 2030.

The university property features 204 acres (83 hectares) divided into two sectors: the West Campus and the East Campus. The West Campus is made up of 42 developed acres (17 hectares), including the old hospital site, and is targeted for academic uses. The East Campus features 162 acres (66 hectares) of developable land, which will include the housing and commercial development. Construction on the East Campus began in October 2000 and was completed in 2006.

CSUCI

Planning, Development, and Entitlements

The CSUCI Site Authority was created in 1998; its mission is to transition the hospital property to university use and to develop additional compatible uses on the site. The site authority is governed by a seven-person board made up of four California State University trustees and three representatives from Ventura County. The board is responsible for managing the purchase and sale of government bonds to fund construction of the university, overseeing the aesthetic integrity of University Glen, and establishing policies that control residents' use of the area. A nonprofit corporation, the University Glen Corporation, was established to handle the

Located in Camarillo, in Ventura County, the campus of California State University Channel Islands was developed on the former site of the Camarillo Mental Hospital. Because of the relative isolation of the University Glen site, there was no significant community opposition to the new residential development.

Of the 414 housing units in University Glen, 316 are market-rate rental units: 60 townhouses and 256 apartments. The units shown here are market-rate rental apartments.

Of the 98 affordable for-sale homes, 36 are single-family homes and 62 are townhouses; the units shown here are townhouses.

The single-family homes range in size from 1,700 to 2,300 square feet (158 to 214 square meters). The two-story units offer three bedrooms with a choice of two-and-a-half or three-and-a-half bathrooms.

day-to-day operations of the residential community and to ensure the continuing affordability of the units.

To develop the housing component, the site authority initially turned Catellus Development Corporation, a San Francisco–based firm. Catellus proposed an all-market-rate development that would have brought a financial return to the university. But because market-rate housing was not likely to be affordable to university faculty and staff, the authority then turned to UniDev LLC, a company based in Bethesda, Maryland, that had extensive experience developing both university housing and affordable housing. In 2000, UniDev was brought on as the owner's representative to manage the planning, design, financing, and implementation of the East Campus redevelopment.

UniDev worked closely with university faculty and staff and with the site authority to craft a plan that would serve everyone's needs. The faculty and staff needed affordable housing, and the site authority needed a dedicated and consistent revenue stream to fund campus expansion and

renovation, and to maintain the affordability of the housing. To ensure a continuous income stream, UniDev proposed that the site authority lease the land to the homeowners. The firm also proposed the incorporation of market-rate apartments that were open to the public: the additional income stream from the apartments could help fund campus renovation and construction work, and could also help sustain the homeownership program. UniDev also proposed developing the project in phases, to stagger the move-in dates and create cash flow that would help fund the affordable units.

Because of the relative isolation of the site, the university has no immediate neighbors to speak of, and there was no significant community opposition to the project. Some stream restoration and wetland mitigation were required, and a recurring problem with groundhog tunneling had to be addressed. Because of the financing sources for the project, prevailing-wage requirements were applicable to all construction.

Financing

Tax-exempt bonds and a 100 percent loan from Fannie Mae and Citibank were used to finance the project. In addition, the Mello-Roos Community Facilities District Act was used to fund site improvements. The California legislature passed the Mello-Roos Act in 1982, in response to Proposition 13, which had limited the ability of developers and local governments to finance new projects; passage was spearheaded by state senator Henry Mello and state assemblyman Mike Roos. Under the act, any county, municipality, special district, school district, or joint-powers authority may establish a Mello-Roos Community Facilities District (CFD), provided that a two-thirds majority of the residents located within the boundaries of the proposed district agree. Once the district is established, a special tax lien is placed against all property within it. The lien may be used to finance streets, sewer systems, and other basic infrastructure, and to provide police and fire protection, ambulance service, schools, parks, libraries, etc. If the CFD issues bonds, the taxes are assessed annually until the bonds are paid off.

Design and Architecture

The Spanish colonial and Monterey architectural styles of the historic hospital buildings that had already been converted to campus uses set the design theme for the new residential construction at University Glen. Stucco walls and red tile roofing enclose modern conveniences, including category 5 wiring for high-bandwidth applications in all bedrooms, family rooms, and living areas. The site of the homes is quite spectacular: located in a secluded area adjacent to the university, and surrounded by rolling hills and colorful orchards, the relatively dense development has pedestrian access to the university but maintains a peaceful residential character. Since most residents will be within walking distance of the 30,000 square feet (2,787 square meters) of retail space, the commercial uses will enhance the pedestrian-friendly quality of the housing.

The market-rate rental apartments range in size from 680 square feet (63 square meters) for a one-bedroom, one-bathroom apartment to almost 1,800 square feet (167 square meters) for a three-bedroom apartment with a den, two-and-a-half bathrooms, a fireplace, and a two-car garage.

The townhouses are available in several configurations and two basic styles: the Arroyo and the Monterey. The two-story, two-bedroom,

The site features extensive landscaping throughout.

The Spanish colonial and Monterey architectural styles of the historic hospital buildings set the design theme for the new residential construction.

Stucco walls and red tile roofing enclose modern conveniences, including category 5 wiring for high-bandwidth applications throughout each unit.

Marketing and Operations

No marketing of the for-sale units is required, as there is currently a waiting list for available units. Little marketing is needed for the market-rate apartments, which are almost fully leased. Two factors account for the low vacancy rate of the apartments: first, rental rates are roughly 10 percent below current market rates; second, the apartments are adjacent to the university, and the next-closest apartment complex is quite a distance from the university.

A nonprofit corporation was created to function as a homeowners' association, and has the additional responsibility of addressing the future affordability of the for-sale units. Each time a house is sold, 6 percent of the sales price (1 percent from the seller, and 5 percent from the buyer) goes into a fund that is controlled by the nonprofit and that will be used to ensure the future affordability of the units. Units must remain affordable, but the nonprofit has some discretion in establishing sales prices upon resale.

Experience Gained

The inclusion of market-rate rental units and retail space can help subsidize affordable units. Another important factor in the success of University Glen was the decision to lease the land under the for-sale units instead of selling it to the homeowners, which created a continuous cash flow that can be used to sustain affordability. Providing a mix of housing-product types was also important, as it permitted the developer to meet the needs of diverse households with a broad range of incomes.

Capping the appreciation of the for-sale units at the CPI is vital to maintaining continued affordability. As of this writing, the rate of appreciation in home prices in California far exceeds the CPI: if units were left to appreciate

The market-rate rental apartments are actually slightly more affordable than other apartments in Camarillo and have been almost fully leased since opening. two-and-a-half bath Arroyo townhouses come in three floor plans, ranging from 1,300 to 1,600 square feet (120 to 149 square meters), and are constructed in groups of two to four units per building. The two-story, three-bedroom, two-and-a-half bath Monterey townhouses, which range from 1,460 to 1,800 square feet (136 to 167 square meters), also offer three different floor plans, and are constructed in groups of two to six units per building.

The single-family homes are available in four floor plans, ranging from 1,700 to 2,300 square feet (158 to 214 square meters). The two-story residences have three bedrooms and a choice of two-and-a-half or three-and-a-half bathrooms. All units have an attached two-car garage.

A number of architects assisted with the development of University Glen, including Lim Chang Rohling & Associates, of Pasadena, California; McLarand Vasquez Emsiek & Partners, Inc., of Irvine, California; WFA Architecture and Planning, Inc., of Laguna Beach, California; William Hezmalhalch Architects, Inc., of Santa Ana, California; and the Withee Malcolm Partnership, Architects, of Torrance, California.

at market rates, they would quickly cease to be affordable to university faculty and staff.

In the realm of "negative lessons," the developer reported that the phasing plan, which allowed large numbers of people to move in at the same time, created stress and complications. Smaller phases and move-ins are recommended. In the area of parking, the developer recommends honestly assessing the requirements of the market, rather than relying on governmental minimum requirements. In California, households are particularly auto-dependent, and most households have at least two cars. Although 1.7 parking spaces per unit were required, this amount proved inadequate, and additional parking had to be added to the original plan.

CSUCI

The University Glen site is nestled in a valley between rolling hills. The flat land presented few obstacles to development.

University Glen

Primary Contact

Jeffrey A. Minter
UniDev LLC
808-536-1110
info@unidevllc.com
www.universityglenhomes.com

Project Team

Master Developer
Unidev LLC
Bethesda, Maryland
301-656-7742
info@unidevllc.com
www.unidevllc.com

Architect
Lim Chang Rohling & Associates
Pasadena, California

McLarand Vasquez Emsiek & Partners, Inc.
Irvine, California

WFA Architecture and Planning, Inc.
Laguna Beach, California

William Hezmalhalch Architects, Inc.
Santa Ana, California

Withee Malcolm Partnership, Architects
Torrance, California

Corcoran & Corcoran
Newport Beach, California

Land Planners
HDR | LCA+Sargent, Town Planning
Oakland, California

Landscape Architects
Ridge Landscape
Irvine, California

Lender
CitiGroup, Global Markets
Philadelphia, Pennsylvania

Market Studies
Robert Charles Lesser & Co., LLC
Los Angeles, California

Development Schedule

Planning started	1999
Construction started	2000
Sales/leasing started	2001
Phase I completed	2002
Estimate project completed	2009

Land Use Information

Total site area   72.5 acres

Land Use	Number of Units (Existing)	Number of Units (at Buildout)
Residential	764	900
Multifamily	764	900
Single-family detached	72	386
Single-family attached	306	204

Land Use	Square Footage (at Buildout)
General retail	9,458
Office	2,985
Restaurant	5,940
Market	5,000
Campus bookstore	6,670
Total	30,053

Residential Information

Multifamily Units

Unit Type	Square Footage	Number of Units Leased	Range of Monthly Rents
Phase IA/Phase IB apartment: One bedroom, one bath	680–842	44	$1,100–$1,269
Phase IA/Phase IB apartment: Two bedrooms, two baths	882–974	140	$1,306–$1,411
Phase IA/Phase IB apartment: Three bedrooms, two baths	1,245	14	$1,756
Town Center studio	654	18	$1,059
Town Center apartment: One bedroom, one bath	854	30	$1,327
Town Center apartment: One bedroom, one bath	1,127	10 $	$1,740
Phase IC apartment	680–974	130	$1,100–$1,411

Single-Family Detached

Unit Type	Square Footage	Number of Units Sold	Sales Prices
Phase IC Alley	1,689–2,282	72	$332,000–$400,000

Single-Family Attached

Unit Type	Square Footage	Number of Units Sold	Sales Prices
Phase IC Alley	1,689–2,282	72	$332,000–$400,000
Cluster townhouses 201	1,315	20	$1,808
Cluster townhouses 202	1,323	10	$1,818
Cluster townhouses 203	1,574	10	$963
Alley townhouses 301	1,462	14	$1,911
Alley townhouses 302	1,638	18	$2,014
Alley townhouses 303	1,795	16	$2,066
Cluster for-sale units	1,303–1,572	98	$231,000–$272,000
Alley for-sale units	1,462–1,795	120	$255,000–$307,000

Affordable Residential Units

All for-sale units in Phases IA, IB, and IC are affordable.

Retail Information

Type of Tenant	Gross Leasable Area (Square Feet)
Mercantile Bank & Trust	3,000
Retail/office space (buildings A and D)	9,458
Office suite	2,985
Bookstore (Building B)	6,670
Café (Building B)	1,817
Tortilla's Mexican (Building C)	1,500
Quick Casual (Building C)	770
The Point Restaurant (Building C)	1,853
Market (Building D)	5,000
Total	30,053

Gross Leasable Area (at buildout)

Use	Square Footage
Office	2,985
Retail	27,068
Total	30,053

Wellington
Breckenridge, Colorado

Project Information

Tucked above the historic mining town of Breckenridge, Colorado, Wellington has creatively provided workforce housing for Summit County, a rapidly growing resort community where affordable housing for permanent residents has become increasingly scarce. Phase I, which consists of 122 units, is a well-planned neighborhood designed to evoke Colorado's Victorian mining towns. Developed on a 22-acre (nine-hectare) site, Wellington has reclaimed and remediated what was once the site of a historic dredge-mining operation. Through a series of covenants, deed restrictions, and purchaser-eligibility standards, 80 percent of Wellington's homes are reserved exclusively for purchase by people who work in Summit County, at about one-third the median purchase price of a home in Breckenridge.

Workforce Housing Information

In Breckenridge, as in many growing resort communities, purchases of second homes and vacation homes have driven up housing prices, forcing a majority of Breckenridge's workforce out of the local residential marketplace. One consequence is "mountain sprawl": for many Breckenridge workers, affordable homeownership opportunities were available only across Hoosier Pass, a 45-minute commute over mountain roads.

Wellington has provided Summit County with attractive and affordable homeownership opportunities for the area's growing workforce. Wellington homeowners include many of those who

are essential to day-to-day life in the town—the town manager and other government employees, a district attorney, shop owners, teachers, and police officers.

Boulder housing developers David O'Neill, John Wolff, and Tom Lyon formed Poplarhouse LLC to build Wellington. They worked closely with the Summit County Housing Authority, as well as with town officials, to devise the project's unique affordability guidelines. During the project's initial planning stages, town officials were concerned that income restrictions would be difficult and costly to administer and enforce. In response to this concern, the development team worked jointly with public officials to devise a straightforward and self-enforcing set of guidelines that will ensure perpetually affordable workforce housing in Wellington.

Under Wellington's affordability restrictions, the 98 units designated as workforce housing have no associated income limitations. Instead, residents are required to sign an affidavit stating that they work at least 30 hours per week in Summit County. To maintain future affordability for the area's workforce, the owners of Wellington's "restricted" homes are required to execute a series of deed and resale restrictions, including a deed of trust and an appreciation-limiting promissory note. These documents are signed at closing, then recorded in the town's land records; together, they create a self-administering mechanism that maintains affordability as properties change ownership.

For the deed-restricted homes, resale appreciation is limited to 3 percent per year, or to the percentage increase in the area median income (AMI), whichever is greater. (In recent

Wellington Neighborhood

Wellington features 12 groups of homes, of approximately ten homes each, that face each other across village-scale greens—or "green courts," as the designers call them. The courts are narrower at their entrances, and widen to 60 feet (18 meters) at their centers.

years, AMI has increased about 5 percent per year. In contrast, the average market-rate home in Breckenridge has appreciated between 10 and 15 percent per year.) In short, the owners of the restricted units accept a reduction in potential appreciation in exchange for gaining a place in the community.

Workforce housing in Wellington has no direct public funding. The town of Breckenridge, however, supported the project through indirect subsidies worth over $1 million, including (1) waiving annexation fees for sewer and water connections, (2) eliminating impact fees and building-permit fees, and (3) excluding the housing from a 1 percent transfer tax per unit.

Twenty percent of Wellington's homes (approximately 24 units) are unrestricted, market-rate homes targeted to second-home buyers.

Site, Surroundings, and History

The Wellington site is located on the outskirts of historic Breckenridge, 1.3 miles (2.1 kilometers) from the town center, in an area known as French Gulch. The neighborhood is located just below the reclaimed Wellington-Oro Mine, which produced gold, silver, and lead until

1972. For over 60 years, dredge boats plowed through the river valley, searching for resources and leaving behind 30-foot- (nine-meter-) high piles of river rock. The Wellington site sits atop 85 acres (34 hectares) of land that had been subject to invasive dredge-mining operations.

During the project's due-diligence period, the developers of Wellington talked extensively with the mining company and with the U.S. Environmental Protection Agency (EPA) to determine whether the site had any residual environmental issues that would make it unsuited for residential development. While the mine tailings in the area were unsightly and difficult to work around, it was determined that the area was indeed safe for residential use.

However, before the developers actually acquired the site, property owners, other citizens, the Colorado Department of Public Health, and EPA officials devised a reclamation plan for the Wellington-Oro Mine and its environs. This group, known as the French Gulch Remediation Opportunities Group (FROG), worked over several years with the Keystone Center, a nonprofit environmental mediation group based in Keystone, Colorado, to assess community concerns, to determine which areas to clean up first, and to obtain the funding needed for the cleanup. Eventually, issues related to contamination and cleanup were resolved to the point where all parties felt comfortable about proceeding with residential development.

Under an agreement between the mining company and the EPA, 80 percent of the revenue generated from the sale of the land was set aside in an EPA "lock box," and will be used to fund environmental remediation throughout the area surrounding the project. Before construction began, a comprehensive scope of work for environmental remediation was prepared by the developers' environmental consultants and approved by the EPA. Prospective homebuyers are provided with a prospective purchaser agreement that addresses on- and off-site environmental conditions.

Planning, Development, and Entitlements

Breckenridge officials and residents were closely involved in shaping the plan and design of Wellington. Although the Wellington property was originally located in the unincorporated portion of Summit County, the development plan called for annexation by the town of Breckenridge. Because the site was initially zoned for a buildout of only four single-family homes, significant rezoning and a transfer of development rights (TDR) were needed to achieve the targeted densities required to make the project financially feasible and to reach the affordability goals set for the development. Using the TDR mechanism embodied within the Breckenridge zoning and subdivision ordinance, the town transferred residential density from a municipal parking lot to the Wellington property.

The developers and the town of Breckenridge also created an annexation agreement that (1) set the targeted densities (for residential, light-commercial, and live/work uses), (2) established the eligibility requirements for the workforce housing and the ratio of restricted to market-rate units, and (3) confirmed that Wellington would receive municipal services and utility connections. Under this agreement, the developers were permitted to convey the unrestricted, market-rate units (representing 20 percent of the project) only gradually, as the buildout and sale of the workforce units progressed over time; specifically, three deed-restricted workforce housing units had to be sold and conveyed before a market-rate unit could be constructed and sold.

Wellington Neighborhood

Because the developers wanted to create a traditional neighborhood design, the design team had to work closely with community stakeholders and planning officials to devise flexible new zoning standards that would allow increased density, smaller setbacks, narrower streets and rights-of-way, and smaller lots. These new zoning standards also encouraged a mix of uses in several planned live/work buildings. As the neighborhood grows and gains critical mass, the developers believe that it will support services such as a coffee shop, a bakery, and a postal substation.

The developers were responsible for extending the sewer and water lines approximately three-quarters of a mile (1.2 kilometers). The required excavation for a nine-inch (23-centimeter) water line and a twelve-inch (31-centimeter) sewer line added considerable difficulty to the initial site work and increased the project's costs.

Wellington's overall planning and permitting process was completed in approximately four years.

As the result of extensive negotiations with town officials, who were concerned about snow removal and access for emergency vehicles, Wellington has wider streets than would ordinarily be found in a new urbanist development.

Wellington Neighborhood

The 98 homes that are designated as workforce housing have no income restrictions; however, they are reserved for purchase by people who work in Summit County. The homes are sold for roughly one-third of the median price of a home in the area, and appreciation is restricted.

Financing

Since the development of Wellington required no direct public funding or debt, development financing for the project was similar to that for many single-family developments. The sellers provided financing for the purchase of the Wellington site through a nonrecourse note secured by the land and the improvements. Development and construction were financed through two separate revolving lines of credit, one for site work and land improvements and one for building construction. The developers demonstrated their commitment to the project by personally guaranteeing development financing.

The developers worked with Fannie Mae to ensure (1) that homebuyers would be able to readily secure mortgage financing and (2) that future lenders would honor the restrictive covenants in cases of foreclosure.

Design and Architecture

Wellington blends traditional neighborhood design with modern methods of production homebuilding. The project's mountainside location and extremely high elevation—9,600 feet (2,926 meters)—meant that the planning and design team had to thoughtfully adapt new urbanist design principles to the development's cultural and environmental characteristics, which are more rural and rugged than is typical for new urbanist communities.

Wellington's design creates a sense of place that draws on the development's historic mountain setting and its human scale. The project's compact plan includes public greens and connections that create a safe and appealing environment for pedestrians. Free public transportation links Wellington to downtown Breckenridge and to neighboring ski areas. Walking and hiking trails give residents access to thousands of acres of open space.

The overall neighborhood plan features a simple grid of connected streets and alleyways. Wellington's planners made a careful study of historic settlement patterns and urban design characteristics, including street patterns and public spaces, in several Colorado communities, among them Chautauqua Park, in Boulder, and downtown Aspen.

Street standards, which had been designed to accommodate snow removal and storage, became the primary focus of site planning and design. To obtain a change in the standards, the designers had to demonstrate that the narrow street network proposed for Wellington would not inhibit residents' safety, access for emergency vehicles, or future road maintenance. After much debate and negotiation with town officials, the development team ultimately settled on a typical street standard for the community, which includes a 50-foot (15-meter) right-of-way, a 20-foot (six-meter) paved cart-way, and a three-foot (0.9-meter) drainage swale or gutter on each side of the street. To allow for easier snow removal and storage, the streets in Wellington do not include a curb; without a curb, however, the streets lack the formal edge often found in traditional neighborhood developments.

Because town planning officials did not initially understand the required dimensions for Wellington's rear-loaded alleys, they requested an enormous (70-foot [21-meter]) right-of-way. The parties eventually compromised on an 18-foot (5.5-meter) paved travel way within a 34-foot (ten-meter) right-of-way. While these dimensions are hardly typical of the cozy streets and alleys found in historic communities, they provide ample room for snow storage and accommodate the sport-utility vehicles and river rafts of Wellington's residents.

The neighborhood site plan features 12 groups, of approximately ten homes each, that face each other across village-scale greens, which the designers refer to as "green courts." The green courts are narrower at their entrances, to create a feeling of intimacy, and widen to approximately 60 feet (18 meters) at their centers; the result is an active, pedestrian-friendly environment. Although they are connected to streets at both ends, these shared open spaces are auto free. Landscaping and fencing details give each green court its own identity.

Homeowners traveling by car access their homes by means of rear-loaded alleyways that are privately maintained by the homeowners' association. Parking for visitors is provided along the public streets near the entries to the green courts.

Homes within Wellington range from approximately 1,200 to 1,900 square feet (111 to 177 square meters). The project includes both duplexes and detached, single-family homes. To maintain affordability goals and ensure economical construction, the developers put a great deal of effort into keeping the homes small and efficient; at the same time, however, it was important to accommodate the needs of an active and relatively diverse target market.

Wellington offers five models, all in traditional styles. The project architecture reflects a "mountain Victorian" theme—but, in order to allow the use of production homebuilding methods, building forms were kept simple. Color, mass-

Wellington Neighborhood

ing, and architectural details (including subtle design considerations such as porches and gables) are thoughtfully mixed to create visual variety and rhythm.

Marketing and Operations

Early in the predevelopment stage, Wellington's developers established a comprehensive marketing plan targeting Summit County's growing workforce. Households with incomes ranging from 80 to 120 percent of AMI have been the project's principal market. Although there was also significant market demand for housing serving lower income ranges, such a project would not have been financially feasible without substantial public subsidies.

Wellington's sales, marketing, and advertising initiatives—newspaper and radio advertisements, and a Web site—were fairly modest but cost-effective, and successfully reached the target market. To reach residents making unnecessarily long commutes, radio advertising was run during

Detached garages are accessed through alleyways behind the homes. Because of the significant snowfall, garages are more important to homeowners than they would be in less rigorous climates.

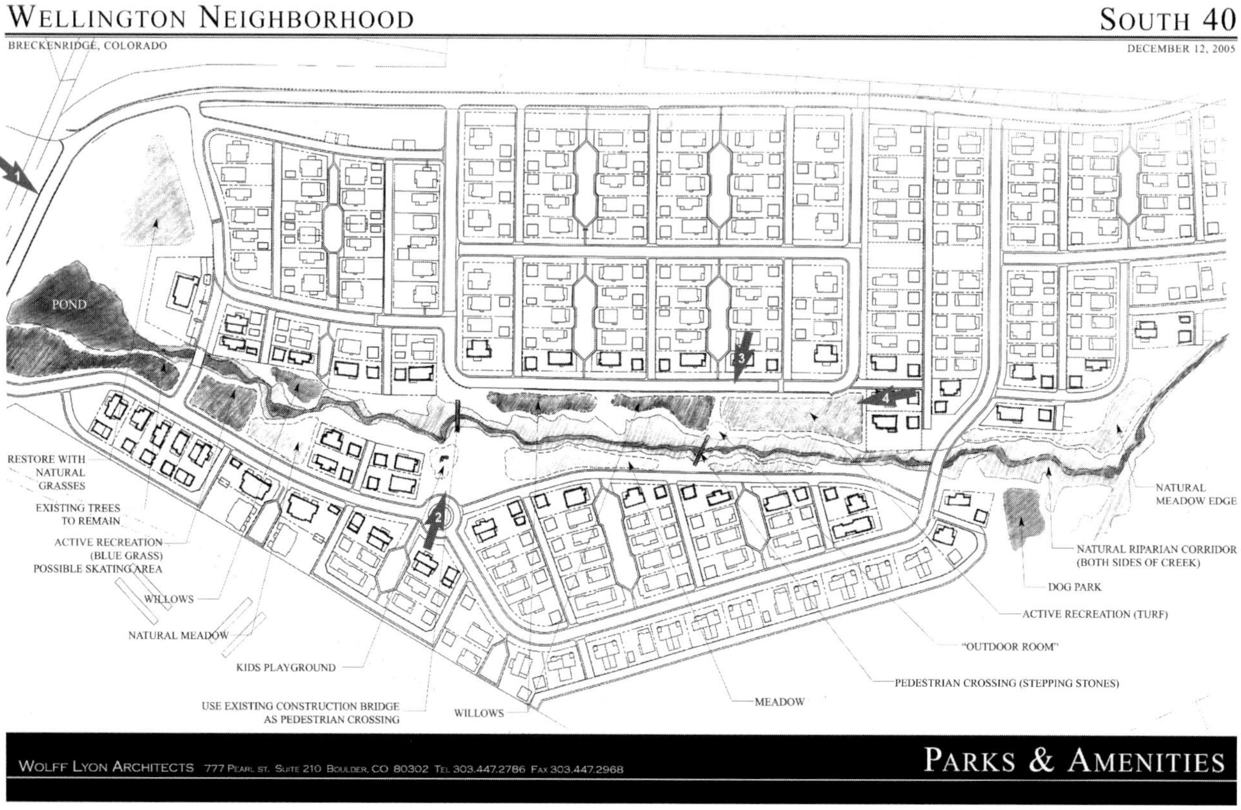

WELLINGTON NEIGHBORHOOD
BRECKENRIDGE, COLORADO

SOUTH 40
DECEMBER 12, 2005

POND

RESTORE WITH
NATURAL
GRASSES

EXISTING TREES
TO REMAIN

ACTIVE RECREATION
(BLUE GRASS)
POSSIBLE SKATING AREA

WILLOWS

NATURAL MEADOW

KIDS PLAYGROUND

USE EXISTING CONSTRUCTION BRIDGE
AS PEDESTRIAN CROSSING

WILLOWS

MEADOW

NATURAL
MEADOW EDGE

NATURAL RIPARIAN CORRIDOR
(BOTH SIDES OF CREEK)

DOG PARK

ACTIVE RECREATION (TURF)

"OUTDOOR ROOM"

PEDESTRIAN CROSSING (STEPPING STONES)

Wellington Neighborhood

WOLFF LYON ARCHITECTS 777 PEARL ST. SUITE 210 BOULDER, CO 80302 TEL 303.447.2786 FAX 303.447.2968

PARKS & AMENITIES

The neighborhood plan features a simple grid of connected streets and alleyways, with a significant amount of active and passive open space.

commuting time. The developers also used strategic public relations efforts, sponsoring local events and working on media placement. Significant leads were also generated through homeowner referrals.

Confident that the targeted demographic for the project was computer literate and likely to have Internet access, all Wellington marketing efforts were directly tied to the project's Web site. Postcards with the project's Web address were distributed in the sales office, through mass mailings, and at special events. The marketing efforts included no printed marketing materials.

The comprehensive, Internet-based marketing plan reduced marketing expenses while providing prospective homeowners with interactive and up-to-date sales and marketing information. The approach also gave the developers a more reliable

and detailed method for tracking and forecasting sales and marketing activity. In fact, Wellington's marketing data indicate a direct correlation between the number of hits on the Wellington Web site and the number of sales contracts.

The Wellington development team also creatively integrated computer technology into the construction-management process: homeowners, the developers, the general contractor, and subcontractors are all linked through the Wellington intranet. The project and construction schedules are posted and regularly updated on the intranet, giving homeowners, construction staff, and the developers ready access to information. In fact, every subcontractor is required to use the intranet daily.

The Wellington intranet has also helped to maintain homeowner satisfaction: for example, it has been used to address post-closing punch-list (minor incomplete) items. Wellington home-owners post their requests on the intranet to the job-site supervisor, who then uses the system to assign various tasks to the responsible subcontractor, copying the homeowner and the developers. The subcontractors then use the system to schedule appointments with homeowners via e-mail. If punch-list items are not addressed within 14 days of being assigned to subcontractors, payments to the subcontractors are withheld. The intranet has created a clear, open, and effective means of communication among all project stakeholders.

Experience Gained

Self-administering covenants and deed restrictions, such as appreciation-limiting promissory notes, can promote the development of workforce housing and help sustain the supply of such housing. Self-administering mechanisms are valuable because they can relieve municipalities of the administrative burdens (including income verification) often associated with workforce housing.

Initially, homes within Wellington were built by means of modular construction, and a local general contractor handled the finish carpentry. However, this approach created several challenges for the developers, including quality control and the difficulty of securing good subcontractors (because of the limited scope of work required). Partway through the project, the developers arranged to have a local general contractor frame the buildings on site. In the future, the developers would use modular construction only for significantly smaller infill projects.

The fact that prospective homeowners often have great difficulty visualizing planned amenities and streetscape improvements adds difficulty to early sales and marketing efforts. Early investment in amenities, open-space improvements (including common greens), and streetscapes can significantly improve sales absorption and net revenues.

Through due diligence and public/private partnerships, environmentally contaminated sites can provide creative development opportunities.

Traditional and new urbanist design principles and street standards can be thoughtfully adapted to unusual sites and environments, including high-altitude areas that receive significant snowfall.

Wellington

Primary Contact

David O'Neil
Poplarhouse LLC
31 Willow Green
P.O. Box 4626
Breckenridge, Colorado
970-453-5303
www.poplarhouse.com

Project Team

Owner/Developer
Poplarhouse LLC
31 Willow Green
P.O. Box 4626
Breckenridge, Colorado
970-453-5303
www.poplarhouse.com

Master Planner/Architects
John K. Wolf and John T. Lyon
Wolf/Lyon Architects
777 Pearl Street
Suite 210
Boulder, Colorado
303-447-2786
www.wlarch.com

Land Planner
John Humphreys
John Humphreys & Associates
Breckenridge, Colorado

General Contractor
Traditional Neighborhood Builders, Inc.
P.O. Box 633
Frisco, Colorado 80443
970-668-5057

Project Engineer
Jim Lenzotti
Tetra Tech/FLO Engineering

Development Costs

Land (finished lot)	$80,000
On-site costs (general requirements, site work, carpentry, roofing, finishes, electrical, and mechanical)	162,750
Soft costs (architecture, engineering, plant investment, fees, developer fee, financing, and insurance)	26,638
Sales and marketing	8,125
Total	$277,513

DEVELOPING HOUSING FOR THE WORKFORCE
Toolkit

Toolkit

THE SHORTAGE OF WORKFORCE HOUSING HAS
affected regional and local economies throughout the country.
As a result, state and local governments have instituted myriad
policies and programs designed to increase the supply of housing that is affordable to moderate-income families. The range of
possible strategies is vast, no two programs are exactly alike,
and no two jurisdictions have implemented the same combination of programs.[1]

Toolkit

For any given jurisdiction, the choice of strategies will depend on a number of factors, including the nature of the local government; the regional and local housing market; and the community's needs, resources, opportunities, and constraints. Similarly, for a developer, choosing which of the available workforce housing programs to use for a given project will depend on the project's characteristics, including its location and eligibility for particular programs.

This toolkit presents a selected array of programs that state or local governments have implemented successfully to promote workforce housing. Of necessity, descriptions are brief, but all include contact information to enable readers to obtain more detail. Information is organized under the following major headings: land acquisition and assembly, planning and regulatory approaches, financing, and maintaining long-term affordability.

Some programs emphasize the production of housing in specific locations; others focus primarily on achieving affordability. Affordable-housing programs are often most cost-effective and politically acceptable when they support the development of mixed-income housing; thus, many of the programs described in this toolkit promote mixed-income housing through, for example, requirements that a certain percentage of the units in a project be set aside for households within specified income ranges. To spur the development of workforce housing, other programs remove regulatory barriers or provide cash subsidies or cost-saving incentives; a few provide information, in-kind assistance, or other facilitating services. Because the combination of programs that is suitable for any given community must be locally determined, the toolkit describes programs separately, but with the understanding that no one program will solve a community's workforce housing needs.

The programs discussed in this toolkit can be undertaken in locations where price and proximity to employment would render projects attractive to moderate-income households. Another option, not specifically addressed in this book, is for cities to revitalize distressed residential neighborhoods that are affordable and well located, but that are not currently desirable places to live. To revive such locations, cities can work with financial institutions, foundations, intermediaries, community groups, nonprofit and for-profit developers, and others to develop strategies that combine federal, state, and local programs. Such programs might target the remediation of brownfields; the removal of blight; the preservation of existing housing; the development of mixed-income housing; mixed-use development; the reuse of vacant and abandoned properties; the protection of existing low-income residents; historic preservation; the provision of infrastructure, services, and amenities; or the redevelopment of distressed public housing. To succeed, efforts to revitalize distressed neighborhoods must include two elements: making the community a safe place to live, work, and raise a family; and improving the local public schools.

Acquiring and Assembling Land

One of the first steps in producing affordable housing is obtaining land for development. Because "workforce housing" refers to housing that is both located near employment and priced to be affordable to moderate-income households, the ability to produce it depends, in part, on finding well-located sites at reasonable prices. Other issues that can arise in urbanized areas include clearing the title; identifying and negotiating with the landowner; addressing encumbrances; and dealing with environmental problems. In many cities that need more workforce housing, the public sector helps developers to find, obtain, and prepare good development sites for that purpose.

A good development site for workforce housing will meet the same criteria that apply to any other real estate development, in terms of location, size, price, access, physical characteristics (such as shape, topography, soils, and drainage), infrastructure, and legal and political considerations (such as zoning status and likelihood of obtaining development approvals). Of course, workforce housing sites must be located where people would want to live—or the developer, in partnership with the local government, must be willing to transform the area into a place where people would want to live. The price must be low enough to make the development of workforce housing feasible, and such housing must be allowable under current zoning regulations. (Alternatively, the developer may feel that a revision of the zoning ordinance is likely to be obtained.)

Finding Good Sites

The best opportunities for developing workforce housing close to employment centers are high-density, mixed-used areas, including urban infill sites, land located near transit nodes or within transit corridors, and urban or suburban activity centers.

Where undeveloped land is readily available, developers can apply the typical criteria for site selection mentioned in the previous section. Where vacant land is scarce, good development sites for workforce housing are not always obvious.[2] For infill development, potential sites include vacant lots; air rights locations above infrastructure or commercial uses; *in rem* properties;[3] and underused land, such as sites occupied by any of the following uses:

- Surface parking lots;
- Marginal or obsolete commercial or industrial uses (including brownfields);
- Transportation facilities, such as old rail yards or excess rights-of-way;
- Older, suburban-style low-density office buildings;
- Low-intensity commercial strips;
- Closed military bases;
- Historic properties.

In some cases, existing buildings can be adapted for use as housing; examples include schools, factories, warehouses, offices, mill buildings, and department stores. In Foster City, California, the city government worked with property owners, tenants, developers, and local community groups to transform declining neighborhood shopping centers into market- and below-market-rate housing, alone or along with commercial uses.[4]

Though sites in developed areas can be more difficult and costly to develop, they are generally closer to places of employment and/or accessible to them by mass transit, minimizing workers' daily transportation costs.[5] Furthermore, such locations are often characterized by higher allowable densities and more flexible development regulations, and tend to include more balanced and mutually supportive use mixes.

How Local and State Governments Can Help

Local governments can help developers obtain good sites for workforce housing in the following ways:

- Identifying and providing information about available sites;
- Negotiating for sites on the developer's behalf;
- Making surplus public land available;
- Using redevelopment authority to help assemble and improve land in desirable locations;

- Assisting in the remediation of brownfield sites;
- Allowing innovative solutions (e.g., development within air rights, transfer of public property to a land bank or land trust for future development as workforce housing).

In addition, local governments can forgive tax liens and help clear title to the property. They can buy the property, write down its cost, and sell it to a developer—or even swap land with reluctant landowners. Local governments can encourage landowners to become partners in the development. In certain cases, public agencies with the power of eminent domain can use that power—directly or indirectly—to obtain sites for development. Local governments can also conduct master environmental assessments or reviews, or pre-engineer sites so that land targeted for development is "permit-ready."[6]

States must pass enabling legislation to allow local governments to take many of the actions just listed; in addition, states can undertake direct efforts to make vacant or underused land available for development or redevelopment. Under the category of enabling legislation, states can make it easier for local governments to exercise powers of condemnation and eminent domain, allow localities to establish land banks, or enable local governments to foreclose on tax-delinquent properties expeditiously. Under the category of direct efforts, states can create voluntary cleanup programs to provide incentives for brownfield redevelopment, and can establish development authorities with the power to levy taxes, issue bonds, and receive public and private funds for redevelopment.[7] In addition, as will be discussed in later sections of this toolkit, states exercise regulatory and financing powers that allow local governments to facilitate the reuse of land.

Land Surveys, Inventories, and Information

By maintaining an inventory of vacant land and properties, a locality or region can not only help developers identify potential sites for housing projects, but can also assist government agencies, citizens' groups, and other interested parties in planning and educational efforts. For example, in the San Francisco Bay Area, the Bay Area Jobs-Housing Footprint Project, spearheaded by the Bay Area Council, has analyzed the amount of land that will be available in the Bay Area to meet projected housing needs through 2020.[8]

Many local governments maintain databases with information on assessed value, tax status, code violations, occupancy, and other characteristics of each property within the jurisdiction. Using geographic information systems (GIS), localities can create maps that provide current information on land use, zoning, and other relevant characteristics, both in the aggregate and for specific sites; they can then make this information widely available through the Internet. If the local government does not have and does not wish to obtain the technical capacity to create such maps, the task can be delegated to a commercial, nonprofit, or university contractor. For example, the University of California at Los Angeles created and maintains the "Neighborhood Knowledge Los Angeles" Web site, which provides information on city properties.[9]

PROGRAMS AND POLICIES

Through the **One-Stop Shop** program, in Emeryville, California, landowners, developers, residents, and other interested parties have access to an online, interactive tool that provides information about any parcel of land in the city: address, size, assessed value, current land use, zoning, property ownership, and environmental status.

For more information, visit
www.ci.emeryville.ca.us/econdev/osiris.html.

Map Milwaukee, a sophisticated Web site created by the city of Milwaukee, provides public access to information about the city as a whole, specific areas, or individual sites. Maps and data allow users to identify sites of interest, such as public facilities and tax-delinquent properties, and to explore overlapping areas such as zoning districts, development zones, and voting districts. Users can also access information about any parcel of land in the city, including its current use, its tax status, and whether it is owner-occupied. The site also provides access to the city's Master Property Record, an inventory of the city's estimated 160,000 properties that includes detailed data on each.

For more information, visit
www.ci.mil.wi.us/display/router.asp?docid=3480.

Washington State's Buildable Lands program, enacted in 1997 as an amendment to the Growth Management Act, requires six counties and the 40 cities within them to gather and analyze data on their available land and growth potential.[10] Each year, the jurisdictions collect data on the amount and density of new development, update their land-supply inventories, determine their capacity to accommodate anticipated growth, and prepare a five-year evaluation report. The first reports were completed in 2002; future reports will be due at five-year intervals thereafter. If the evaluations reveal problems with density or capacity, the communities must address them.

For more information, visit
www.cted.wa.gov/site/419/default.aspx. To view
King County's 2002 report, visit
www.metrokc.gov/budget/buildland/bldlnd02.html.

Property Disposition or Acquisition Programs

Most local governments and many private institutions have excess real estate. Programs for the disposition of surplus properties can make available prime sites for workforce housing. Under California law, local governments planning to sell surplus properties must offer first right of refusal to public and nonprofit entities that might want to develop housing on the properties.

In some cases, jurisdictions that want to promote affordable-housing development may purchase and then donate or write down property expressly for that purpose. Localities can obtain land for affordable housing in other ways as well: for example, in jurisdictions that have inclusionary zoning requirements, developers may have the option of donating land for affordable housing, paying a fee, or providing affordable units on site. When a public or nonprofit entity develops housing on donated land, the elimination of the land cost may permit the construction of units that are even more affordable, or the construction of a larger number of units.[11]

⚒ PROGRAMS AND POLICIES

Initiated in 1998, **Boston's Home Again Program,** administered by the Department of Neighborhood Development (DND), promotes the construction of owner-occupied housing developments on city-owned vacant land. The program supports affordable-housing developments, which have an income limit of 80 percent of area median income (AMI); market-rate housing developments, in which buyers must earn at least 80 percent of AMI; and mixed-income developments, in which houses are for sale to both income groups. Development is undertaken by non-profit or for-profit developers selected through a request-for-proposals process.

The city and the Neighborhood Housing Trust have pledged $6 million from the city's housing linkage program to the Home Again Program —which, when combined with other city resources, is expected to result in the construction of 200 new homes.[12] Other city resources include technical assistance, environmental assessments, site surveys, land acquisition (for as little as one dollar), and direct capital subsidies from linkage or HOME funds.[13]

The city is working with BankBoston to provide construction loans with favorable rates and reduced, predictable costs. For income-qualified buyers, the DND provides information about, and access to, various home mortgage products, as well as help with downpayments and closing costs.

For more information, call the Department of Neighborhood Development (617-635-3880), or visit www.cityofboston.gov/DND/D_Home_Again.asp.

Philadelphia's Neighborhood Transformation Initiative (NTI) was created in 2001 to enable the city to gain control of derelict residential properties, preserve neighborhoods within the city, and encourage redevelopment by removing blight, stimulating investment, and improving delivery of city programs and services.[14] As part of the initiative, the city worked with the Reinvestment Fund to analyze housing and economic data, then organized the city's census tracts into six categories on the basis of characteristics such as housing values, rate of appreciation, and physical condition. Ultimately, the city will design a redevelopment strategy based on the specific requirements of each category.

Under the auspices of NTI, the city is assembling land for redevelopment and land banking, demolishing vacant and blighted struc-

tures, "cleaning and greening" vacant lots, investing in housing preservation and development, and stepping up code enforcement. The city also selects developers and assists them to acquire and develop properties. Through NTI, the city has been able to float some $295 million in tax-exempt government-purpose bonds; tax-exempt private-activity bonds; and taxable bonds, all of which have helped stimulate investments that will return idle land and derelict buildings to vital residential use.

For more information, visit www.phila.gov/nti/.

Development Authorities

Development and redevelopment authorities are quasi-municipal corporations created and authorized by state legislation for a specific purpose, such as providing housing for lower-income households or for a specific geographic area— a designated redevelopment area, for example. Development authorities typically have the power to levy and collect taxes, receive grant monies, issue bonds, and acquire and dispose of real property (in some cases through eminent domain); they can also revitalize blighted areas through actions such as master planning, land and property acquisition, demolition of blighted or obsolete structures, and provision of infrastructure and amenities.

Housing authorities focus specifically on housing production; to that end, they can raise money and can enter into partnerships with local governments, developers, and others to achieve their goals.[15] General-purpose redevelopment authorities may also control funds that can (or must) be used for affordable-housing development. For example, in California, at least 20 percent of local redevelopment authorities' funds must be set aside to help fund the development of low- and moderate-income housing; in some jurisdictions in the state, the percentage has been increased to 30 or even 50 percent.

In recent years, the closing of military bases has made available large tracts of land in desirable locations, presenting opportunities for development authorities to create substantial amounts of workforce housing. For example, the Fort Ord Reuse Authority's plans for the redevelopment of the Fort Ord Air Force Base, near Monterey, California, include 10,350 housing units, 20 percent of which will be affordable to low- and moderate-income households.

PROGRAMS AND POLICIES

The **Urban Redevelopment Authority** (URA) of Pittsburgh, created in 1946 to fight blight through urban renewal, now implements the city's major development programs and activities. Though many of the URA's projects result in commercial or cultural developments, more than half create housing, and the authority's mixed-use and residential developments have produced homes for households with a wide range of incomes. In particular, through partnerships with the city, the county, private developers, and others, the URA has made possible the development of new neighborhoods on brownfield sites throughout Pittsburgh. The URA typically acquires the land and assumes responsibility for environmental assessment and cleanup, demolition of structures, infrastructure development, and other site improvements. In addition, the URA funds housing and adaptive use projects in distressed neighborhoods; operates various programs to provide income-qualified homebuyers with below-market mortgages; and helps finance the construction or rehabilitation of income-restricted for-sale and rental housing.

For more information, call Jessica Smith, development manager (412-155-6688), or visit www.ura.org.

After the closure of the **Lowry Air Force Base,** in Colorado, the two nearest cities—Denver and Aurora—negotiated two intergovernmental agreements that established the Lowry Economic Recovery Project and the Lowry Redevelopment Authority. When fully redeveloped, the 1,800-acre (728-hectare) site will contain economic uses that will generate 10,000 jobs; it will also feature business parks; educational facilities; parks and recreational facilities; and 4,000 housing units in a wide variety of product types.[16]

The Lowry Redevelopment Authority requires that 20 percent of the housing units constructed on the property be set aside as affordable housing.[17] Under the auspices of the Lowry Community Land Trust Affordable Living Program,[18] 15 percent of the for-sale homes built on the site (about 300 homes) will be built for households that earn no more than 80 percent of AMI, on land owned in perpetuity by the Lowry Community Land Trust.[19] These homes will include condominiums, townhouses, duplexes, and single-family homes scattered throughout the community. The Lowry Redevelopment Authority will donate the land for these homes and fund a portion of the soft costs; it will also provide funding for the trust's initial operating costs. The total value of these contributions is approximately $4.5 million. As construction proceeds, homebuilders, the cities, and equity partners will need to provide the remaining $4.5 million in funding for the completion of the affordable homes.

For more information, call the Lowry Redevelopment Authority (303-343-0276) or the Lowry Community Land Trust (303-340-1954), or visit www.lowry.org/homes/affordable_living.htm.

The **San Jose, California, Redevelopment Agency,** which was created to redevelop and upgrade blighted areas of the city, has used land assembly, infrastructure development, and tax-increment and bond financing to assist in the construction of approximately 2,400 housing units in downtown San Jose and surrounding areas. By 2010, the agency intends to have produced 8,000 housing units at prices that are affordable to households earning a wide range of incomes.

For more information, call the San Jose Redevelopment Agency (916-448-8760), or visit www.sjredevelopment.org.

Brownfield Redevelopment

Brownfields are abandoned, idle, or underused industrial or commercial properties where redevelopment is complicated by real or perceived contamination. According to a Rutgers University study, "Most Northeastern and Midwestern cities are fully built-up and brownfield sites represent the only land available to redevelop."[20] Because brownfields are often located near major employment centers or public transportation, they offer potential opportunities for the development of workforce housing; thus, it is often in local governments' interest to return brownfields to economically viable use.[21]

Though brownfield sites often have strong market potential for residential use and are often priced well below similarly located properties that do not have associated environmental concerns, complicated legal requirements and other issues affecting reuse can be major obstacles to development. Not only must the sites be remediated (cleansed of dangerous chemicals), which can add significantly to development costs, but it must be determined who is responsible—and legally liable—for cleanup. In addition, some governmental programs designed to help clean up brownfields for productive use do not apply to residential properties. (Because cleanup standards for residential use are more stringent, most brownfield redevelopment programs target commercial, public, recreational, or open-space uses.)

The complexity of brownfield redevelopment typically requires a public/private effort and cooperation from every level of government. Because more than 15 agencies are involved in brownfield cleanup at the federal level alone, in 1997 the federal government created the Brownfields National Partnership to coordinate the resources of these agencies and to address local cleanup and reuse issues. Most states have voluntary cleanup programs that offer incentives for returning brownfields to productive use. Massachusetts's Brownfields Redevelopment Fund, for example, has earmarked funds to transform brownfields into developable sites for housing. Through California's Mello-Roos Districts program, communities can abate property taxes and issue bonds to capitalize revolving loan funds for assessment and cleanup of designated sites.

Local governments can facilitate brownfield redevelopment in a number of ways: by finding reusable sites, helping to fund cleanup on sites targeted for redevelopment, assisting developers to work with federal and state environmental agencies, and assuming legal responsibility for certifying remediation. Even with such assistance, however, developers should proceed with caution: the costs of preparing brownfield sites for residential development are difficult to predict and may make workforce housing infeasible, especially without additional financial help. Under the 2002 federal Small Business Liability Relief and Brownfields Revitalization Act, voluntary participation in federally qualified cleanup programs protects property owners from further liability under federal law.[22] Nevertheless, the uncertainty of financial returns and the risk associated with legal liability may remain.[23]

Self-insured brownfield-remediation companies are often willing to purchase contaminated property and assume all responsibility for cleaning it up; such firms provide environmental insurance and remove all other entities from the chain of title, and either develop the property or resell it to a developer.[24] Working with government agencies and private developers, these firms can often develop or facilitate the development of brownfields for housing.

PROGRAMS AND POLICIES: STATEWIDE

Pennsylvania's Land Recycling Program is a voluntary cleanup program that revamped the state's cleanup standards and review process. It offers a variety of financial incentives to encourage environmental studies and cleanup, and the redevelopment of industrial sites. Any entity that uses one of the program's designated cleanup options (including property owners and developers; financiers, lenders, and fiduciaries; and economic development agencies) gains liability relief.[25]

For more information, call 717-783-7816, or visit www.depweb.state.pa.us/landrecwaste/cwp/view.asp?a=1243&Q=462045&landrecwasteNav=|.

Minnesota's Voluntary Investigation and Cleanup (VIC) Program, a fee-for-service technical assistance and advisory service operated by the Minnesota Pollution Control Agency (MPCA), limits the liability of successor developers and property owners for cleanup as long as they perform an appropriate level of cleanup and do nothing to exacerbate the problem. The program was made possible by the Land Recycling Act of 1992, which stipulates that entities that are not otherwise responsible for the contamination and who voluntarily investigate and clean up properties in accordance with MPCA regulations may be eligible for future liability protection. Furthermore, participation in the VIC Program is a requirement for eligibility for certain environmental cleanup grants.

The VIC program, which has won awards from the Kennedy School of Government at Harvard University and from the Ford Foundation, assisted more than 1,000 parties during its first six years, from 1988 to 1994.[26]

For more information, call Barbara Jackson, VIC program supervisor (651-296-7217), or visit www.pca.state.mn.us/cleanup/vic.html.

The **Clean Ohio Revitalization Fund** is a $400 million bond program, half of which funds preservation of open space and half of which funds brownfield reclamation. Funding in the form of grants or low-interest loans is available to local governments, port authorities, conservation districts, and nonprofit and for-profit groups working in cooperation with a governmental entity; it can be used for demolition, environmental cleanup, or infrastructure development. Projects are selected by the Clean Ohio Council, which gives special consideration to mixed-use projects.

For more information, visit www.odod.state.oh.us/ud/CORF.htm.

PROGRAMS AND POLICIES: LOCAL

Identifying brownfields is the first step in finding sites suitable for redevelopment—and, as noted on the Fort Worth government's Web site, "one of the city's most difficult tasks is to create a complete brownfields inventory." Through its **Bust a Brownfield!** program, the city's Department of Environmental Management asks residents to help city staff pinpoint brownfield sites, including abandoned gas stations and idle or abandoned commercial or industrial properties. To date, more than 340 potential sites have been identified, 262 of which are profiled in the city's database.

For more information, call Kathryn Hansen, manager, Brownfields Program (817-392-8136), or visit www.fortworthgov.org/dem/bust_brownfield.asp.

To address land and groundwater contamination and incompatible land uses, Emeryville, California, created a comprehensive program for cleaning up brownfields in older industrial areas. Because groundwater contamination often crosses property lines, the city employs a cooperative approach, rather than providing assistance to individual landowners.

The **Emeryville Brownfields Pilot Project,** funded by a grant from the federal Environmental Protection Agency, involves collecting information on existing land uses and contamination problems and organizing workshops with key stakeholders to resolve the problems that are identified. In addition, the city coordinates the environmental and planning approvals process, acting as an intermediary between developers and regulatory agencies.[27] Through its One-Stop Shop program (described in the "Land Surveys, Inventories, and Information" section of this toolkit), Emeryville provides information on the contamination of sites in the city and maintains an environmental GIS map of the city.[28]

For more information, call 510-596-4350, or visit www.ci.emeryville.ca.us/bf/bf-finalstatus.html.

New York City's New Venture Incentive Program (NewVIP), an initiative of Mayor Bloomberg, provides predevelopment loans for projects that may involve environmental contamination. The program is designed primarily for manufacturing sites that have been or will be rezoned for residential use, and gives preference to proposals for the development of

housing that is affordable to low-, moderate-, and middle-income households.[29]

Over a five-year period, a total of $200 million dollars will be invested to encourage project development—including the development of 10,000 units of low-, moderate-, and middle-income housing. The city will invest $40 million in the program, and pool of capital from city financial institutions will make up the difference. The city has committed $8 million and obtained $40 million in bank commitments for the first year, and NewVIP is currently selecting projects. Projects that receive NewVIP loans have priority in obtaining construction and permanent financing through other city programs.

For more information, call Heather Jacksy, Department of Housing Preservation and Development (212-863-6334), or visit www.nyc.gov/hpd.

The **Brownfields Program** in Dallas combines private, state, and federal resources to help clean up and redevelop brownfields. In one two-year period, Dallas leveraged more than $109 million in private investments and $1.9 million in federal funds to facilitate brownfield development, helping to reclaim more than 1,200 acres (486 hectares) of land for commercial and residential redevelopment. Dallas was designated a Brownfields Showcase Community by the Brownfields National Partnership.[30]

For more information, call the Dallas Economic Development Department (214-670-1686), or visit www.dallas-edd.org/brownfields.html.

Abandoned or Tax-Delinquent Properties

Abandoned or tax-delinquent properties provide opportunities for the development of modestly priced apartments, condominiums, cooperatives, or mixed-use projects. However, to protect property owners, jurisdictions adopt careful procedures for foreclosing on such properties, allowing a period of time for taxes, penalties, and interest to be paid prior to foreclosure (or even after a foreclosure sale). As a result, the foreclosure process may take years—during which time the properties continue to deteriorate.[31]

The power of eminent domain (the authority to take property for public purposes), depends upon state and local laws. Thus, for some jurisdictions, eminent domain is a useful tool for acquiring land for redevelopment, while in other jurisdictions, the law significantly restricts the local government's ability to obtain title to properties and transfer them to development entities.

Some states, such as Maryland and Michigan, have quick-take laws that enable localities to take possession of vacant properties that are carrying significant tax liens. In Missouri, the power of eminent domain can even be delegated to private developers, if exercise of that power is consistent with a locally approved redevelopment plan. In St. Louis, for example, McCormack Baron & Associates used eminent domain to acquire certain parcels during the development of the Westminster Square project.[32]

✖ PROGRAMS AND POLICIES

In 1999, **Michigan's tax-foreclosure process** was reformed to make it simpler and faster, and to ensure that the process would result in a clear and marketable title. The revised process also enables counties to foreclose on tax-delinquent properties with minimal state involvement. Changes included the elimination of annual tax-lien sales, which were replaced by an annual forfeiture and judicial foreclosure process; strengthened due-process and notification procedures; and expedited handling of tax-reverted properties. As a result of these improvements, the tax-reversion process now takes three years rather than six.[33]

For more information, visit www.waynecounty.com/treasurer/tax_reversion.htm.

New York City's Third Party Transfer (TPT) Program, enacted in 1996 and administered by the city's Department of Housing Preservation and Development (HPD), allows the city to transfer title of tax-delinquent residential properties directly from the delinquent owners to new owners, through the *in rem* foreclosure process, without the city taking title itself. Attached to the transfer is the requirement that the new owners correct housing code violations and rehabilitate the properties soon after they take ownership. In cases where rents and tenant incomes are insufficient to support market-rate financing, the program also provides low-interest rehabilitation loans through HPD's Participation Loan Program.

Neighborhood Restore, a nonprofit entity created by the Enterprise Foundation and the Local Initiatives Support Corporation, controls the property and takes ownership while a suitable for-profit or nonprofit owner is selected through HPD's request-for-qualifications process, and provides technical assistance to the new owner after the property is transferred. Depending on the project and the new owner's needs, a variety of other city programs may also be used to support the redevelopment of transferred properties.

For more information, call the Department of Housing Preservation and Development (212-863-6562), or visit www.nyc.gov/html/hpd/html/developers/third-party-ownership.shtml.

Land Banking

Land bank authorities are nonprofit entities established to acquire and hold publicly owned or tax-delinquent properties in advance of development; properties can either be held for future use or transferred to for-profit—or, more typically, nonprofit—developers for redevelopment.

Typically, land bank authorities can forgive property taxes owed on the properties they acquire. A land bank authority also has the power to assemble sites, remove environmental contamination, clear title encumbrances, and otherwise prepare properties for redevelopment. Land bank authorities can sell land to produce funds for affordable housing—and, to ensure that the land is developed for the intended use, can attach restrictions to it at the time of sale.

PROGRAMS AND POLICIES

The **Fulton County/City of Atlanta Land Bank Authority** (LBA) is a nonprofit corporation created in 1995 to acquire abandoned and deteriorated property in the region and return it to productive use. The LBA can acquire clear title to a property on behalf of a nonprofit or for-profit developer during the foreclosure process; alternatively, a developer may acquire a tax-delinquent property directly. In either case, the developer must apply to the LBA for tax forgiveness—which the LBA has the authority to grant, provided that the project meets specified criteria.

The LBA has supported commercial projects, parks, gardens, recreation centers, and affordable single- and multifamily housing projects. More than 900 housing units have been built on land obtained through the LBA, and 240 more are under construction.[34]

For more information, call the Fulton County/City of Atlanta Land Bank Authority (404-525-9336).

Cleveland's Land Bank, established in 1976, was one of the first land banks created to reclaim tax-delinquent properties. The land bank works in partnership with county and local agencies to acquire properties, pay the foreclosure costs, forgive back taxes, and transfer the properties to nonprofit or for-profit developers. State legislation passed in 1988 expedited the tax-foreclosure process by establishing a tax-abatement policy for properties entering the land bank and eliminating the existing *in rem* proceedings; these changes made the land bank an efficient vehicle for returning delinquent properties to productive use.[35] Property owners may also donate tax-delinquent properties to the land bank.

Land is priced for sale at fair-market value, though the city may impose restrictions if it chooses, and those restrictions may affect the sales price. According to one source, 90 percent of all new residential construction in the city, for-profit and nonprofit, involves bank lots.[36]

For more information, call Evelyn Sternad, manager, Cleveland Land Bank (216-664-4126), or visit www.city.cleveland.oh.us/government/departments/commdev/cdneigdev/cdndlandbank.html.

Planning and Regulatory Approaches

Planning and regulatory approaches are the primary means of encouraging private-market provision of workforce housing development. The production of housing for moderate-income households cannot rely primarily on public or private subsidies. For one thing, given the high cost of producing housing, "even extraordinary sums of money can produce a limited number of units."[37] Moreover, persuading half the nation's population to contribute extraordinary sums to subsidize housing for the other half would be an uphill battle.

Though the effects of government regulation of land use and development are difficult to document with precision, many developers believe that such regulation increases the cost of producing workforce housing by (1) limiting the supply and locations of land for housing; (2) constraining the amount and types of housing that can be built; and (3) imposing requirements, procedures, fees, and delays that complicate the development process and add directly and indirectly to construction costs. Nevertheless, most governments use their planning and regulatory powers to encourage certain desired types of development, including affordable housing.

Local governments are the entities primarily responsible for regulating the use of land. They can encourage (or discourage) the development of workforce housing through comprehensive planning, zoning, subdivision regulation, building codes, issuance of development permits, and so forth. However, states and the federal government also use their regulatory powers to encourage the production of moderate-income housing.

The federal government has long recognized and sought to lower regulatory barriers to development. The 1991 report of the Advisory Commission on Regulatory Barriers to Affordable Housing, *Not in My Backyard: Removing Barriers to Affordable Housing,* details the major regulatory barriers affecting affordable-housing development and suggests ways to remove them. In June 2003, the U.S. Department of Housing and Urban Development (HUD) announced America's Affordable Communities Initiative, a department-wide effort to encourage the removal of regulatory barriers to affordable housing. Under the initiative, HUD awards additional "rating points" to funding applications that involve the removal of such barriers.[38]

In addition, HUD requires local governments applying for federal funds to have a strategy for providing affordable housing; undertakes research and promotion of cost-cutting technologies, including manufactured housing; and maintains an online clearinghouse that provides guidance on ways to streamline, speed up, and rationalize the development process.

States plan and regulate affordable-housing development in various ways—for example, by creating the legal framework for local governments' regulation of land use, and by establishing statewide building and fire codes. Some states impose planning and affordable-housing "fair-share" requirements on local governments or create state-level zoning-appeals mechanisms for housing. State involvement in other activities—such as the provision of transportation and other infrastructure and the protection of environmental resources—can also affect housing supplies, locations, and affordability.

An individual local government's regulatory approaches to the provision of workforce housing will depend on its housing needs, economy, physical form, legal structures, and other characteristics. Generally speaking, however, the process begins with the creation of a comprehensive plan that sets forth a vision of the community's future in the form of goals and objectives. Policies and strategies based on the comprehensive plan describe how the community's goals will be translated into physical form over the years ahead.

A comprehensive plan gives a community an opportunity to balance its various needs and values—in particular, to achieve a quantitative and qualitative balance between the community's employment base and housing that is affordable to the people who make up that base. Ideally, the comprehensive plan clearly sets forth the community's intent to provide housing for its workforce, and ensures that all elements of the plan—including infrastructure development and commercial land uses—work together to enable the community to achieve its workforce housing goals.[39]

This section describes some of the most useful state and local regulatory approaches to encouraging the production of workforce housing, arranged according to type of program:

- Inclusionary housing policies and programs;
- Zoning designed to allow more housing and more housing types;
- Targeting specific locations;
- Master planning large sites;
- Development standards;
- Parking;
- Density incentives;
- Transfer of development rights;
- Revisions to building codes and rehabilitation subcodes;
- Improvements to the development permitting process;
- Waivers or reimbursement of development fees.

Inclusionary Housing

Inclusionary housing policies and programs rely on private sector housing developers to create affordable housing as they build market-rate residential developments.[40] Local governments adopt inclusionary *policies* to set broad goals for increasing the supply of affordable housing; inclusionary *programs* are the mechanisms for achieving those goals. One of the most common inclusionary housing programs is inclusionary zoning (IZ), which encourages or mandates the inclusion of a set proportion of affordable units in each new market-rate housing development above a certain size.

Because inclusionary housing programs apply across the board to housing developments that meet threshold criteria, create a range of housing choices in dispersed locations, and may not require public subsidies, they are currently among the most popular approaches that state and local governments are using to encourage the production of affordable housing. Research sponsored by the Urban Land Institute indicates that between 300 and 400 communities across the nation have enacted IZ or other inclusionary policies, and that many other communities impose inclusionary requirements on a case-by-case basis. Many of the programs focus on units affordable to households earning no more than 60 percent of AMI, but a significant number provide for units that are affordable to households earning between 60 and 120 percent of AMI. A number of inclusionary programs target both workforce housing and lower-cost units that may be subsidized by developers or public funds.

Inclusionary policies and programs require political will to establish and administrative expertise to implement. Nevertheless, their increase in popularity has provided a rich store of knowledge and experience on which communities can draw. One of the most important lessons is that inclusionary programs—like other individual workforce housing programs—are most effective when they are combined with other approaches, as part of a multifaceted strategy for generating and improving workforce housing.

State and Regional Inclusionary Housing Programs

Resistance to adding lower-income households to existing neighborhoods is one of the most troublesome barriers to the creation of affordable housing. To help overcome the NIMBY ("not-in-my-backyard") syndrome, some states—such as California, Florida, New Jersey, and Oregon—require each municipality to accommodate a fair share of the state's affordable-housing needs.[41]

One effect of these state initiatives has been to encourage local governments to enact inclusionary housing policies and laws. According to Douglas Porter, president of the Growth Management Institute, "Most jurisdictions administering inclusionary policies and regulations are located in California and New Jersey, both states that require local governments to promote production of affordable housing in the exercise of planning and regulating development."[42] California's law is especially supportive of workforce housing production because it allows local governments to target up to half the required allocation of affordable units to households earning 80 to 120 percent of AMI.

In addition, some regional entities—such as metropolitan Portland, Oregon; Westchester County, New York; Cape Cod, Massachusetts; and Minneapolis–St. Paul, Minnesota—have taken steps to allocate shares of responsibility for affordable-housing production to their member jurisdictions.

✴ PROGRAMS AND POLICIES: STATEWIDE AND REGIONAL

The 1975 and 1983 Mt. Laurel decisions of the New Jersey Supreme Court, which enabled judges to overturn local zoning decisions that effectively excluded affordable housing, set the stage for the **New Jersey Fair Housing Act of 1985.** The act created the Council on Affordable Housing (COAH), which sets numerical affordable-housing goals for each of the state's 566 municipalities and promotes adherence to those goals: if a jurisdiction's affordable-housing plans are certified by COAH, it will not be subject to litigation under the Mt. Laurel decision. Though local governments are not legally required to create such plans, about half did so in 2001.[43] Also, by mutual agreement, a local government can transfer up to half of its affordable-housing obligation to another municipality within its housing region, in return for a negotiated per-unit fee.[44] COAH estimates that the act has stimulated private-sector production of 26,800 new affordable units and 10,400 rehabilitated units, none of which received public subsidies.

For more information, visit www.state.nj.us/dca/coah.

Under **California's Housing Element Law,** each regional council of government (COG) must conduct an analysis of its housing needs. On the basis of that analysis, the California Department of Housing and Community Development determines each region's "fair share" of affordable housing for four separate income tiers. Since 1980, each local government in California has been required to include in its general or comprehensive plan a housing element that describes how the jurisdiction will meet its fair share. Local governments must also (1) zone sufficient land for residential development by right, and (2) ensure, through density and development standards, that the projected housing needs of all four income tiers can be met.

As of August 2002, all COGs had conducted analyses of regional housing needs, and more than half of California's local governments had complied with the requirements of the law. A 2003 survey determined that 107 of the 527 counties and cities in California had adopted inclusionary programs.[45]

While the law has encouraged planning for affordable housing, and inclusionary programs have generated over 34,000 affordable units, the law's power to require implementation is weak. As a result, only a fraction of the planned housing has actually been built.[46]

For more information, visit www.hcd.ca.gov/hpd/hrc/plan/he/status.pdf.

Florida's Growth Management and Land Development Regulation Act, enacted in 1985, requires local jurisdictions to adopt affordable-housing goals as part of the housing element of their comprehensive plans, and to enact programs to achieve those goals. Although the state cannot enforce implementation (that is, it cannot require local governments to achieve the goals that they have set), and although the law has not led local governments to adopt inclusionary housing ordinances, the law has, according to Douglas R. Porter, "assisted affordable housing developers to obtain incentives such as impact fee waivers as well as state and local housing funds to build thousands of affordable units in virtually every area of Florida."[47]

For more information, visit www.dca.state.fl.us/ fdcp/dcp/compplanning/index.cfm.

State Appeals Boards

To ensure that local governments do not exclude proposed housing developments with affordable components, some states, such as Illinois and Massachusetts, have created state-level housing appeals boards that have the power to overturn local zoning decisions that effectively deny developers the right to build affordable housing.

⚒ PROGRAMS AND POLICIES

Massachusetts's Comprehensive Permit Law, also known as the "anti-snob zoning" law, enables the state to override local exclusionary decisions under certain circumstances. Originally enacted in 1969, the law specifies that 10 percent of all housing in Massachusetts cities and towns should be affordable to households that earn less than 80 percent of AMI. If a jurisdiction has not met that threshold, and a public agency, a nonprofit, or a limited-dividend organization proposes a residential project in which at least 25 percent of the units are affordable to low- and moderate-income households, an adverse decision by the local zoning board can be appealed to the local board of adjustment and, if necessary, to the state housing appeals board. Since the law was passed, in the early 1970s, it has stimulated the production of approximately 20,000 affordable homes.[48] Most units were subsidized, however, and only 1,200 were generated by inclusionary programs.[49] Connecticut and Rhode Island have since adopted similar laws.[50]

For more information, call Fred Habib, deputy director, Massachusetts Department of Housing and Community Development (617-727-7765), or visit www.mass.gov/dhcd/.

Under **Illinois's Affordable Housing Planning and Appeal Act,** which was modeled after the Massachusetts Comprehensive Permit Law, the state housing appeals board can overturn local zoning decisions affecting developments in which at least 20 percent of the units are affordable to households earning 80 percent of AMI or less. By July 1, 2004, communities in which less than 10 percent of the housing was affordable were required to adopt a plan for increasing the stock of affordable housing. The law has been criticized because (1) it does not include a comprehensive permitting process; (2) the developer carries the burden of proof in the appeals process; (3) the legal standards of affordability are vague; and (4) the appeals board cannot hear any cases until 2009.[51]

For more information, call Business and Professional People in the Public Interest (312-641-5570), or visit www.bpichicago.org/ rah/pubs/hb625.pdf.

Local Inclusionary Housing Programs

Local inclusionary housing programs may be mandatory or voluntary. Both generally provide incentives such as density bonuses or reductions in fees, development standards, or parking requirements. Voluntary programs usually provide more incentives.[52] Incentives are intended to compensate, at least partially, for the inclusion of low-priced units in market-rate projects. One advantage of IZ programs is that they can generate a geographically dispersed supply of affordable housing in developing areas, produced (and, in the case of rental properties, managed) by the private sector.[53]

After 30 years of collective experience, IZ programs are likely to feature similar requirements; however, program particulars—such as the size and type of projects affected, the percentage of units set aside for income-qualified families, the income range of the households served by the program, and the duration of affordability controls—vary widely among communities. For example, according to a survey of IZ programs conducted by two housing advocacy groups, set-aside requirements ranged from less than 10 percent to over 20 percent.[54]

IZ programs are most likely to succeed where demand is strong—which is also where workforce housing tends to be most needed. However, operating costs and condominium fees can make it difficult to impose IZ on high-rise rental or condominium projects. To address this problem, some communities allow high-rise developers to pay a fee in lieu of providing actual units; however, this approach does not necessarily help achieve the goal of creating a geographically distributed supply of affordable units.

Income ranges vary widely among programs. In Montgomery County, Maryland, for example, the units included in the Moderately Priced Dwelling Unit program must be affordable to households that earn no more than 65 percent of the county's AMI.[55] California's Housing Element Law, in contrast, defines "moderate-income" units as affordable to households earn-ing 80 to 120 percent of AMI—a range that is suitably priced for workforce housing.

⚒ PROGRAMS AND POLICIES

Under the **Below Market Rate Program** established in San Mateo, California, at least 10 percent of all newly constructed residential units, newly subdivided residential parcels, or condominium conversions that contain 11 or more units must be reserved for moderate- or lower-income households. The below-market units offered for sale must be affordable to households earning no more than 120 percent of AMI; rental units must be affordable to households earning no more than 80 percent of AMI. Preference is given to people who live or work in San Mateo, and every third unit must be offered to an eligible city employee. The program includes a maximum density bonus of 25 percent. Thirty-year resale restrictions preserve the affordability of the for-sale units.

For more information, visit www.ci.sanmateo. ca.us/downloads/planning/bmr_inclusionary_ program.pdf.

Under **Denver's Inclusionary Housing Program,** enacted in 2002, developers constructing projects with more than 30 for-sale units must ensure that at least 10 percent of the units are affordable to households earning 80 percent or less of AMI, for at least 15 years. Some developments are subject to different income requirements. For example, for-sale projects that have more than three stories, that include elevators, and in which at least 60 percent of the parking is structured can offer units priced to be affordable to households earning up to 95 percent of AMI.

The program also offers a number of incentives to developers: rebates of between $5,000 and

$10,000 on the fees incurred for affordable units (depending on the income level of the targeted households); reduced parking requirements; expedited permitting; and, in certain zones, a 10 percent density bonus. More than 300 new affordable units were created during the first six months of the program, in addition to the 766 created through negotiated agreements prior to program adoption. Because state law prohibits rent control, participation by developers of rental projects is voluntary.

For more information, call Beth Truby, acting housing manager, Department of Housing and Neighborhood Development Services (720-913-1533), or visit www.milehigh.com/housing/homeownership-opportunities/affordable-housing.

Boston's inclusionary housing program was initiated in February 2000, by an executive order of Mayor Thomas Menino. The program applies to residential developments of more than ten units that require a zoning variance or that involve city or redevelopment authority land or financing. Under the program, 10 percent of the units in such developments must be affordable: of those, half must be targeted to households earning less than 80 percent of AMI, and half to households earning between 80 and 120 percent of AMI. In return, the city provides property-tax abatements and an increase in the project's allowable height or floor/area ratio.

For more information, visit www.bostonhomecenter.com./dnd/.

A program initiated in **Somerville, Massachusetts,** in 2003 allows developers to obtain density bonuses, fast-track permitting, and fee waivers in return for ensuring that 12.5 percent of projects are affordable. The program is voluntary for projects with eight or more units (but mandatory for projects needing special

permits), and eligible occupants include households earning up to 80 percent of AMI, or 81 to 110 percent of AMI. Prices and rents are controlled in perpetuity. By the end of 2003, the program had generated 25 units.

For more information, visit www.ci.somerville.ma.us.

Zoning Designed to Allow More Housing and More Diverse Housing Types

Local zoning ordinances may discourage affordable-housing development by limiting the amount and location of residential development; specifying excessively large lot sizes, floor areas, setbacks, or road widths; separating different land uses and housing product types; and disallowing certain housing types, such as manufactured homes or accessory units. In addition, many traditional zoning codes are not suited to the higher-density, mixed-use development forms that can allow people with different incomes and lifestyles to live in the same community. Depending on local circumstances, zoning changes may help remove barriers to the production of workforce housing.

Zoning for Residential and Mixed Uses

Many communities fail to zone enough land to meet current and future housing needs. Others require lengthy hearings or conditional-use permits—both of which add to development costs—before residential development can proceed. One way to encourage affordable-housing development is by zoning appropriate locations for "by right" housing development—especially for medium- and high-density residential projects—in amounts that are consistent with the community's housing needs.

Traditional zoning segregates land uses, disallowing mixed-use projects. Instead, local governments can amend zoning ordinances to allow higher-density residential development in certain commercial areas, thereby fostering the construction of housing that is conveniently located for workers. For example, Austin, Texas's Traditional Neighborhood Development (TND) Code promotes compact, mixed-use projects by allowing residential, retail, workplace, civic, and recreational uses and a range of housing types within designated TND zones. Use mixes can also be permitted more broadly, through performance-based or flexible zoning ordinances, which set forth goals and criteria for land development instead of listing specific permitted uses.[56]

✂ PROGRAMS AND POLICIES

Pittsburgh's Urban Zoning Code was adopted in 1998 because existing regulations—including setbacks and requirements for large lot sizes—made it difficult for developers to create innovative, mixed-use projects that would be compatible with the city's urban character. The new regulations created a series of use and development subdistricts that developers could use in combination, to gain more flexibility in designing projects that fit the city's urban context. The regulations separate use from development characteristics, control a development's appearance and impact on nearby uses, and address traffic and parking issues.[57]

For more information, call Pittsburgh City Planning (412-255-2200), or visit www.city.pittsburgh.pa.us/cp/.

Boulder, Colorado, a city where raw land is scarce, established **Mixed-Use Zones** in 1997 to encourage a mix of uses within redevelopment projects. The Mixed-Use Redeveloping Zone, for example, allows residential, retail, and office development in the same project or lot within a mixed-use zone, and encourages developers to include housing by waiving reviews and reducing parking requirements.

The Business Main Street Redeveloping Zone encourages artists, craftspeople, and small-business owners to live and work near one another, or in the same building, in locations between commercial and service industrial uses. To create a transition between commercial centers and residential neighborhoods, the Residential Mixed-Use Redeveloping Zone allows the development of live-work spaces.[58]

For more information, call the Boulder Planning Department (303-441-3270), or visit www.bouldercolorado.gov/index.php?option=com_ content&task=view&id=1415&Itemid=507.

Zoning to Permit Alternative Housing Types

Local governments can consider amending zoning ordinances to allow the development of nontraditional housing and higher-density housing types—such as manufactured homes, accessory dwelling units, duplexes, and zero-lot-line homes—that can help meet affordable-housing needs.

Manufactured housing, which must meet the requirements of a national, performance-based building code (commonly known as the HUD Code), can be constructed more quickly and more cheaply than stick-built homes, and can be sold to consumers at lower prices. According to the Manufactured Housing Institute, the per-square-foot cost of a new manufactured home is typically 10 to 35 percent lower than the cost of a comparable site-built home.[59]

Historically, localities have not welcomed manufactured-housing communities. Manufactured homes are typically not allowed "by right" in residential zones and instead require a conditional-use permit, which is difficult to obtain. Some localities effectively exclude manufactured housing by establishing requirements for characteristics such as roof pitch, minimum floor area, and dimensions. Others require minimum lot sizes or huge setbacks that raise land costs.[60]

Toolkit

However, a number of states—including California, New Mexico, Ohio, Utah, Vermont, and Wisconsin—forbid local governments to exclude permanently sited manufactured homes from single-family zoning districts, as long as the homes meet the HUD Code and the uniform requirements of the zoning district.

Accessory or secondary units are self-contained housing units that are typically attached to existing homes, although they may be constructed separately on the same lot. By allowing accessory units, local governments can foster a modest and low-cost increase in the supply of affordable housing throughout the community without changing the character of existing neighborhoods.

Many jurisdictions use zoning—especially density limits, building codes, and parking requirements—to prohibit or constrain the construction of accessory units. Neighborhoods willing to accept accessory units can be rezoned to allow them, with appropriate design restrictions to ensure the continued integrity of the neighborhood character. Building codes should be reviewed to eliminate or amend requirements that are not truly needed for this type of structure.

Although parking can be an issue for accessory units, extra parking may not be necessary if the intended occupants are elderly, or if the unit is near mass transit and retail uses. If additional off-street parking is needed, tandem compact parking (a group of two or more parking spaces arranged one behind the other, so that one space blocks access to the other space) may be a good option.

✴ PROGRAMS AND POLICIES

In 2002, **California** passed a law requiring local governments to allow accessory units without requiring a special permit, as long as the units meet locally determined criteria such as size, and setbacks from the street and neighboring properties. As a result of this law, local governments throughout the state have been revisiting their requirements for accessory units. In Sacramento, local ordinances were changed to allow by-right construction of secondary units that meet certain size, setback, and occupancy criteria.

In addition, manufactured homes built under the HUD Code and designed to be placed on a foundation may be situated on lots zoned for single-family residential use. The homes must conform to the same development standards as traditional single-family homes in terms of setbacks, parking, etc., but may be subject to additional requirements for roof overhang, roofing material, and siding material. California law forbids local governments from adopting development standards that effectively exclude manufactured housing.

For more information, visit www.hcd.ca.gov/.

The zoning code of **Cary, North Carolina,** permits accessory dwelling units in all single-family homes. In this fast-growing town near Research Triangle Park, the builder of a new townhouse project in the neotraditional planned community of Carpenter Village has included a 300-square-foot (28-square-meter) suite in each of the homes.

For more information, call Shawn McNamara, senior planner, Cary Planning Department (919-469-4086), or visit www.townofcary.org/depts/planning/planninghome.htm.

Orlando, Florida, allows tandem single-family housing (more than one home on a single lot) as a conditional use in various zoning districts.[61] Tandem housing is especially encouraged within the city's overlay district, where it can be built by right in certain residential, mixed-use, office, and commercial zones. The ordinance requires at least ten feet (three meters) of separation between structures, with no less than five feet (1.5 meters) on each side of the property line. Design requirements ensure that tandem houses will be compatible with existing neighborhoods.

For more information, call the "planner on call" at the Current Planning Section of the City Planning Division (407-246-2269), or visit www.cityoforlando.net/PLANNING/.

Targeting Specific Locations

Municipalities use a number of geographic designations to encourage the development of affordable housing in targeted locations, including specific plans, area plans, overlay zones, floating zones, housing enterprise zones, transit-oriented development zones, and planned unit development zones. These various zones and districts may be defined—and operated—somewhat differently by different jurisdictions.

Specific plans—detailed plans for specific areas within a jurisdiction—focus governmental resources and requirements in order to direct, control, and encourage certain kinds of growth. This flexible approach involves public participation, and typically includes zoning changes, environmental impact reports, design guidelines, and standards and criteria for project development and implementation. When zoning changes are part of the process, specific plans "can help reduce the development permitting process by 6–12 months . . . [and] minimize neighborhood opposition, avoid lawsuits, and ensure that community needs are met."[62] In California, proposed developments that are consistent with specific plans (which means that they are also consistent with the jurisdiction's general plan, zoning ordinance, and other local land use regulations) need not obtain separate general plan, zoning, subdivision, or other discretionary approvals.[63]

Precise plans, also known as small-area plans, are legislative tools for coordinating public and private investments to support the development of specific properties for certain uses that a juris-

diction would like to encourage.[64] Precise plans replace traditional zoning with specific design and development requirements, and are used to facilitate mixed-use or higher-density development in areas such as transit nodes.

Overlay zones are designated geographic areas superimposed on the zoning map to protect specific resources or to promote certain types of development within their boundaries. Overlay districts are popular because they do not require a major rewrite of zoning codes; they can "simply be grafted onto an existing law."[65]

Overlay zones can permit certain uses by right; allow variations from the zoning ordinance in order to encourage certain uses; and impose additional or more restrictive development standards or criteria. For example, an overlay zone might permit higher-density residential development by right; allow flexibility in height, massing, or setbacks to facilitate the construction of mixed-use developments; or set forth minimum as well as maximum density requirements to encourage more intense use of land. Overlay zones can also be used to encourage affordable housing by allowing it as a by-right use. The Town of Corte Madera, California, for example, has created an affordable-housing overlay zone in which affordable housing is mandatory on some sites and voluntary on others.[66]

✂ PROGRAMS AND POLICIES

Mountain View, California, has used precise plans since the 1960s to intensify land use around transit facilities and to promote higher-density, mixed-use development. In place of the original zoning designations, the plans set forth detailed development guidelines. Mountain View's precise plans have resulted in the development of small- and medium-lot single-family homes and low- and medium-density housing.

For more information, call the Planning and Zoning Division, Community Development Department (650-903-6306), or visit www.ci.mtnview.ca.us/city_hall/community_development/planning/default.asp.

The Livable Centers Initiative of the **Atlanta Regional Commission** (ARC), established in 1999, targets public investment to specific districts to encourage privately developed residential, mixed-income, and transportation-oriented development in activity centers and town centers in the Atlanta region. Through this program, ARC awards $1 million a year (provided by ARC and matching federal funds) for five years for planning studies; it has also allocated $350 million for investment in specific projects undertaken by local governments and by nonprofit organizations whose work is focused on activity centers or town centers. Though the program is not specifically designed to foster the private production of workforce housing, it does encourage the creation of diverse, mixed-income residential neighborhoods within town centers that include employment, shopping, recreation, and access to a range of travel modes.

For more information, call Tom Weyandt, director, Comprehensive Planning Department, ARC (404-463-3101), or visit www.atlantaregional.com/cps/rde/xchg/.

Land development regulations in **Teton County, Wyoming,** include a planned unit development district overlay zone for affordable housing; because the standards of the traditional zoning districts are not strictly applied within the overlay zone, developers can create mixed-income neighborhoods within it. The county also awards density bonuses for developments in which 66 percent of the units are affordable to households that earn 120 percent of AMI or less. (In certain circumstances, the minimum

percentage of affordable units may be reduced to as low as 50 percent.)[67] Finally, the county requires that 15 percent of the homes in new developments be affordable, although the developer is also permitted to build the required affordable homes off site, or to pay an in-lieu fee to an affordable-housing fund.[68]

For more information, visit www.tetonwyo.org/plan/docs/ComprehensivePlan/Comp-Chapter5.pdf.

Master Planning Large Sites

There are many different approaches to master planning large development sites to allow a mix of housing types and densities. Through flexible tools such as development agreements, vesting subdivision maps, and floating zones, local governments can encourage private development that is consistent with community goals. Such tools also benefit developers, by providing greater certainty about obtaining entitlements and/or simplified or expedited development approvals.

Development agreements bind local governments to an agreed-upon plan, thereby giving developers assurance that the project can proceed as planned, even if the composition of the governing body changes. Vesting subdivision maps guarantee developers that they can complete their development over time as agreed, as long as they comply with the governing ordinances, policies, and standards in effect at the time the vesting subdivision map was approved.[69] Floating zones—zoning districts that are not tied to specific sites on a map—permit certain types of development, such as mixed-income housing or multifamily development, in designated locations as long as the projects are consistent with specified performance standards.

Perhaps the most popular tool for guiding the development of large sites is the planned development (or planned unit development—PUD) designation. Because standards for PUDs are typically performance based, such designations give developers substantial control over project design, allowing a range of housing choices that small developments cannot provide. PUD laws generally set forth specific criteria regarding density, the number and kinds of units, allocations for other uses, etc., within which the developer is allowed to proceed according to flexible development standards. PUDs allow more innovative spatial arrangements, including the clustering of development; more efficient use of land; a wider mix of uses; and more variety in uses and housing types.

✖ PROGRAMS AND POLICIES

Timberleaf, in Orlando, Florida, is a 188-acre (76-hectare), 1,800-unit, mixed-use, mostly affordable-housing development that resulted from a development agreement between the developer and the city. The negotiated agreement, which took more than a year to hammer out, set the parameters of the project's master plan in terms of scale, timing, facilities, and density. As a result of the agreement, the city grants approvals for different stages of the development within 30 days of application. A design review committee, which includes bankers and developers, manages the streamlined permitting process and is the focal point for actions by all participating city agencies.[70]

For more information, call Leila Allen, director of housing (407-246-2708).

Homan Square, in Chicago, is a 300-unit mixed-income, mixed-use project undertaken as a planned development by the Shaw Company in partnership with Sears, Roebuck, and the city of Chicago. Located in the distressed and largely minority community of North Lawndale, on the west side of Chicago, the project features public amenities and uses, including a community center, parks, and gar-dens; commercial space; and a range of mostly affordable for-sale and rental-housing products.

Homan Square was developed under a "planned development" designation, which gave the developer the flexibility to make changes within an approved overall plan. The city retained the right to review each phase, give its administrative approval, and set performance benchmarks as conditions for continued designation, but having the designation reassures the city and the developer that the plan will go forward in a certain way. The fixed items in the planned development designation included the ultimate unit count, use limits for each type of land use, and the amount of site coverage and open space.

For more information, visit www.homansquare.org/.

Development Standards

Development standards incorporated into a local government's zoning ordinance determine, to a large extent, the amount, type, and location of different uses that can be developed on a site. Since the 1980s, a number of communities have replaced traditional prescriptive development standards with performance standards (also known as flexible zoning) to help depoliticize the development process, make it more efficient, and facilitate more creative land use solutions. Unlike prescriptive standards, performance standards do not list permitted or excluded land uses or set specific requirements. Instead, they set forth desired outcomes, such as density and environmental impacts. Projects developed under performance standards must be consistent with approved plans, complement existing land uses, and meet other community objectives, but they give developers more flexibility in project design. Performance standards can apply to an entire project or to specific project components, such as lot sizes, streets, parking, utilities, parks, open space, walkways, curbs and gutters, drainage systems, sewers, utilities, and amenities.

Over time, several of the communities that had adopted performance standards have returned to more conventional approaches, primarily in response to the administrative complexity associated with performance standards, and to address citizens' desires for more predictability in development outcomes; however, most of these communities have retained the key elements of performance standards, in order to preserve some flexibility in decision making.

✗ PROGRAMS AND POLICIES

Largo, Florida, adopted a comprehensive development code in 1983 that incorporated considerable flexibility in land use and design. Rather than specifying requirements for setbacks, lot sizes, and building heights, the ordinance based approvals on floor/area ratios and impervious-surface ratios. As the city developed, and concern shifted to infill and redevelopment projects, "the expanding cadres of longtime residents assured a constant watch over development proposals, leading finally to desires for more protection from unexpected consequences of development."[71] Perceiving performance standards as unreliable in this regard, the city revised its ordinance to return to a more conventional approach—and, in particular, to require developers to meet with neighborhood residents and to mitigate the negative impacts of development.

For more information, call Rick Goss, planning director (813-587-6749), or visit www.largo.com/index.cfm?action=dept&drill=community&type=development.

In 1981, **Fort Collins, Colorado,** adopted the Land Development Guidance System, a performance-based system that included provi-

sion for negotiated planned unit developments and set forth extensive criteria for rating proposed projects. In 1997, it revised the ordinance to eliminate negotiable guidelines in favor of mandatory requirements. The new ordinance includes most of the performance criteria and standards of the 1981 law, as well as its design and amenity incentives. The city retains flexibility through the use of "alternative compliance options"—and, although the revised ordinance sets minimum requirements, they can be exceeded at the city's discretion. Moreover, allowable densities in residential zones are based on the project's average density, which permits developers to vary densities within a site.

For more information, call Cameron Gloss, director of current planning (970-221-6750), or visit www.ci.fort-collins.co.us/building/.[72]

Parking

Even where higher densities are allowed, parking requirements often determine the number of housing units that can actually be built on a given site—and thus the land costs per unit. In many communities, parking requirements associated with housing developments, particularly multifamily developments in infill locations, create a significant cost barrier to the provision of affordable housing. The provision of parking is expensive and consumes land and financial resources that could, potentially, be used to develop more housing—or less expensive housing—in locations near employment. Depending on land costs, surface parking can cost developers $5,000 or more per space, and underground or structured parking can cost between $20,000 and $50,000 per space.[73]

Parking requirements are often inflexible, set without regard to factors such as vehicle ownership rates, development density, or transit access.

Incorporating flexibility into a jurisdiction's parking requirements can help to encourage workforce housing. Several jurisdictions, including Austin, Denver, Los Angeles, and San Diego; and the cities of Milpitas, Mountain View, and San Jose, in the San Francisco Bay Area, have reduced parking requirements for affordable housing and/or housing near transit. To serve a number of public policy objectives, including making urban housing more affordable, Portland and Eugene, Oregon; Cambridge, Massachusetts; and Gainesville, Florida, have all imposed *upper* limits on the number of parking spaces developers can provide in their projects.[74]

Local governments can build in flexibility and avoid burdening occupants with parking costs by "unbundling" parking spaces from units, and by establishing the parking requirement separately from the total unit count. Under such arrangements, parking costs are subtracted from rental rates and home prices, and parking spaces are sold or rented separately. Thus, parking requirements are based on likely need rather than on a set standard. For example, for a development situated where street parking is available, less parking would be required. Palo Alto, California, has built in the flexibility to make these kinds of decisions: the planning director has the discretion to partially waive parking requirements if the amount of parking called for seems unnecessary (and if it can be added later if needed).

✖ PROGRAMS AND POLICIES

Portland, Oregon, sets maximum parking requirements in order to promote efficient land use, encourage the use of mass transit, and protect environmental quality. The specific requirements vary by type of use and location within the city. Lower maximum requirements apply in areas that are zoned for more intensive development or that have easy access to mass transit; higher maximums apply to developments located more than a quarter-mile (0.40-kilometer) walk from a bus stop or more than a half-mile (0.80-kilometer) walk from a light-rail or streetcar stop.

For more information and a table of specific requirements, visit www.portlandonline.com/auditor/index.cfm?c=28197.

On the basis of statistical evidence that lower-income households tend to own fewer cars, **Los Angeles** lowered parking requirements from 2.0 to 1.5 spaces per unit for affordable (rent-restricted) units that have four or more habitable rooms. If the affordable unit is also located within 1,500 feet (457 meters) of mass transit or a major bus line, the minimum parking requirement is reduced to one space per unit.[75]

For more information, visit cityplanning.lacity.org/.

The development code of **Pinellas County, Florida,** allows reductions in parking requirements for certified affordable-housing developments (those whose occupants earn less than 80 percent of AMI).

For more information, visit www.pinellascounty.org/housingpinellas/.

Density Incentives

Especially in high-demand markets, the cost of land is a major barrier to housing affordability. Increasing allowable densities, and thereby increasing the number of housing units, can make housing less expensive to produce by reducing per-unit land costs. In San Francisco, for example, BRIDGE Housing has used this technique to create enough value to develop mixed-income housing developments.[76]

To make possible higher-density housing development, local governments can include higher-density single-family and multifamily development districts within their comprehensive plans, at a level consistent with the jurisdiction's projected housing needs and in locations that enable workers to live near jobs, public transportation, or both. Local governments can also use density bonuses to promote the development of affordable housing and to encourage more housing development in specific locations. Because higher density translates to lower per-unit costs, governmental entities that impose affordable-housing requirements often incorporate density "sweeteners"—that is, allow developers to build at higher densities—to offset the cost of the affordable units.

States can take a lead role in encouraging higher-density residential development, especially as a means of promoting affordable-housing development.[77] California, for example, requires all communities to offer a 25 percent increase in allowable density to developers of projects in which at least 20 percent of the units are affordable.[78] Through the Transit Village Development Planning Act, the state also provides incentives that encourage local governments to plan transit-village development districts within a quarter-mile (0.40-kilometer) radius of transit stations; such districts are eligible for a 25 percent density bonus.[79]

✖ PROGRAMS AND POLICIES

San Rafael, California, provides density bonuses and other incentives for housing developments located in areas designated for medium- and high-density land use that make a certain percentage of the units affordable to low-, very low-, or moderate-income households for at least 40 years. City zoning rules provide for height bonuses of one to two stories for mixed-use projects that add residential units; exempt downtown housing developments from limits on floor/area ratio; and reduce parking requirements for downtown apartments.[80]

For more information, call Jean Frietas, Planning Department (415-485-3085), or visit www.cityofsanrafael.org/Government/ Redevelopment_Agency/Affordable_Housing/ Affordable_Housing_Requirements_for_ Developers.htm.

The Affordable Housing Density Bonus Program of **Collier County, Florida,** awards density increases to developers who guarantee that a portion of a given housing development will be affordable to moderate-, low-, or very low-income households. The county also offers expedited permit processing for affordable-housing developments.

For more information, call the Collier County Financial Administration and Housing Department (239-403-2330), or visit www.colliergov.net/Index.aspx?page=469.

Portland, Oregon, has devised a number of small, unobtrusive ways to increase density— for example, by allowing construction of new duplexes and attached homes in locations such as corner lots, as long as they are compatible with surrounding houses. The city also allows increased densities in transitional areas between residential zones and nonresidential zones that buffer residential uses, thereby promoting additional housing opportunities without changing the character of established single-family neighborhoods.[81] Finally, increased densities are allowed within the city's Alternative Design Density Overlay Zones for accessory units, well-designed developments, attached residential units on vacant lots, and single-family and multifamily housing.

For more information, visit www.portlandonline.com/planning/ index.cfm?c=28534.

Minneapolis, Minnesota, passed a law in 2003 that offers a 20 percent density bonus to developers of multifamily projects of five units or more, in which one-fifth of the units are affordable.

For more information, call the Housing Development Division (612-673-5095), or visit www.ci.minneapolis.mn.us/cped/housing_home.asp.

Transfer of Development Rights

Transfer of development rights (TDR) is a means of shifting the development potential of one site to another site in a different location. The resulting increase in allowable density in the "receiving location" may, in some cases, make possible the development of workforce housing. First used in New York City in 1968, TDR is now used by at least 134 communities nationwide.[82]

The transfer takes place voluntarily, as a result of market forces, and does not require direct public funding. Property ownership is unaffected by the transfer of development rights: the owner of the site from which the development rights are transferred retains ownership of the land, and sells only its development rights. After the sale, a deed restriction limits future development on the transferring owner's site. After paying the sender a mutually agreed upon price, the owner of the receiving site gains the right to develop the property at a higher density.

TDR is typically used to preserve agricultural land or open space and to encourage more intense development in urbanized areas. The technique work best when tailored to local circumstances. Santa Fe County, New Mexico, for example, uses TDR to protect areas such as scenic highways. Bainbridge Island, Washington, allows density transfers from farmland and "critical areas" to its Mixed Use Town Center and its Neighborhood Service Centers.[83] San Francisco's Transferable Development Rights Ordinance can be used to transfer unused floor/area ratio from sites containing landmark or other historically significant buildings to proposed development sites in the same zoning district.

✗ PROGRAMS AND POLICIES

Montgomery County, Maryland, adopted a TDR program in 1980, to encourage the preservation of farmland in the northern portion of the county and to direct growth to the southern half, which abuts Washington, D.C. The county rezoned a 110,000-acre (44,515-hectare) area in the northern portion as an Agricultural Reserve, within which 90,000 acres (36,422 hectares) were designated as a Rural Density Transfer Zone. Before the rezoning, allowable density in the area was one unit per five acres (two hectares); thereafter, it was one per 25 acres (10 hectares). The county also designated receiving areas where additional development rights could be accommodated. As of 2002, landowners in the Rural Density Transfer Zone had sold development rights to 40,000 acres (16,187 hectares), ensuring permanent preservation of the land for agricultural use.[84]

For more information, call the Montgomery County Planning Board, Montgomery County Department of Parks and Planning (301-495-4610), or visit www.mcparkandplanning.org/.

The TDR program enacted in **Boulder County, Colorado,** in 1995, preserves open land in unincorporated areas by transferring development rights to sites in incorporated cities. Though the program is not specifically intended to foster the development of workforce housing, a participating municipality could add an affordable-housing element to a receiving site by, for example, allowing increased density on the site or subsidizing the TDR lots.

For more information, call Graham Billingsley, director, Land Use Department (303-441-3930), or visit www.co.boulder.co.us/lu/tdr.

Revisions to Building Codes and Rehabilitation Subcodes

Many local governments employ strict building codes, including fire codes, that are largely designed to meet the needs of office structures. Such codes are sometimes excessive for residential construction, and may particularly impede the development of affordable housing. In addition, building codes designed for new construction may be unrealistic for rehabilitation projects, and use restrictions can limit both the availability of land and the variety of allowable residential units. Such considerations are especially worrisome in cities, where rehabilitation is the dominant type of construction.[85]

When a single building code applies both to new construction and rehabilitation, redeveloped older buildings must typically be brought up to current code requirements. Although preservation and adaptive use are important goals from the perspective of historic preservation, sustainability, and meeting market demand, the costs associated with bringing some older buildings up to current standards may render redevelopment economically infeasible. While there may be good reasons for the current building standards, those standards were not anticipated when many of the older buildings were created. As a result, changes in building codes for rehabilitation are taking place at the local, state, and federal levels.[86]

To help facilitate the construction of desired housing developments, jurisdictions can build some flexibility into their building codes and help developers work with state requirements. For example, St. Petersburg, Florida, allows building officials to modify code provisions that create practical difficulties. In Denver, a tool known as Chapter 31 enables developers to obtain variances or waivers when standard codes impose unintended and unreasonable burdens on housing redevelopment projects. Rochester, New York, helps developers obtain state waivers that make renovations less costly.

In 1997, HUD set forth Nationally Applicable Recommended Rehabilitation Provisions (NARRP), which are based on New Jersey's rehabilitation subcode. Intended as a model for state and local governments, the NARRP is designed to create a predictable, clear environment for redevelopment in which code requirements are directly linked to the extent of the rehabilitation.[87]

✕ PROGRAMS AND POLICIES

In 1998, New Jersey enacted an entirely separate set of building codes to govern construction on existing buildings.[88] The new code—technically known as the **Uniform Construction Code, Rehabilitation Subcode** ("the New Jersey Subcode"), follows a "ladder system," in which the requirements for compliance increase with the extent of the changes to the building structure. The law encompasses three types of projects (rehabilitation, change of use, and additions) and four categories of rehabilitation (repairs, renovations, alterations, and reconstruction).

New Jersey's rehabilitation subcode has stimulated an increase in rehabilitation and reduced the cost of redeveloping old buildings by an estimated 10 to 50 percent, depending on the scope of work and type of project.[89] States that have adopted variations of the New Jersey subcode include Maryland, Rhode Island, and Vermont.[90]

For more information, call John Terry, supervisor, Code Enforcement, New Jersey Department of Community Affairs (609-984-7609), or visit www.state.nj.us/dca/codes/rehab/index.shtml.

Maryland's Smart Code legislation, enacted in 2000, includes model rehabilitation codes and guidelines for local governments to adopt (Maryland does not have a statewide building code), and features incentives to encourage such adoptions. The legislation also provides jurisdictions with free training to help them get underway. Among the incentives offered to jurisdictions that adopt a rehabilitation code are priority access to certain state funding programs, including the state's rural legacy, neighborhood conservation, mortgage, and transportation-enhancement programs, as well as other initiatives of the state department of transportation.[91] Maryland's Building Rehabilitation Code Program, part of the Smart Code legislation, is targeted to buildings that are more than one year old and encourages private investment in existing buildings and communities by "streamlining and harmonizing" code requirements for rehabilitation work.

For more information, visit www.dhcd.state.md.us/ Website/programs/smartcodes/smartcodes.aspx.

The **Traditional Neighborhood Development Code** adopted by Austin, Texas, in 1997 aligns zoning regulations and building codes to encourage compact, mixed-use developments on sites of 40 to 250 acres (16 to 101 hectares). The code encourages walkable neighborhoods where housing, retail, employment, civic uses, and recreation are developed in close proximity, and allows a mix of housing types.[92]

For more information, call 512-499-2146, or visit www.ci.austin.tx.us/planning.

Improvements to the Development Permitting Process

In many jurisdictions, what impedes housing development—and the development of affordable housing in particular—is not specific regulatory requirements but the complexity, uncertainty, and cost of the entire permitting process. In some cases, the effects of excessively onerous regulations can be compounded by fragmented, inefficient, uncoordinated, and sometimes uninformed administrative processes, adding even more time, risk, and cost—not to mention a significant emotional toll.

A number of resources are available to state and local governments that want to identify and address regulatory barriers, including permitting processes, that may interfere with affordable-housing development. For example, HUD maintains a Web site (www.regbarriers.org) where users can search for information by topic or by geographic location. The American Planning Association, through its Growing Smart program, offers a model statute for a unified development-permitting process; among the statute's features are set time periods for the acceptance of permit applications and for decisions on applications, and authorization for a single, all-inclusive master permit that allows a developer to go forward with a project.[93]

Some of the techniques commonly recommended in these and other information sources to streamline the entitlement process include the following:

- Creating a one-stop shop for development permits;
- For each project, assigning a project coordinator/expediter within the local government staff;
- Clarifying procedures;
- Holding preapplication conferences or reviews to give developers early feedback;
- Creating multiagency review committees;
- Allowing concurrent processing of permit applications;
- Limiting the number of public hearings;

- Establishing by-right zoning for developers that meet zoning requirements, and permitting more by-right uses;
- Preparing master environmental impact reviews for areas where the local government would like to encourage housing development;
- Establishing clear design guidelines;
- Using computers and other technological innovations;
- Cross-training staff to promote consistency and efficiency;
- Building flexibility into the review process;
- Using benchmarking and customer feedback to evaluate performance.[94]

States can take a number of steps to facilitate affordable-housing production by streamlining the approvals process. Oregon, for example, requires local governments to adopt clear, objective review standards, and to make decisions no more than four months after an application is filed. The state also ensures that its Land Use Board of Appeals hears appeals and makes decisions quickly. Florida law mandates that local governments provide expedited reviews for projects that meet broad definitions of affordability, even if such reviews delay decisions on other development proposals.[95] In Washington State, legislation requires local governments to limit processing time for permits and to integrate the project review, environmental review, and permitting processes.

Many jurisdictions have instituted cost-cutting improvements in their development process. For example, in the case of new construction based on standard designs, Chicago and New York City allow builders to self-certify for building permits, significantly reducing permit reviewing time. Anchorage, Alaska, allows contractors to purchase building permits and request inspections over the Internet. Gilroy, Milpitas, Santa Clara, and Sunnyvale, California, provide cross-departmental review of residential projects. Sunnyvale's one-stop permitting center, established in 1984, gives builders a schedule for reviews (about two months); for many minor building permits, electronic permitting is available.[96] Seattle, Washington, shortened permit times, simplified requirements, and reduced parking requirements for affordable-housing developments.[97] San Jose, California, and Fort Collins, Colorado, also offer expedited reviews for affordable-housing developments.

⚒ PROGRAMS AND POLICIES

The **Smart Permit** project uses technology to help local governments improve and streamline their development review and permitting processes. Initiated in 1994 by the nonprofit Silicon Valley Network, working in conjunction with high-tech firms, the pilot program has helped eight jurisdictions make the change from manual to integrated, Internet-based permitting systems. Each jurisdiction has taken a different approach: for example, Milpitas is implementing a new "smart" permit system, based on GIS maps, that will facilitate the delivery of city services, and Mountain View is working with nearby Sunnyvale to create a completely computerized permitting process.[98]

For more information, visit www.jointventure.org/programs-initiatives/smartvalley/overview.html.

Tampa, Florida, streamlined its permitting process and follow-up monitoring process by collaborating with homebuilders, and the city continues to work with builders to resolve ongoing issues. As a result of these efforts, Tampa has consolidated operations in a one-stop permitting center. Its inspection system is fully electronic: inspectors furnished with cell phones and laptops can set up instant lines of communication between project sites, builders' offices, and the central permitting office. Many routine applications for permits can be submitted and approved electronically. A plan review checklist is posted on the Internet, and the city is working to develop an electronic system for submission, review, and approval of project proposals.[99]

For more information, call Theresa Meyers, residential services manager, Construction Services Center (813-259-1774), or visit www.tampagov.net/ dept_Construction_Services/.

The expedited review process developed by **Orange County, Florida,** reduces by at least 60 days the time required to review affordable-housing projects, thereby lowering developers' carrying costs.[100] For projects certified by the Division of Housing and Community Development, developers receive expedited review and improved coordination from the board of zoning adjustment, the planning department, the zoning department, and the development review committee.

For more information, call the Orange County Housing Development Section of the Orange County Housing and Community Development Department (407-836-4240), or visit www.orangecountyfl.net/cms/DEPT/growth/ housing/default.htm.

Waiver or Reimbursement of Development Fees

To pay for the marginal cost a proposed project will impose on local facilities and services (such as schools, roads, and utility lines), many communities impose fees on developers, including development impact fees, capital facility fees, and utility connection fees. Fees vary widely among jurisdictions, but may account for up to 20 percent of the cost of a new home.[101] To help facilitate the development of affordable housing, some jurisdictions, such as Fremont, California, and San Antonio, Texas, waive all or part of such fees.[102]

⚒ PROGRAMS AND POLICIES

In May of 2000, Austin, Texas, established the **S.M.A.R.T** ("safe, mixed-income, accessible, reasonably priced, transit-oriented") **Housing Initiative** to encourage the construction of affordable housing. The program offers incentives to developers whose housing developments meet certain criteria: a location on a proposed major bus route or light-rail line; adherence to specified green building standards; and prices that are affordable to households earning no more than 80 percent of AMI. In return, developers can obtain full or partial fee waivers for up to 1,000 units per year, depending on the percentage of affordable housing; expedited permitting and zoning reviews; reduced parking requirements; and staff advocacy on behalf of the project during the development process, especially with respect to neighborhood groups.[103]

For more information, call the Neighborhood Housing and Community Development Department (512-499-3154), or visit www.ci.austin.tx.us/ahfc/smart.htm.

Albuquerque, New Mexico, provides fee rebates and density bonuses to developers of for-sale low- and moderate-income housing in infill areas and areas with water service. Rebates can be given for design review fees, utility expansion charges, parks and dedication fees, and building permit fees; the maximum density bonus is 20 percent. The developer must allocate the value of the fee rebates and density bonus to the buyer in the form of a deferred loan, which the buyer must agree to repay, along with a percentage of the appreciation in the unit's value, when the unit is sold.[104]

For more information, visit www.huduser.org/ rbc/search/rbcdetails.asp?DocId=83.

The **Administrative Construction Fee Exemption** program of Fort Collins, Colorado, waives certain construction fees, inspection fees, right-of-way construction-license fees, and street-cut fees for housing developments in which more than half the units are affordable to households that earn 80 percent or less of AMI. For projects in which at least half the units are affordable to households earning 80 to 95 percent of AMI, half the fee amounts are waived.

For more information, call the Fort Collins Engineering Department (970-221-6605), or visit www.fcgov.com/affordablehousing/other.php.

Fort Collins also grants priority processing to expedite the development review and permitting process for qualified affordable-housing projects, and its **Development Impact Fee Payment Delay Program** enables the developer of an affordable-housing project to delay paying impact fees until a certificate of occupancy is issued.

For more information, call the Affordable Housing Planner (970-221-6758).

Financing

Workforce housing is often scarce because developers cannot produce it profitably, especially in high-growth areas where market demand is strong and average home prices are high. In some cases, the prices (or rents) affordable to moderate-income households are too low to enable a developer to make a reasonable profit, given the project's land and development costs. In other cases, developers can generate greater profits by producing high-end housing or other kinds of developments instead. As a result, subsidies and incentives—both financial and nonfinancial—are often used to encourage developers to produce workforce housing. Incentives come in many forms, and different jurisdictions use varying combinations of financial and nonfinancial incentives to achieve their housing goals.

As is clear from the examples offered in this toolkit, housing programs vary greatly in origin, scale, and purpose.[105] HUD alone operates dozens of different housing programs, and a number of other federal agencies also provide assistance to encourage certain kinds of housing development. There are more than 1,000 state and local government housing agencies, and each operates a number of separate housing assistance programs —some drawing on federal funds, and some using funding from other sources. In addition, many private sector investors, lenders, and organizations participate in funding programs designed to assist with the production of affordable housing.

Most housing assistance programs, however, are not targeted to workforce housing. Instead, they are usually designed to increase the supply of housing that is affordable to households that earn no more than 60 percent of AMI (or in some cases up to 80 percent). Relatively few of these programs help produce housing for the workforce—that is, moderate-income households whose incomes are between 80 and 120 percent of AMI; those that do sometimes specify that only a small percentage of the housing produced can be affordable to households whose incomes are within this range.

This section describes some of the financial programs and funding partnerships that have been created to encourage the development of workforce housing. The case studies in this book provide examples of how financial and nonfinancial assistance can be combined to facilitate successful workforce housing developments.

Federal, State, and Local Government Programs

A number of HUD programs administered by state and/or local entities can be used to encourage workforce housing development.[106] The income limits attached to federal programs are generally too low for this book's definition of workforce housing, but the programs warrant mention because of their role in helping make possible mixed-income housing projects that include a workforce housing component.[107] The major HUD programs that can be used to help produce workforce housing in this way include the following:

■ The Community Development Block Grant (CDBG) program, enacted in 1974, is a federal program that passes funding through the states to local governments. The funding is intended to alleviate poverty and eliminate blight, but it can be used for a variety of purposes, including predevelopment work, site acquisition and improvement, housing acquisition and rehabilitation, and downpayment and closing-cost assistance for first-time buyers. Seventy percent of CDBG funds must be used to benefit low- and moderate-income households.

■ The HOME Investment Partnership Act, enacted in 1990, provides funds, in the form of block grants to states and localities, for affordable-housing development, including land acquisition and improvement and the construction, acquisition, or rehabilitation of non-luxury housing. HOME funds may also be used to assist homebuyers with downpayments and closing costs. The program requires that states and localities set aside a certain percentage of HOME funds for nonprofit community housing development organizations.

■ The Section 8 program provides rental assistance to qualified low-income tenants, prima-rily in the form of vouchers. The tenant pays only the difference between the value of the voucher and the actual rent charged.

■ The HOPE VI public housing transformation program has been used by public housing authorities to leverage funding from other sources to transform distressed public housing projects into well-designed, amenity- and service-enriched mixed-income communities through public/private partnerships.[108]

The federal government also operates tax-credit programs that can be used to encourage the development of workforce housing. The Low-Income Housing Tax Credit (LIHTC) program provides tax credits for private investment in affordable rental-housing developments.[109] Though LIHTC developments are targeted primarily to households earning no more than 60 percent of AMI, some of the tax-credit projects are developed as mixed-income developments that incorporate housing for moderate-income households and/or market-rate units. The federal Historic Preservation Tax Credit program (also known as the Rehabilitation Investment Tax Credit), enacted in 1981 and amended in 1986, provides investors with a 20 percent tax credit for the rehabilitation of income-producing residential and nonresidential properties,[110] and has been described as "the most significant single incentive for historic preservation and the production of housing (including affordable units)."[111] Historic tax credits can be combined effectively with LIHTCs to create low- and moderate-income housing.[112] The Environmental Protection Agency also operates programs that may be used by states, localities, and individual developers to help build residential projects on brownfield sites or in other locations with real or perceived environmental issues.[113] The federal Community Reinvestment Act (CRA), which requires federally insured depository institutions to meet the credit needs of the communities in which they are chartered, has stimulated private investment (including investment in housing development) in low- and moderate-income communities.

The Federal National Mortgage Association (Fannie Mae) and the Federal Home Loan Mortgage Corporation (Freddie Mac) provide a secondary market for the purchase and sale of residential mortgages and for the guarantee of mortgage-backed securities—and, as part of their mission, are required to serve low- and moderate-income households and locations, according to goals set by HUD.[114] Though best known for helping modest-income households purchase homes, Fannie Mae and Freddie Mac also have programs to help facilitate the production of affordable for-sale and rental housing. These two agencies, along with the Federal Housing Administration (FHA), the Government National Mortgage Association (Ginnie Mae), the Rural Housing Administration, large corporations, and sometimes local governments may guarantee mortgage loans for subsidized housing developments through mortgage insurance or risk-sharing arrangements, making it possible for project owners to borrow money at reduced interest rates.

States and localities may help administer federal programs, and most also operate their own housing assistance programs, either alone or in partnership with other public and private entities. They may also administer certain funds that can be used to finance the construction of affordable housing, such as tax-exempt and taxable bonds, mortgage-revenue bonds, housing trust funds, and linkage program fees. As noted earlier, states and localities can also use tax waivers or abatements to encourage affordable-housing production.

Housing Trust Funds

Housing trust funds (HTFs) are flexible state, regional, or local partnership-based public funds created by legislation, ordinance, or resolution to receive specific, dedicated revenues for affordable-housing development. According to the Housing Trust Fund Project of the Center for Community Change, a housing trust fund has a dedicated source of ongoing revenue; is committed to the production and preservation of housing affordable to lower-income households, including the homeless; and makes available funds that would not otherwise be used to address housing needs.[115]

The first HTFs were established in the mid-1970s, and as of 2001 there were more than 275 housing trust funds in cities, counties, and states nationwide, providing at least $750 million each year to meet important housing needs.[116] HTFs provide grants and loans for a wide range of entities and housing project types, depending on the fund's individual goals. HTFs support activities such as predevelopment financing, site acquisition, construction, and rehabilitation; many HTFs also offer buyer-assistance programs.[117] Typically, HTF resources are used to leverage funds from other sources.

Though most HTFs target only low- or very low-income households, some will help fund housing for moderate-income earners as well. For example, in 2001, of 53 city housing trust funds that responded to a survey by the Center for Community Change, 34 reported that their income targets included at least some households earning more than 60 percent of AMI.[118]

Trust funds have been funded by more than 40 kinds of sources, typically taxes or fees. For state trust funds, the most common revenue source is the real estate transfer tax; for city trust funds, it is a linkage program (linkage programs are described in the next section); and for counties, it is the document recording fee.[119] Fees collected by the country's various HTFs range from less than $100,000 to $180 million per year.

HTFs are administered by government entities, such as a housing department, and distribute funds through a competitive request-for-funding process. Many HTFs will fund for-profit as well as nonprofit developers; however, some limit their support to nonprofits or to organizations whose missions are compatible with the HTF's goals.

⚒ PROGRAMS AND POLICIES

In 1992, through the **William E. Sadowski Affordable Housing Act,**[120] Florida created a dedicated source of funds to help local governments meet the affordable-housing development requirements set forth in the Housing Element of the state's Growth Management and Land Development Regulation Act. The Sadowski Act increased the documentary stamp tax paid on real estate transfers and allocated the revenues from that increase to state and local housing trust funds—30 percent to the state trust fund and about 70 percent to local funds. The local monies are allocated to Florida local governments through the State Housing Initiatives Partnership (SHIP) program. There are some requirements: 30 percent of the funds must be used for households earning no more than 50 percent of AMI, and 30 percent for households earning no more than 80 percent of AMI; the remaining 40 percent may be used for households earning up to 120 percent of AMI; in addition, 65 percent of the money must be spent on initiatives that promote homeownership. The act generates more than $175 million each year and, since its inception, has leveraged more than $2.4 billion in private and public investment.[121]

For more information, call the Florida Department of Community Affairs (904-488-4197), or visit www.dca.state.fl.us/fdcp/DCP.

The **Housing Trust Fund of Santa Clara County, California,** is a public/private partnership created in 1999 by the Santa Clara County Board of Supervisors, the Silicon Valley Manufacturing Group, the Santa Clara County Collaborative on Housing and Homelessness, and the Community Foundation Silicon Valley. Capitalized largely by the private sector, the housing trust operates a revolving loan fund (and occasionally provides grants) to leverage affordable-housing funding from other sources.

Employers such as Hewlett-Packard, Adobe, and Intel have contributed more than half the money (51 percent); the rest comes from the county (13 percent); municipalities within the county (24 percent); and private foundations, community organizations, and individuals (12 percent). The $20 million that the housing trust has raised since its inception will leverage approximately $180 million in development.

The trust offers three primary products: (1) predevelopment loans for nonprofit developers; (2) gap financing for special projects, typically for the homeless; and (3) buyer assistance to households earning up to 120 percent of AMI. Buyer assistance is the largest program, and includes $6,500 in closing-cost assistance (repayable when the home is sold or refinanced), a forgivable second mortgage for up to 6 percent of the purchase price, and a below-market-rate mortgage for 97 percent of the purchase price.

For more information, call Roccie Hill, executive director, Housing Trust Fund of Santa Clara County (408-436-3450), or visit www.housingtrustscc.org/.

The **Fairfax County Housing Trust Fund,** established in 1988 in Fairfax County, Virginia (a suburb of Washington, D.C.), is funded by developer contributions and targets households earning less than 120 percent of AMI. As of fall 2003, the fund had provided more than $18 million to assist in the development of more than 1,000 units of affordable housing. In addition to supporting housing development by both for-profit and nonprofit developers, the fund also participates in the county's Employee Homeownership Assistance Program, which helps moderate-income county and school employees buy their first homes.

For more information, call Louise Milder, senior real estate finance officer, Redevelopment Housing Authority (703-246-5255), or visit www.co.fairfax. va.us/gov/rha/housingtrustfund/main.htm.

Housing Linkage Programs

Some local governments use housing linkage programs to help the workforce housing supply keep pace with job growth. Generally, the local government requires the developer to construct a certain number of affordable-housing units, depending on the amount of commercial square footage being developed, or to pay an in-lieu fee to a specified entity, which will then use the funds to assist with affordable-housing development (developers often prefer this alternative). Because housing linkage programs increase the cost of developing new commercial projects, they can be implemented only where the commercial development market is robust. In weaker markets, commercial developers may take their developments elsewhere rather than be subject to the linkage fee. Linkage fees are especially popular in luxury resort areas, where new commercial developments stand to benefit directly from the creation of housing for their workers.

✗ PROGRAMS AND POLICIES

In 1986, Boston initiated a housing linkage program that requires developers who are seeking rezoning in order to develop large commercial,

retail, hotel, or institutional projects to pay a per-square-foot fee for the off-site development of affordable housing. Fee payments go into the city's **Neighborhood Housing Trust,** and payment may be made either in advance (based on the property's current value), or over an extended period. Extended payments begin when the building permit is issued, and may be made over a seven-year period for a downtown project or over a 12-year period for a neighborhood project. Extending the payment schedules enables developers to pay the fees out of operating revenues, thereby reducing their upfront project costs.

For more information, call the Boston Redevelopment Authority (617-722-4300), or visit www.cityofboston.gov/bra/.

The **San Francisco Jobs/Housing Linkage Program** (successor to the city's Office/ Affordable Housing Production Program, enacted in 1985) requires developers of large-scale entertainment, hotel, office, or retail projects to build housing units;[122] contribute land or funds to a partnership or joint venture that will build housing units; or pay an in-lieu fee into a fund that helps finance the city's affordable-housing program.[123] Projects of more than 25,000 square feet (2,320 square meters) are subject to the program requirements. Developers who opt for direct provision of housing must ensure that the average prices of for-sale homes are affordable to moderate-income households (that is, households earning no more than the AMI). Rental housing must be affordable to low-income households. Most developers have opted to pay the fee.

For more information, call the San Francisco Department of City Planning (415-558-6377), or visit www.sfgov.org/site/planning_index.asp.

The **City of Aspen** and **Pitkin County, Colorado,** require every residential or commercial development to contribute to the city's or the county's affordable-housing stock, either through deed-restricted housing, donated land, or in-lieu fees. Requirements are complicated and are based on:

- The type of project, which determines which section of the land use code would apply;
- The zoning district where the project is located, which determines whether the county or city has jurisdiction and which specific requirements would apply;
- For commercial projects, how many jobs would be generated by the completed project.

The required housing is targeted to people whose household incomes fall within seven categories, ranging from low- to middle-income.[124]

For more information, call Cindy Christensen, operations manager, Aspen Housing Office (970-920-5050), or visit www.aspenhousingoffice.com.

Bond Financing

Proceeds from the sale of municipal bonds issued by state or local governments provide flexible funds that can be used to support workforce housing development. Taxable revenue bonds can be used to help fund revenue-generating developments (such as multifamily rental projects) and are underwritten by the project's expected revenues. General-obligation bonds must be used for a public purpose, require state or local voter approval, and are backed by a jurisdiction's tax base; thus, property taxes can be used to repay general-obligation bonds. Tax-exempt revenue bonds, which are issued by state and local housing-finance authorities,[125] can be used to help finance multifamily rental-housing developments that meet affordability guidelines;

to qualify for financing through tax-exempt revenue bonds, developers must generally set aside a certain percentage of units for low-income or very low-income households.[126] Because issuing bonds is a complicated and expensive proposition, bond financing is not appropriate for small developments.[127]

PROGRAMS AND POLICIES

The **New Homes Land Acquisition Fund** of Westchester County, New York, uses bond proceeds to fund for-profit and nonprofit developers' acquisition of land for the construction or rehabilitation of workforce housing. Located just north of New York City, Westchester County is one of the highest-cost areas of the country: in 2002, the AMI was $91,400, and the median single-family home price was over $570,000. Several years ago, the county put in place two multimillion-dollar bond issues. Through the first, the New Homes Land Acquisition Program, the cost to a developer of acquiring land for affordable housing is written down to zero. The second program, the Housing Implementation Fund, pays for infrastructure costs. To be eligible for funding, projects must be for-sale housing offered only to first-time buyers whose incomes are at or below 80 percent of AMI.[128] The units constructed so far have all been townhouses. There are 40-year affordability restrictions that require resale to another qualified household; however, the seller is permitted to receive appreciation on the equity he or she puts into the home over the years, including capital improvements made during occupancy.

For more information, call Nancy Hadley, deputy commissioner, Division of Housing and Community Development, Westchester County Department of Planning (914-995-2404), or visit www.westchestergov.com/planning/housing/FactSheets.htm#NHLA.

The **Economic Development and Housing Revenue Bond Program** of Portland, Oregon, is administered by the Portland Development Commission. The program raises capital through the issuance of bonds to help finance development projects that incorporate public benefits. The bonds are not backed or guaranteed by the city, but can help make projects feasible by giving developers access to lower interest rates than they would generally be able to obtain through private commercial sources. (Because bond purchasers receive tax-free interest income, they can accept a lower interest rate on their invested capital.) To obtain bond funding, a developer must meet certain Internal Revenue Service requirements.[129]

For more information, visit www.pdc.us/ housing_serv/hsg_development/private-bonds.asp.

New York City's New Housing Opportunities Program (New HOP), which is administered by the New York City Housing Development Corporation (HDC), uses proceeds from taxable bonds to provide long-term, fixed-rate, permanent financing for rental developments that are affordable to households earning up to 250 percent of AMI. The program also provides subsidies of up to $30,000 per unit—and, for projects that meet certain criteria, such as high land costs, lower rents, or larger units, may provide up to $45,000. Developers can use the subsidies for subordinate financing or can combine them with the proceeds from taxable bonds to produce a below-market-rate first mortgage. Subsidy funds and bond proceeds can also be used during construction, with appropriate third-party credit enhancement. Eligible projects include new construction, substantial rehabilitation, and the conversion of nonresidential buildings into at least 20 units developed by right. The developer's fee is limited to 10 percent of the nonsubsidized development cost.

Between April 30, 2003, and December 31, 2003, New HOP provided $30.8 million in financing, creating 680 units. By the end of calendar year 2004, HDC had committed another $37.4 million in New HOP funds to create 837 more housing units.

For more information, call Aaron Koffman, project manager, Housing Development Corporation (212-227-9470), or visit www.nychdc.com/pdf/ developers/new%20hop%20termsheet%20June %202006.pdf

Taxation Programs

Communities can use their power to levy taxes to create incentives for affordable-housing development and to help fund such development. For example, the Portland Development Commission (PDC) provides ten-year tax abatements, along with other incentives, to facilitate the development of workforce housing. The PDC used land writedowns, tax-increment financing, and tax abatements to support workforce housing in the Pearl District, just north of downtown Portland. In that district, 36 percent of the 2,032 new housing units built since 1999 are affordable to households earning no more than 80 percent of AMI, and another 9 percent are affordable for those in the 81 to 120 percent income range.[130]

Tax-Increment Financing. Special taxing districts, such as tax-increment financing (TIF) districts or public-improvement districts, enable local governments to fund public improvements that support desired forms of development, including affordable housing, within the designated districts. Under a TIF arrangement, a local government issues bonds to fund infrastructure and other improvements within the TIF district. The improvements are intended to stimulate new development, which will increase property taxes within the district. The bonds are then repaid through the tax revenue increases generated within the TIF district.

TIFs require state enabling authority, but are currently offered in 48 states and the District of Columbia (the exceptions are North Dakota and South Dakota). Two risks are associated with TIF: first, there may not be a market for the bonds; second, in order to attract investors, the interest rate offered on the bonds may have to be so high that the project becomes financially infeasible. Moreover, TIF alone may not achieve the desired results; it may need to be used in tandem with incentives.[131]

✕ PROGRAMS AND POLICIES

Chicago's TIF program, authorized by state legislation in 1977 to promote private investment in blighted areas and expanded in 1985, has become a popular tool for generating gap financing and funding infrastructure improvements throughout the city. In addition, the city offers a Streamlined TIF Program, which provides expedited grants for the renovation, expansion, or redevelopment of commercial, retail, or mixed-use (including residential) properties in TIF districts.[132] Grants range from $25,000 to $1 million, may cover up to 25 percent of project costs, and are paid after project completion.

Chicago also operates the Public Housing Transformation TIF Financing Program, through which the city will borrow money from Fannie Mae and its partners to obtain front-end funding for the construction of eligible new homes built as part of the Chicago Housing Authority's plan to transform public housing developments into mixed-income communities. The loans, which are guaranteed by the MacArthur Foundation, will be repaid by taxes generated from the new homes, the city's share of the development profits, and recaptured subsidies for certain affordable units.[133]

For more information, call the Department of Planning and Development (312-744-2489), or visit http://egov.cityofchicago.org/ and click on Your Government\City Departments\Planning and Development\Programs and Services\Tax Increment Financing Program.

In San Antonio, Texas, **Tax Increment Reinvestment Zones** (TIRZs) are TIF zones that can be used to generate funds for infrastructure improvements to support new city housing. Most are intended to facilitate the development of low- and moderate-income housing by nonprofit developers, but for-profit developers are also developing homes in TIRZs. The city uses the expected property tax revenues from development within a TIRZ as security to obtain a bridge loan to fund initial infrastructure improvements; future revenues can be used to fund additional facilities and amenities.[134]

For more information, visit www.sanantonio.gov/nad/DevDiv/TIF/Tif.asp.

Tax Credits. Programs that provide tax benefits to investors can create valuable financing sources for workforce housing development. As noted earlier, federal historic tax credits can provide an incentive for developers to preserve and rehabilitate properties located within historic districts, in some cases as affordable housing. States, and some local jurisdictions, offer historic preservation tax programs that complement and enhance the federal program.[135] While such programs are not specifically designed to stimulate the production of affordable housing, they have in some cases made developments possible that included units affordable to workforce households.

⚒ PROGRAMS AND POLICIES

Under **North Carolina's State Historic Rehabilitation Tax Credits** program, enacted in 1998, properties that receive the 20 percent federal historic tax credit for investment in historic preservation are eligible for an additional 20 percent credit on state taxes for any expenditures that qualify for federal credits. The state credit is granted at an annual rate of 4 percent over five years. Thus, the combined federal and state tax credits lower by 40 percent the cost of rehabilitating a certified income-producing historic structure. Though the program is not specifically targeted to affordable housing, many projects, especially those involving adaptive use, have yielded affordable housing; moreover, a number of the projects also used LIHTC financing.[136]

For more information, call Tim Simmons, preservation tax credit coordinator, Restoration Branch, State Historic Preservation Office, North Carolina Division of Archives and History (919-733-6547), or visit www.hpo.dcr.state.nc.us/tchome.htm.

Tax Waivers or Abatements. Waivers or abatements of property taxes can promote development in specific locations, or of particular types; however, because there is a public cost involved, the use of waivers and abatements should be tied to the creation of public benefits that would otherwise be unlikely to occur. Tax waivers and abatements are typically time-limited, apply to improvements and not to land, and require specific statutory authority.

Tax abatements can be used to encourage the development of affordable urban housing, especially where development costs are high or in the early stages of a housing renaissance, when a jurisdiction wants to stimulate new housing development. Seattle, for example, provides tax abatements for multifamily developments within the city. Local governments can also offer homebuyers time-limited property tax abatements, under which property taxes are typically phased back in over a specified time period.

⚒ PROGRAMS AND POLICIES

To encourage the development of multifamily housing in its 14 designated mixed-use centers, **Tacoma, Washington,** offers eligible property owners a property-tax exemption on improvements made within these districts. The purpose of the program is "to make housing projects more appealing to investors by freeing up capital and reducing operating costs."[137] The exemption is available to owners of new, rehabilitated, or converted properties; in the case of existing buildings, the rehabilitation or conversion must correct one or more code violations, and no tenant may be displaced as a result of the improvements. If the building is sold after the city has granted the tax exemption, the exemption passes to the new owner. Between 1996 and 1999, the program resulted in the development of more than 700 housing units and stimulated the investment of more than $33 million.

For more information, visit www.cityoftacoma.org/Page.aspx?nid=456.

In 1975, **Portland, Oregon,** established a ten-year tax exemption to encourage new construction of low-, moderate-, and middle-income multifamily housing in the central city, where land costs are high, and in districts where the city wanted to encourage redevelopment. The tax exemption applies only to the value of improvements to eligible developments. To be eligible, projects must (1) contain at least ten units, (2) be located within designated areas of the city, (3) require the tax exemption to be economically feasible, and (4) include a feature that creates public benefits. Eligible features include affordability to households with a broad range of incomes, and amenities such as recreational facilities, open space, public meeting rooms, child care facilities, and arts facilities. For projects in which units are offered for sale individually, the property-tax exemption is available only for units with initial sales prices that are no greater than 95 percent of the median purchase price for a condominium unit in Multnomah County,[138] and must be sold to households earning 100 percent or less of AMI.

For more information, call the Housing Section of the Portland Bureau of Planning (503-823-7838), or visit www.pdc.us/housing_serv/.

Georgia's State Preferential Property Tax Assessment Program for Rehabilitated Historic Property,

enacted in 1987, freezes property-tax assessments for eight-and-a-half years. The program can be used for either commercial or residential historic properties that have undergone substantial rehabilitation.

For more information, call Martha Marcille, tax incentives coordinator (404-651-5566), or visit www.gashpo.org.

Other State and Regional Programs

States and private entities have created a varied menu of affordable-housing programs, including a number that can be used to develop workforce housing. Some states provide useful inventories of such programs. For example, California's Department of Housing and Community Development operates the Clearinghouse for Affordable Housing and Community Finance Resources, which provides information on more than 200 public and private programs, as well as other sources of grants and loans for affordable housing. The listings include information on goals, types of assistance, eligible uses, application deadlines, and currently available funding.[139]

✖ PROGRAMS AND POLICIES

New Jersey's Balanced Housing Program provides gap financing for affordable-housing developments that meet certain criteria for location, cost, price, and design. Funds are awarded to municipalities for their own use, or for use by local housing authorities, nonprofit organizations, or for-profit developers, and can be used to develop a wide range of low- and moderate-income rental or for-sale housing. Affordability controls of ten to 30 years apply to units funded through this program.[140]

For more information, call the New Jersey Department of Community Affairs, Division of Housing and Community Resources (609-633-6258), or visit www.hcdnnj.org/funding/state.htm.

California's Workforce Housing Reward Program does not fund workforce housing production. Instead, it provides financial incentives to encourage municipalities and counties to do so. The program offers grant funds according to a formula based on the number of permits issued for new affordable housing and the level of affordability achieved. To be counted, housing must be for low- and very low-income households. Rental units must be rent-restricted for at least 55 years, and public funds used to produce for-sale units must be recovered and reused for affordable housing for at least 20 years.[141] Grants may be used to construct or acquire capital assets such as traffic improvements, parks, school facilities, playgrounds, community centers, and police or fire stations.

Through its Jobs-Housing Balance Program, adopted in 2003 to encourage all types of housing production, the state awarded $25 million in one-time grants to municipalities and counties that, during 2001, could demonstrate a significant increase (more than 112 percent) in residential building permits over the previous three years. Grants were based only on the percentage increase in residential building permits, regardless of affordability.

For more information on both programs, contact Linda Nichols, Housing and Community Development Department (916-323-3175), or visit www.hcd.ca.gov.

The **Florida Affordable Housing Guarantee Program** is a credit-enhancement program designed to encourage lending for affordable housing by guaranteeing part or all of a developer's loan, which lowers the risk for lenders and may also lower interest rates for borrowers. Created in 1992 as part of the Sadowski Act, the program is open to nonprofit or for-profit entities for the development, acquisition, or rehabilitation of multifamily rental projects targeted to households earning 120 percent or less of AMI.[142]

For more information, call the Florida Housing Finance Corporation, Finance and Guarantee Programs (850-488-4197), or visit www.floridahousing.org/Home/default.htm.

Other Local Government Programs

Local governments across the country have devised a wide range of additional programs to encourage the development of workforce housing. The particular mix of programs reflects the characteristics of the jurisdiction, including its housing needs, market attributes, and political and economic climate. Though most programs offer funds, regulatory incentives, or both to encourage housing development, there are other ways for jurisdictions to help direct funds to the production of affordable housing. Loudoun County, Virginia, for example, links a proportion of the county's deposits in local financial institutions with the affordable-housing initiatives of those institutions.

⚒ PROGRAMS AND POLICIES

The **New Homes for Chicago Program** is designed to encourage developers to provide condominiums and for-sale single-family and two-family homes for households earning between 60 and 120 percent of AMI. Incentives include construction subsidies of $10,000 per single-family income-restricted home or condominium ($30,000 for a two-flat structure), for up to 24 homes per year. Buyers earning less than 90 percent of AMI are also eligible for a purchase-price subsidy, which takes the form of a second mortgage that is forgiven after four years.

The program also offers a simplified design-review process, faster development approvals, and waived or reduced building-permit and utility-connection fees. Through the City Lots program, the city may also provide city-owned vacant lots for one dollar. Since its inception, in 1992, the program has facilitated the construction of more than 1,600 affordable new for-sale homes in Chicago.

For more information, call the Department of Housing (312-744-5000), or visit http://egov.cityofchicago.org/ and click on Your Government\City Departments\ Housing\DOH Partnerships\New Homes for Chicago.

New York City's Cornerstone Program, an initiative operated by the city's Department of Housing Preservation and Development (HPD), will stimulate the production of almost 3,000 new middle-income and market-rate multifamily apartment buildings and townhouses on vacant city-owned land. The for-sale and rental units will be financed largely through private sources, without direct city subsidies. The city identifies sites; obtains development approvals; discounts the cost of the land; and, depending on the needs of the individual project, may provide financial subsidies through the New Housing Opportunities Program (New HOP, described in "Bond Financing"). Developers are selected through a competitive request-for-proposals process.

As of January 2004, HPD had completed four projects through the Cornerstone Program, and had about a dozen more under construction, for a total of approximately 1,500 units, and it had selected development teams for 15 more sites that will yield nearly 1,500 additional units.

For more information, call Syreeta McFadden, Division of Multifamily New Construction, HPD (212-863-6091) or Aileen Gribben, deputy housing commissioner (212-863-5875), or visit http://www.nyc.gov/html/hpd/html/developers/large-scale-cornerstone.shtml.

The **Affordable Housing Program** of Fort Collins, Colorado, provides various incentives to private, public, and nonprofit developers to create and preserve housing for households of all income levels. Incentives include waivers of the city's development impact fee and development plan fee; funding assistance through private-activity bonds; authorization to delay payment of the development impact fee; priority processing for qualified affordable-housing projects; and buyer assistance and development subsidies through the federal HOME Investment Partnership and CDBG programs.[143]

For more information, call Joe Frank, city of Fort Collins (970-221-6376), or visit http://fcgov.com/affordablehousing/.

Private Funding Sources and Programs

Private lenders include foundations and other charitable organizations, which generally prefer to assist nonprofit organizations; traditional institutional investors; banks and savings institutions; and private investment funds.

Bank investment in affordable housing has been invigorated by the mandate included in the Community Reinvestment Act, which requires financial and depository institutions to help to meet the credit needs of the communities in which they operate. As a result, many large banks now have community lending arms that invest in affordable-housing developments, especially in low- and moderate-income neighborhoods. Because of their resources and national scope, the scale of investment of some private funding sources, including those highlighted below, is huge compared with that of public-sector programs.

Through their Community Investment Cash Advance (CICA) programs, Federal Home Loan Banks offer grants and other low-cost, long-term funds that member lenders (banks and thrifts) can use to help finance targeted projects. Through one such program, the Community Investment Program for Housing, member banks provide low-cost loans or letters of credit to fund the purchase, construction, or predevelopment financing of for-sale housing, rental housing, or manufactured-housing parks in which more than half the units are affordable to households earning no more than 115 percent of AMI.[144]

Generally, lending institutions will invest in workforce housing developments on an individual basis, working with developers that they know and trust; they may also make investments in partnership with other lenders, as described in "Financing Partnerships and Lending Consortia." Pension funds and certain other private funds also operate investment programs that support workforce housing.

✴ PROGRAMS AND POLICIES

Fannie Mae's **American Communities Fund,** operated by the Fannie Mae Foundation, a private foundation supported by Fannie Mae, provides funding for-profit, nonprofit, or public projects involving workforce housing. Projects must either be located in redevelopment areas, as defined by specific criteria, or must supply and/or preserve affordable housing. The affordability requirements for any given project are flexible, but half of the fund's business must serve households earning no more than 100 percent of AMI. The fund works in one of three ways: in partnership with a lender, to participate in acquisition, development and construction financing; by investing equity, also through a partnership vehicle; or by providing bridge financing to public entities, which those entities can use to make loans or grants for specific projects.[145]

(The Fannie Mae Foundation ceased operations in April 2007. To determine the status of the American Communities Funds, please contact Fannie Mae's Office of Community and Charitable Giving: the E-mail address is community_giving@fanniemae.org.)

For more information, call Phil Weber, executive director (202-752-2256), or visit www.fanniemae.com/housingcommdev/ commdev/acf.jhtml.

Bank of America, through its community development division, invests billions of dollars each year in workforce and affordable-housing developments through construction lending, investments in LIHTCs, and strategic investments in mission-based real estate funds and individual development projects. Decisions to invest in real estate developments are made on an individual basis; preference is given to projects located in geographically focused, top-tier markets where there is a demonstrated need that no other product of the bank's can fill. Though the bank's community development activities do not include investment in market-rate housing, there are no income parameters limiting its housing investment decisions.

The bank also operates a real estate development arm, the Banc of America Community Development Corporation (BACDC), which works in partnership with public sector agencies, community-based nonprofit organizations, and for-profit developers to produce affordable and workforce housing while also fostering revitalization. The projects in its Workforce Housing Development Program are typically new or rehabilitated multifamily developments (and sometimes mixed-use projects) located in low- or moderate-income areas within markets where the bank has a strong presence. Most of the multifamily developments are mixed-income, and serve households whose incomes are between 50 and 100 percent of AMI. The BACDC generally has between 2,000 and 2,500 multifamily rental units under development each year, in addition to 3,300 for-sale homes.

For more information on fund investments, call Mary Campbell, senior vice president (314-607-5466); for information on the bank's CDC and Workforce Housing Development Program, call Jim Grauley, president, BACDC (404-607-5466), or visit www.bankofamerica.com.

The **California Public Employees Retirement System** (CalPERS), a statewide pension fund, is the single largest investor in the United States and the second-largest in the world. CalPERS invests in workforce housing primarily through its California Urban Real Estate Initiatives (CUREI) program. The CUREI program, initiated in 1995, now includes ten partners and has led to $1.1 billion in investment in California's urban areas.

Through one CUREI program, the Affordable Multi-Family Housing Program, CalPERS has provided, among other things, $150 million in equity capital for the development of affordable multifamily housing. For this program, CalPERS is working with three partners: Klein-Steadfast, LLC, a mezzanine debt partner that has allocated $50 million; Legacy Partners 1002, LLC, an equity partner that has allocated $60 million; and the Related Companies, a credit-enhancement partner that has allocated $30 million for reserves toward bond-financed development. The Affordable Multi-Family Housing Program will support projects that have a 70/30 or 80/20 ratio of market-rate to affordable housing.

Besides CUREI, CalPERS operates numerous other programs, including an Acquisition and Development program to obtain and develop residential lots in California for single-family homes, and a Single-Family Housing program that provides construction financing and equity investment in single-family developments targeted to first-time buyers.

For more information, call Brad Pacheco, CalPERS Office of Public Affairs (916-326-3991), or visit www.calpers.ca.gov.

Financing Partnerships/Lending Consortia

In response to CRA requirements, various entities have formed financing partnerships to enable participants to pool funds for affordable housing, community development, or both, and to share associated risks and administrative burdens. These partnerships have been formed by various groups of participants: among lenders; between employers and lenders; between governments and lenders; and among employers, lenders, and public entities.

Though varying in size, composition, income targets, and scope of activity, most financing partnerships are independent nonprofit organizations, and most lend to both nonprofit and for-profit developers, typically for the development of new or rehabilitated multifamily housing.[146] The partnerships are capitalized by member institutions, and their operations are funded through points, interest-rate spread, and loan origination and servicing fees. In most cases, all members participate in all loans, according to a formula that takes into consideration their percentage participation in the lending pool or the relative size of their deposits or assets within the state.

Lending consortia are usually governed by a member (or member and nonmember) board and employ a small staff; some also have advisory committees made up of representatives from the community and from nonprofit organizations, which keep them informed about community needs and help maintain community support. Because lending consortia often securitize their portfolios, they seek ways to fund loans that meet the needs of both borrowers and investors.[147]

⚒ PROGRAMS AND POLICIES

The **Genesis Workforce Housing Fund** is the product of a collaboration between Genesis LA Economic Growth Corporation and the Phoenix Realty Group. The $100 million private equity fund has financed the development of about 3,000 homes and apartments in urban areas of the greater Los Angeles region.[148] Managed by the Phoenix Realty Group, the fund encourages the development of for-sale homes for workers earning between 80 and 200 percent of AMI by providing equity and mezzanine financing for construction and land acquisition. The fund assists nonprofit and for-profit developers of townhouses, condominiums, live/work units, mixed-use projects, rental communities, and single-family homes that serve the target population. The initial investors included Bank of America, Citicorp, Far East National Bank, Washington Mutual, and Northwestern Mutual. The fund was fully capitalized at $100 million in April 2005. A similar fund, the San Diego Smart Growth Real Estate Fund, operates in San Diego County.

For more information, call Jay Stark, fund manager (323-936-9699), or visit www.phoenixrg.com.

The **Greater Minnesota Housing Fund** (GMHF), a private nonprofit organization established in 1996, provides resources to address affordable-housing needs in the 80 counties outside the Twin Cities metro area. The GMHF was established through a $26 million grant from the McKnight Foundation and the Blandin Foundation;[149] state, regional, and local funding organizations also participate.

The fund assists with, and invests in, nonprofit and for-profit development of new affordable housing; encourages and facilitates the participation of employers, communities, lenders, local officials, and others in affordable-housing development; sponsors research on cost-cutting development techniques; and serves as an education and advocacy resource for affordable-housing issues. The GMHF's programs are targeted to households earning 80 percent of AMI, and include a multifamily housing-development program, a single-family homeownership program, an employer-assisted housing program, a rehabilitation program, a supportive housing program, and the Building Better Neighborhoods program. Since its creation, the GMHF has helped to produce more than 4,800 units.

For more information, call Warren Hanson, president and chief executive officer (651-221-1997), or visit www.gmhf.com.

The **Long Island Housing Partnership Regional Lending Consortium** is an unincorporated committee of the Long Island Housing Partnership (LIHP) that offers construction and permanent financing for the development of various affordable-housing products that meet the consortium's social goals and credit standards. The LIHPRLC lends money to nonprofit and for-profit entities for new construction, acquisition, rehabilitation, predevelopment work, and bridge financing. Member banks participate in loans at their own discretion, but each member bank must participate in at least one consortium loan per year.

The LIHP is a collaboration among federal and state funding agencies, local governments, businesses, and nongovernmental social-service agencies to develop and promote affordable-housing opportunities in the expensive housing market of suburban Long Island. LIHP programs are targeted to households that earn 80 percent of AMI or less; in addition to engaging in housing development and rehabilitation, the LIHP has an employer-assisted housing program, provides technical assistance to nonprofit developers, and offers mortgage and financial-counseling services for homebuyers. Established in 1991, the LIHP has participated in the development of 826 units of affordable housing.

For more information, call Andrew Buonantuono, regional lending consortium administrator (631-435-4710), or visit www.lihp.org/.

The **Community Preservation Corporation** (CPC) of New York City is a nonprofit mortgage lender specializing in financing multifamily housing in low-, moderate-, and middle-income communities. Created in 1974 to help improve neighborhoods that were experiencing housing deterioration and abandonment, CPC has financed more than 100,000 units, representing public and private investments of over $3.7 billion. Through its approximately 90 member banks, CPC offers a range of financial programs and services, including financing for new construction of rental and ownership housing, construction financing for moderate or total rehabilitation of vacant buildings, permanent financing, small-building loans, preservation financing for cooperatives, refinancing for financially troubled cooperatives, and refinancing of existing debt.[150] CPC also works with pension funds, as well as with Fannie Mae and other institutions in the secondary market.

CPC works in New York and New Jersey; funds both nonprofit and for-profit developers; and targets its investments to neighborhood needs rather than to specific income groups.

For more information, call Brenda Ratliff (212-869-5300, ext. 568), or visit www.communityp.com.

Employer Housing-Production Programs

Many public and private employers, recognizing that affordable housing is essential to their ability to attract and retain employees, operate programs intended to increase the supply or affordability of housing for their workforce. Most employer-provided benefits and services take the form of buyer assistance; such initiatives are discussed later in the toolkit, in the section "Demand-Side Programs." Less frequently, however, employers directly assist with housing production by providing land or construction financing, making contributions to defray construction costs, or purchasing guarantees that lower the builder's risk.[151]

Employer-produced housing is more common in places such as resorts, which have extremely high housing costs and strong demand for service employees. In some cases, employers pool resources to produce more workforce housing; in others, they act alone to make more housing available specifically for their own workers. In Fullerton,

California, for example, Ambling Companies and California State University, Fullerton, teamed up to develop University Gables, a 7.9-acre (3.2-hectare), 86-unit project consisting of attached and detached homes for university employees who earn 120 percent of AMI or less.

✖ PROGRAMS AND POLICIES

First Homes, of Rochester, Minnesota, is a partnership of the Rochester Area Foundation, the Greater Minnesota Housing Fund (described earlier, under "Financing Partnerships/Lending Consortia"), the Rochester branch of the Mayo Clinic, and other area employers. The partnership promotes housing development for families earning up to 80 percent of the state median income by (1) providing information about, and access to, local and state funding programs, and (2) helping projects navigate the political process. Since its inception in 2000, First Homes has facilitated the development of more than 340 single-family homes and 229 rental units and has raised a total of $13.1 million in local contributions.

First Homes supports, through a variety of educational and financing programs, single-family developments for a mix of household types with a range of income levels (though it will assist in funding only for homes affordable to households earning less than 80 percent of the state median income). It also assists in the construction of new multifamily developments (or, in some cases, in the rehabilitation of existing developments) that meet its program criteria.

Finally, First Homes offers a gap financing program that provides homebuyers with up to $7,500 to back a second mortgage, which need not be repaid until the home is sold. For homes built on land owned or acquired by First Homes, long-term affordability is ensured through the First Homes Community

Land Trust (see the later section "Community Land Trusts").

For more information, call Sean Allen, executive director (507-287-7117), or visit www.firsthomes.org.

Dartmouth College, in Hanover, New Hampshire, developed the 55-unit Grasse Road development to make for-sale, single-family homes available to college employees at below-market prices. All full-time Dartmouth College employees are eligible to purchase the homes, but preference is given to employees who do not currently own a home and to those with the longest tenure at the college. So that Dartmouth can continue to offer the homes at affordable prices to future generations of employees, the college retains an option to repurchase each property at a predetermined price.

For more information, call Susie Weider, Dartmouth College Real Estate Office (603-646-2186), or visit www.dartmouth.edu/realestate/.

The **Summit County Housing Authority,** in Colorado, in partnership with the town of Breckenridge and the WSG Development Company, of Miami Beach, Florida, has developed Gibson Heights, a 38-unit subdivision for local teachers, firefighters, and others who earn 80 percent of AMI or less. The project's single-family homes, duplexes, and townhouses are deed-restricted to local workers who meet the income criteria. Appreciation is limited to approximately 3 percent, or the percentage growth in AMI, whichever is less. Gibson Heights is adjacent to WSG's Vista Point project, a 56-unit development that includes 18 deed-restricted units for households with incomes between 90 and 110 percent of AMI.[152]

For more information, call the Summit County Housing Authority (970-453-3555) or the WSG Development Company (970-453-2855), or visit www.co.summit.co.us/housing/index.cfm.

The **Military Housing Privatization Initiative** of the U.S. Department of Defense (DoD) was established in 1996, and enables the military to form partnerships with private developers to build housing for armed-forces families in high-cost housing markets.[153] Through this initiative, the DoD can use a variety of financial tools to assist housing development, including direct loans, loan guarantees, equity investments, and provision or leasing of property. As of January 2004, the department had contracted for 27 privatization projects, which together will yield more than 55,000 units.

In San Diego, for example, where the median housing price was $304,000 in 2002, the Navy, the Marine Corps, and Lincoln/Clark San Diego, LLC, formed a partnership to build, renovate and/or manage over 3,200 housing units for military personnel in the area. The partnership recently developed the Village at NTC (so named because it is on the site of the former Naval Training Center), a $260 million project that provided 500 townhouses for Navy and Marine families.[154]

For more information, call Lisa Tychsen (703-607-3207), or visit www.acq.osd.mil/housing.

Demand-Side Programs

Programs that help purchasers buy homes are key pieces of the housing-affordability puzzle.[155] Demand-side programs focus on assisting prospective homebuyers by lowering their purchase costs—for example, through reductions in downpayments or closing costs; fee waivers; matched savings programs; forgivable loans; subsidized ("soft") mortgages; below-market-rate mortgages; mortgage guarantees; or flexible financing qualifications or terms. Most of the programs also offer homebuyer education or counseling.

Demand-side programs are effective, and offer a number of advantages that make them popular with both governments and employers: they can easily be targeted to specific income groups, neighborhoods, or employees; incur comparatively low administrative costs; do not arouse the concern of neighborhood groups (and therefore tend to be politically acceptable); and are easy to change over time.

Demand-side programs may be offered by public or private entities; as noted earlier, some are provided by employers, in which case the initiative is referred to as employer-assisted housing (EAH). EAH programs typically help employees obtain below-market mortgages, or help fund closing costs or downpayments through grants, forgivable or deferred-payment loans, or matched savings. In addition, employers may provide homebuyer or financial counseling, or may guarantee all or part of an employee's mortgage.[156]

Some states, such as Florida and Mississippi, operate programs to enable teachers or other public employees to purchase homes; some encourage corporate EAH programs. Connecticut enacted a corporate tax credit for EAH programs in 1994. Maryland has created a matching fund for EAH programs. Illinois supports EAH programs by matching the forgivable home-purchase loans that employers make to their employees; the Illinois Housing Development Authority also provides companies with tax credits at the rate of 50 cents for every dollar provided to employees. In 2002, the program's first year, the state awarded $60,800 in tax credits for 20 homes purchased through EAH programs.[157]

✕ PROGRAMS AND POLICIES: STATEWIDE

California's Extra Credit Home Purchase Program is designed to help attract and retain qualified public-school teachers, administrators, and staff. The program, which is administered by the California Housing Finance Agency, offers tax credits or below-market-rate mortgages to qualified staff who agree to serve for three years in low-performing California schools. Through the tax credits, participants can save approximately $37,000 over the life of a 30-year, $150,000 mortgage; in addition, participants are guaranteed a minimum of $7,500 in local downpayment assistance. The program, which is funded by allocations of tax-exempt bond authority, was initiated in September 2000.

For more information, call Theresa Parker, executive director, California Housing Finance Agency (916-324-4638), or 1-800-789-2432; or visitwww.calhfa.ca.gov/homebuyer/programs/ectp.htm.

The Municipal Mortgage Program offered by **MassHousing** (formerly the Massachusetts Housing Finance Agency), the state's affordable-housing bank, provides zero-downpayment loans to police officers, firefighters, teachers, and other municipal employees to help them buy homes in the communities where they work. MassHousing also offers low-interest loans for first-time buyers who meet income and purchase-price qualifications, and requires no downpayment from households whose incomes are below 80 percent of AMI. Finally, MassHousing offers transit-oriented loans to encourage people to live near mass transit, and provides homebuyer counseling.

MassHousing programs are funded through the sale of bonds to private investors; the agency works with more than 100 banks across the state to deliver its affordable mortgage loans. Banks working with individual borrowers make the loans, and MassHousing purchases the loans from the banks. Since 1970, MassHousing has provided more than $7.8 billion in financing for projects, including over 9,000 units of mixed-income rental housing and more than 43,000 mortgage loans for first-time buyers.[158]

For more information, call Tom Gleason, executive director (617-854-1000), or visit www.masshousing.com.

✗ PROGRAMS AND POLICIES: LOCAL

HouseHartford, a partnership of the city of Hartford, Connecticut; Fannie Mae; and local mortgage lenders, helps households earning no more than 80 percent of AMI to purchase one- to four-family homes. Through this program, buyers may obtain an interest-free downpayment loan of between 5 and 7 percent of the purchase price, and an interest-free loan of up to $3,000 to cover closing costs; both are forgivable over five to ten years (depending on the total amount borrowed), as long as the buyer continues to live in the home. The incomes of purchasers of two-, three-, or four-family homes can exceed 80 percent of AMI, as long as a family earning no more than 80 percent of AMI occupies one of the units.

For more information, call the Department of Housing and Community Development (860-757-9005), or visit www.hartford.gov/Development/housing/ha-hmbuy-househart.htm.

Boston's Soft Second Loan Program combines a conventional first mortgage with a subsidized second mortgage to help first-time homebuyers who earn up to 100 percent of AMI to qualify for a mortgage. Program participants also benefit from low downpayment requirements (3 percent of the purchase price); downpayment assistance; favorable underwriting; elimination of "points"; reduced closing costs; elimination of mortgage-insurance requirements; free legal assistance; and homebuyer education programs. The city estimates that over the life of the mortgage, buyers can save up to $30,000 through this program.

Initiated in 1990, the Soft Second Loan Program is a joint undertaking by the city of Boston, MassHousing, the Massachusetts Housing Partnership, the Massachusetts Department of Housing and Community Development, and a number of private lending institutions.

For more information, call the Massachusetts Housing Partnership (617-330-9955), or visit www.mhp.net/homeownership/softsecond.php.

Chicago's Partnership for Affordable Neighborhoods (CPAN) program, a joint effort on the part of developers and the city, works in tandem with the New Homes for Chicago program (see "Other Local Public Programs") to enable moderate-income homebuyers to purchase homes in market-rate developments.[159] Under the program, developers reduce the purchase price of a certain percentage of homes in a market-rate development, and the difference in value is recaptured as a second mortgage that is assigned to the Chicago Low-Income Housing Trust Fund. The second mortgage is payable only if the buyer sells or refinances the home within 30 years. In that event, the subsidy reverts to the city for use in affordable-housing development. Participating developers receive permit-fee waivers of up to $10,000 per affordable unit, expedited permitting, and a supply of mortgage-ready prospective buyers for the affordable units.

To be eligible for this program, purchasers must be first-time homebuyers (or buyers who have not owned a home within the past three years), with incomes below 100 percent of AMI. The level of assistance depends on the buyer's income and financial need. After the buyer has maximized his or her purchasing power through the private mortgage market, the program will provide a zero-interest deferred loan, which is forgiven over a ten-year period according to a declining scale (the longer the seller owns the unit, the greater the portion of the loan that is forgiven).

For more information, call the Chicago Department of Housing (312-744-5000), or visit http://egov.cityofchicago.org and click on Your Government\City Departments\Housing\DOH Partnerships\Chicago Partnership for Affordable Neighborhoods Developer.

✖ PROGRAMS AND POLICIES: PRIVATE SECTOR

The **HIT HOME Program** of the AFL-CIO Housing Investment Trust is a national homeownership initiative implemented in partnership with Fannie Mae and Countrywide Financial.[160] The program offers qualified union members and municipal employees a $500 credit toward closing costs in high-cost markets (Boston, Los Angeles, Chicago, Washington, D.C., and New York City) and a $250 credit elsewhere. Countrywide Financial provides fast loan approvals; a product known as the Working Family Mortgage, which features a flexible payment schedule and shorter terms, resulting in lower interest rates; a wide selection of competitively priced home loans (including zero-downpayment loans); and homebuyer education and support. Fannie Mae provides money for the downpayments and closing costs; it also buys the mortgage loans and packages them into securities, many of which are purchased by AFL-CIO HIT. As of 2003, the program had assisted 2,000 union members and provided more than $345 million in home mortgages.

For more information, call 1-866-HIT-HOME, or Carol Nixon, HIT chief investment officer, Single-Family Finance; or visit www.hithome.org.

The **Yale University Homebuyer Program,** in New Haven, Connecticut, offers university

employees ten-year grants of $2,000 per year, plus a $5,000 bonus in the first year for assistance with closing costs and home repairs. The home must be in one of six target neighborhoods near the university, and buyers must occupy the unit for at least two years. Participating employees can also use state and city home-financing assistance programs. The university, the city, and various nonprofit organizations work together to provide homebuyer education programs.

For more information, call Jim Paley, Neighborhood Housing Services of New Haven (203-562-0598), or visit www.yale.edu/ hronline/hbuyer/index2.htm.

The **Coastal Housing Partnership of Santa Barbara,** California, is a consortium of 15 public and private employers who obtained favorable financing from a local lender for their employees in return for certain corporate banking arrangements. Employees who purchase a home through the consortium must make at least a 5 percent downpayment. The lender then provides the buyer with an 80 percent mortgage loan at a favorable interest rate, and a second mortgage for up to 15 percent of the purchase price. Employers incur no direct costs.[161]

For more information, contact Corby Gavin Gage, executive director (805-969-1025), or visit www.coastalhousing.org/index.html.

Maintaining Long-Term Affordability

Expanding the supply of workforce housing involves not only producing housing that can be purchased or leased by households with modest incomes, but also ensuring that the housing will remain affordable over time.[162]

For-Sale Homes

It is challenging to produce workforce housing, especially in high-cost areas, and units that revert to market rate are not easily replaced. In some cases, affordability can be maintained in perpetuity. More commonly, affordability restrictions are time-limited; at the end of a specified "control period," the restrictions expire. Depending on the specifics of the program, all or part of the subsidy may be forgiven at the time of sale, depending on the length of time the seller has owned the unit. Under some programs, the seller and the program sponsor share the unit's appreciated value according to a predetermined formula.

Strategies for maintaining the affordability of for-sale homes typically involve restrictions that are part of the buyer's mortgage or that are written into the deed of sale. If affordability is controlled through the mortgage, the agency providing the housing assistance gives the buyer a subsidy to purchase the home, then recaptures the subsidy at the time of resale. Deed restrictions, on the other hand, specify the terms and conditions of the unit's occupancy and resale. Long-term affordability can also be achieved through ownership arrangements such as community land trusts and limited-equity housing cooperatives.

Selecting and crafting affordability controls can be difficult, and decisions will depend on a number of factors, including the values and goals of the sponsoring entity; the legal framework; the available administrative resources; political considerations; the controls' potential effects on the targeted buyers' ability and willingness to purchase; the tax consequences for the buyer; and the controls' possible effects on lender participation. Whether purchasers should be permitted to benefit from the appreciation in the value of their homes, as other homeowners do, is particularly controversial. In the view of some observers, allowing purchasers to benefit is equivalent to awarding profits from the sale of subsidized homes. Nevertheless, from a legal standpoint, it is unclear to what extent the program sponsor can share in the value of appreciation.

The following four sections describe some of the most commonly used mechanisms for preserving the affordability of for-sale housing: mortgage controls, deed restrictions, limited-equity housing cooperatives, and community land trusts.

Mortgage Controls

Mortgage instruments, the most commonly used means of controlling affordability, are typically part of buyer-assistance programs. They are simple to administer, and can be used to recapture the unit's subsidy and/or to require that the home be sold to another income-qualified buyer.

The mortgage instrument most commonly used to ensure that a home remains affordable for a period of time is the soft second mortgage. Typically, the funding entity provides the buyer with money for a downpayment and/or closing costs, then places a zero-interest or low-interest second mortgage on the property for the amount of the subsidy. (The first mortgage is typically a conventional loan.) For a set period—ten years, for example—the homeowner does not have to repay the second mortgage unless the home is sold.[163] If the purchaser sells the home during this period for the original purchase price or more, a portion of the second mortgage must be repaid; the repayment level depends on how long the owner has owned the home.[164] The funding agency can then use the recaptured funds to subsidize other prospective homeowners. If the home is not sold during the set time period, the second mortgage is forgiven. This mechanism is used in many of the employer-assisted housing programs and other demand-side programs discussed in the "Financing" section.

The advantages to this approach are that it enables lower-income buyers to purchase a home they could not otherwise afford, and to realize at least a portion of the appreciation when they resell it. The disadvantages are that the homes do not remain affordable to the target income group in perpetuity; and, in markets where home values are appreciating rapidly, homeowners have an incentive to resell early, to capture a portion of the home's increased value.

Other kinds of mortgage instruments can also be used. For example, lenders making low-interest loans can require the homeowner to repay all or some of the mortgage interest discount if and when the property is sold during the control period.

✂ PROGRAMS AND POLICIES

The subsidy provided by **Boston's Soft Second Loan Program** (see "Demand-Side Programs") is secured by a mortgage. Participants who sell within five years of purchasing a home through the program must repay the full amount of the subsidy that was applied to interest payments on the second mortgage. After five years, the repayment requirement is either the amount of the subsidy or 20 percent of the net appreciation on the home at the time of sale, whichever is less. In either case, the repayment requirement, combined with the buyer's other secured debt, cannot exceed 97 percent of the value of the property.

If the homeowner refinances the second mortgage, the subsidy cannot be applied to the monthly payment, and the repayment requirements remain the same. However, if the total secured debt is less than 85 percent of the property's current value (according to a current appraisal), the Massachusetts Housing Partnership, which administers the program, may defer repayment of the subsidy until the homeowner sells the home.

For more information, call the Massachusetts Housing Partnership (617-338-8274), or visit www.mhp.net or www.cityofboston.gov/ dnd/hhs/C_Soft_Second.asp.

The **First Time Buyer's Financing Program,** operated by the Santa Clara, California, Redevelopment Agency, provides eligible first-time buyers with a second mortgage to fill the gap between the maximum mortgage loan CitiMortgage will provide and a home's purchase price. Homebuyers must put 3 percent down, and the maximum second mortgage amount is $50,000. To be eligible, a household must earn no more than 110 percent of AMI.

The redevelopment agency issues the second mortgage, which has a 15-year term with no payments due during the first five years. During the next ten years, the buyer must make fixed monthly payments on principal only. In lieu of charging interest, the agency retains a contingent interest in the form of shared appreciation, payable at the time the principal is paid off.[165] The entire unpaid principal and shared appreciation are due if the home is sold or refinanced.

For more information, call Donald Kwong, Santa Clara Housing and Community Services Division (408-615-2490), or Carolyn Henry, lending consultant, CitiMortgage (408-777-0479, ext. 203); or visit www.ci.santa-clara.ca.us/ plan_inspection/first_time_buyer.html.

Deed Restrictions

Deed restrictions, affordability agreements, or covenants attached to the deed may subject homebuyers to certain resale restrictions, such as a limitation on the home's sales price; a requirement to give the program sponsor the right of first refusal if the home is put on the market (or an option to purchase the home at a fixed price at a specified future time); or a requirement that the homeowner resell only to an income-qualified buyer.

Right-of-first-refusal restrictions generally specify that the program sponsor has the right to purchase the property either by matching an accepted offer made by a qualified buyer, or by paying an agreed-upon price (usually based on a property appraisal). In some cases, the program sponsor reserves the right to assign its purchase option to another buyer within a set period of time—presumably, another income-qualified buyer whom the project sponsor will assist to purchase the home. Right-of-first-refusal restrictions are always used in tandem with some other form of resale control that limits the sales price.[166]

Resale restrictions can be very effective but must be crafted carefully to avoid legal issues.[167] In addition, such restrictions can be difficult to administer and enforce, and may make homes harder to sell.

✖ PROGRAMS AND POLICIES

The **Purchase and Home Resale Program** of Monterey, California, helps first-time homebuyers purchase homes at below-market prices. The program is targeted to households who live or work in Monterey and earn up to 120 percent of AMI. Homes are made available through a city ordinance that requires developers to sell 15 percent of homes in each project at below-market prices, as set forth in a development agreement between the city and the developer.

The homebuyer purchases the unit under affordable-housing deed restrictions and must notify the city before selling or transferring title to the home. The deed restrictions give the city right of first refusal to buy the unit when the owner wishes to sell. If the city does not choose to buy the home (which is unlikely), the homeowner is free to sell it on the open market. If the city chooses to buy the home, the price is either the home's current appraised value or the home's current

value according to the Consumer Price Index, which depends on the original purchase price and how long the owner has held the unit.

The city also offers downpayment assistance to eligible buyers.

For more information, call the Housing and Property Management Office (831-646-3995), or visit www.monterey.org/housing/purchaseprog_details.html.

The **Stapleton Workforce Housing Program** is the affordable-housing component of the redevelopment taking place on the former site of Stapleton International Airport, near Denver, Colorado. Under the auspices of the Stapleton Development Corporation, a private nonprofit developer, Forest City Enterprises, a publicly traded for-profit development company, has begun a 20-year process that will transform the airport site into a mixed-use urban development that will include housing for low- and moderate-income households. The Stapleton Workforce Housing Program specifies that 10 percent of the 8,000 planned for-sale homes and 20 percent of the 4,000 rental apartments will be affordable to households earning no more than 80 percent of AMI. In addition, Forest City has donated land for 200 housing units for households earning between 20 and 50 percent of AMI.

Long-term affordability will be maintained by the following means: The deed to each affordable unit includes a 30-year resale restriction that permits the owner to capture a portion of the home's appreciation at the time of sale, but that requires the sales price to remain within specified limits. At the end of 30 years, if the homeowner chooses to sell the home, the sale must be made at a restricted price to a nonprofit entity created for the purpose of maintaining the homes' affordability. If the nonprofit declines to buy the home, the owner may sell it at the current market rate, but the designated nonprofit will receive the difference between the market price and the home's restricted price. This arrangement ensures that the homes will remain affordable to their target group for at least 30 years.

For more information, call Denise Gammon, senior vice president for Residential Development (303-355-9600), or visit www.stapletondenver.com/homes/incomequalified/default.asp?pgID=6.

Limited-Equity Housing Cooperatives

A limited-equity housing cooperative (LEHC) is a shared ownership arrangement for multifamily housing.[168] Individuals purchase a share in the cooperative that gives them certain rights: the right to occupy a designated housing unit through a lease or occupancy agreement; the right to sell the use of that unit; and the right to participate in governing the cooperative. Shareholders do not finance their individual units; instead, all units are financed through a single blanket mortgage. Each shareholder pays a portion of the operating costs and debt service.

Restrictions on resale of the shares, which are written into the cooperative's bylaws and individual occupancy agreements, typically include limits on buyers' incomes and the share's resale prices and specify that, at the time a share is offered for sale, the LEHC has the right of first refusal. Resale arrangements are typically complicated, and include a formula for dividing the appreciated value of the unit between the shareholder and the cooperative, and some protection against losses for the shareholder.

Though LEHCs are legally complicated and require owners of shares to participate in governance, this form of ownership is popular in cities like New York City and Washington, D.C.

✖ PROGRAMS AND POLICIES

The **Townhouses of Capitol Hill,** in Washington, D.C., is a mixed-income limited-equity cooperative for households earning up to 115 percent of AMI; the project was built by Corcoran Jennison Companies for the Ellen Wilson CDC and the Telesis Corporation, under HUD's HOPE VI program. Of the 134 units, 34 are for households earning less than 25 percent of AMI; 33 for households earning between 25 and 50 percent of AMI; and 67 for those with incomes between 50 and 115 percent of AMI. The architecturally distinctive Victorian rowhouse project was completed in 2000 and has won a ULI Award for Excellence.

HUD owns the land underlying the project and gave the cooperative the right to occupy the land, with certain use restrictions, for 99 years. Under HUD guidelines, the buyer's income determines the amount that must be paid to purchase a unit, as well as the monthly carrying charges. When a unit is sold, repayment varies based on the length of tenancy, with reduced appreciation for units sold less than three years from purchase.

For more information call David Perry, Ellen Wilson CDC (202-223-4560), or visit www.thcapitolhill.com/thcb.htm.

Maple Court, in the Harlem section of Manhattan, is a 135-unit limited-equity co-op developed with public financing assistance on land purchased from the city. The development was the area's first for-sale, middle-income residential construction in many years. Shareholders are required to use the units as their primary residence; no subletting is allowed. Resale restrictions will apply for at least 30 years, and limit the resale price of shares to 110 percent of the New York City median purchase price for existing housing. Share-holders are required to pay the city a portion of any profits gained from the sale of their share in the cooperative corporation.

For more information, see "Maple Court," ULI Development Case Study 27, no. 2 (January–March 1997), available at www.casestudies.uli.org (subscription service).

Community Land Trusts

Community land trusts (CLTs) are private non-profit corporations that are established to obtain and acquire property for affordable housing or other community needs, such as parks, gardens, or economic development activities. Because CLTs are created in response to local needs, they vary in their organizational structure and mis-sion, the roles they assume, and the types of projects they promote; however, ownership of real estate and community-based control are characteristic features of all CLTs.[169] Typically, a CLT operates within a defined geographic area and is governed primarily by people who live in that area. CLTs can obtain land through donation or purchase from a variety of sources—typically local governments, but also individuals, institu-tions, corporations, and other entities. CLTs can take a flexible approach to community develop-ment: depending on its mission, a CLT might, for example build, acquire, or rehabilitate vari-ous housing types, facilities used for neighbor-hood businesses, or recreational amenities, either alone or in partnership with nonprofit, for-profit, or governmental partners.

A CLT's ownership of the land is separate from ownership of the structures; thus, it can control the development, price, and use of the structures that occupy the land. The land-lease arrange-ment also gives the CLT control over the struc-tural and financial integrity of the property that is constructed on the land, enabling it to inter-vene and force repairs, or, in the event of default, to correct the problems and avert foreclosure.

CLTs have become an increasingly popular mechanism for creating a continuing supply of affordable housing. Though there are exceptions, CLTs typically serve households earning 80 per-cent or less of AMI—that is, the lower end of the income range for workforce housing. Fund-ing comes from the same kinds of sources that fund other affordable-housing programs—public and private program monies in the form of loans and grants, donated property, and in-kind con-tributions. Ground-lease fees typically cover operating costs.

Because CLTs retain ownership of the land underlying the housing they help to create, the land-cost component of the housing price is permanently eliminated, ensuring that the homes will remain affordable in perpetuity. In the case of a multifamily housing (or commer-cial) structure, the CLT may retain ownership of the building, or it may sell it to another non-profit, to a resident cooperative, or to individual households through a condominium structure; no matter what the arrangement, however, the CLT retains ownership of the land to ensure long-term affordability.

CLTs generally sell homes only to income-qualified owner-occupants, and only on a land-lease basis, often with a 99-year renewable lease. CLTs have enabled buyers to obtain "leasehold mortgages," which are insured by the FHA, and which Fannie Mae and some state housing fi-nance agencies will buy.[170]

An owner must sell the home if he or she no longer intends to occupy it. When the home-owner sells the house, the land trust may pur-chase the home at a price determined by an agreed-upon formula recorded in the ground lease; then the CLT resells it to another income-qualified household. At the time of sale, the homeowner realizes profits from the increase in the value of the structures and some return on cash investment, according to a predetermined equity-sharing formula.[171] Though the specific agreements and formulas may differ among CLTs, the ground-lease arrangement provides the homeowner with security and privacy, inheritance rights to the home,[172] and the ability to acquire some equity, while ensuring that the land and structures will be used for affordable housing in perpetuity.

The concept of community land trusts was created in the 1960s by the Institute for Creative Economics (ICE), which has nurtured it ever since. ICE is a national organization that provides information and financial and technical assistance—including a revolving loan fund—to support CLTs. According to ICE, there are now 118 CLTs in 31 states and the District of Columbia, and the CLT movement has created more than 5,000 permanently affordable homes for lower-income households.

Obtaining land for housing and funding for operating costs are the key issues in the creation and operation of CLTs. Because the dual-ownership arrangement is unusual, recruiting and educating homebuyers can be challenging, especially when the land trust is attempting to market to ethnic communities with strong feelings about property ownership.

✖ PROGRAMS AND POLICIES

The **Portland Community Land Trust** (PCLT) in Portland, Oregon, was created in 1999 with financial and technical assistance from ICE, in order to stem displacement in gentrifying neighborhoods in the northern parts of the city. Working in partnership with nonprofit and market-rate developers,[173] the PCLT targets households earning between 50 and 80 percent of AMI. Because the land trust retains ownership of the land, buyers can purchase homes at lower cost, and long-term affordability is ensured.

For more information, call Allison Handler, executive director (503-493-0293), or visit www.pclt.org.

Created in 1984 with $200,000 in seed money from the city of Burlington, Vermont, and some private land donations, the **Burlington Community Land Trust** (BCLT) is a nonprofit organization with more than 2,500 members—the largest, and one of the oldest, of the community land trusts.[174] As of fall 2003, the BCLT had developed and sold approximately 270 rental apartments and 370 shared-appreciation condominiums and single-family homes. The trust has also developed a neighborhood park, community facilities, and a retail store, and redevelops blighted industrial and commercial properties (brownfields) in low-income neighborhoods.

Families that purchase a home on BCLT land must earn no more than 85 percent of AMI. When homeowners sell their dwellings, the prices are set according to a predetermined limit; owners receive all the principal they have paid, plus the value of any improvements they have made, plus one-quarter of any appreciation in the home's value. The CLT, of course, retains ownership of the land.

For more information, call Brenda Torpy, executive director (802-862-6244), or visit www.champlainhousingtrust.org/.

First Homes Community Land Trust, in Rochester, Minnesota (described earlier, in "Employer Housing-Production Programs"), facilitates the production of workforce housing and assists homebuyers in purchasing homes. The homes are built on land that the trust already owns or purchases later. Taking the land out of the transaction can cut the price of a home by $30,000.

First Homes works closely with developers to build starter homes, and offers homebuyers financial assistance in the form of gap loans (low-interest deferred loans of up to $7,500) that enable homeowners to reduce their mortgage amount. Gap loans are repayable when the home is sold.

Homes are sold to income-qualified buyers, and the ground is leased to eligible families for 99 years under a renewable agreement. First Homes retains the option to purchase the homes at the time of resale. When a home is sold, the seller receives the amount of the downpayment, plus half the appreciation in the home's value; the other half of the appreciated value goes to the land trust.

For more information, call Sean Allen, executive director (507-287-7117), or visit www.firsthomes.org.

Rental Housing

Concerns about preserving the long-term affordability of subsidized rental housing are most commonly associated with HUD-subsidized housing.[175] The strategy is typically straightforward and involves financial incentives tied to an agreement that requires the for-profit developer/owner (and subsequent for-profit owners, if the property is sold) either to maintain affordable rental rates for a specified period of time, or to sell the property to a nonprofit or public agency.[176] Two key issues are the duration of the controls (typically between 15 and 40 years) and the need to accommodate changes such as redevelopment, refinancing, or foreclosure. Alternative means of ensuring long-term affordability of rental housing include community land trusts (discussed in the previous section) and rent control, which is intended to limit rent increases for all tenants within a delineated market area.

Rent Control

Rent control, also known as rent stabilization, is a controversial mechanism for preserving the affordability of privately owned rental housing in high-cost urban housing markets. Rent control limits rent increases for a controlled apartment during the entire period of time that the existing tenants reside in it. When the tenant leaves, the unit reverts to market rent. In addition to holding down rents, rent control thus exerts a powerful incentive for tenants to remain in their units. Rent-control laws may also contain other provisions that protect tenants from capricious eviction or that ensure access to services such as parking, laundry facilities, or storage space.

Though rent control dates from World War II, the idea gained momentum during the 1970s as a means of protecting low-income renters from displacement in gentrifying neighborhoods. By the time the housing-price inflation that began in the 1970s had reached its peak in the mid-1980s, more than 200 municipalities—which, together, contained 20 percent of the country's population—had rent-control laws in place. Today, only about 140 jurisdictions—including Fremont, Oakland, San Francisco, and San Jose, California; Washington, D.C.; New York City; and Hoboken, New Jersey—maintain rent-control ordinances. As a result of a statewide referendum, Boston, Cambridge, and Brookline, Massachusetts, did away with their rent-control ordinances in the mid-1990s.[177]

Advocates believe that rent control enables lower-income residents to remain near jobs and services even during periods of inflation, or when the areas they live in become highly desirable—and expensive—in the housing marketplace. Opponents point out that rent-control benefits do not require an income qualification; that the burden of the subsidy is borne by landlords and by other renters, who must pay higher prices for their units; and that such laws can discourage landlords from properly maintaining and re-investing in their units, and can also discourage the development of new rental housing.

⚒ PROGRAMS AND POLICIES

New York City's rent controls were originally imposed during World War II; today, the law "generally applies to residential buildings constructed before February 1947 in municipalities that have not declared an end to the postwar rental housing emergency" (a total of 151 municipalities within the state, including New York City).[178]

Under rent control, landlords can charge a maximum base rent, which is adjusted every two years to reflect changes in operating costs. Rent increases may also be permitted if the owner is providing more services or has substantially improved the building, or for certain other considerations. The law ensures tenants the right to receive required services and to have their leases renewed for either one- or two-year terms, at their preference; it also specifies the grounds for eviction.

Rent control applies to units occupied by tenants who have lived continuously in the controlled apartment since before July 1, 1971. Once vacated, the apartment either becomes rent stabilized—or, in the case of buildings with fewer than six units, decontrolled. Rent stabilization applies to buildings with six or more units that were constructed between July 1, 1947, and January 1, 1974, and to tenants in buildings built prior to 1947 who moved in after June 30, 1971.

Initially intended to help lower-income households, the city's rent-stabilization law often benefits more affluent residents, although apartments renting for $2,000 or more that became vacant after 1994 are now exempt under the Rent Regulation Reform Act of 1993 and Local Law No. 4.[179] As is true in other cities that have rent-control ordinances, a significant portion of the city's rental-housing units (27 percent) are exempt from rent control; and, because of the price constraints on much of the rental-housing supply, rental rates for the exempted portion of the housing market are much higher than they would be otherwise. As a result, newcomers to the city (and people who wish to move out of rent-controlled apartments) typically have difficulty finding a new apartment.[180]

For more information, call the general information number of the New York State Division of Housing and Community Renewal (1-866-275-3427) or the Rent InfoLine (718-739-6400); or visit www.dhcr.state.ny.us.

San Francisco's rent-control law, which is administered by the San Francisco Rent Board, limits rent increases for most of the city's renters to a set, inflation-dependent amount each year.[181] Tenants can challenge the increase for "failure to repair and maintain" the unit, and have the right to petition for rent decreases if the landlord fails to provide an agreed-upon service. In addition, tenants can be evicted only for "just cause"; the 14 specified causes include failure to pay rent, creating a nuisance, and lease violations.

For more information, call the San Francisco Rent Control Board (415-252-4600), or visit www.sfgov.org/site/rentboard_index.asp.

Notes

1. For example, San Jose, California, which is located in high-priced Silicon Valley, directs local funds, policies, and programs toward increasing the supply of moderately priced housing. Between 1989 and 1999, through partnerships with public and private entities, the city facilitated the production of 6,000 affordable new and rehabilitated housing units. San Jose has received numerous awards for its efforts. Department of Development Services, Town of Cary, *1999 Town of Cary Affordable Housing Toolkit* (Cary, N.C.: Department of Development Services, 1999), 31.

2. For examples and case studies describing the creative use of unlikely sites for successful housing (including a former parking lot, hotel, meat-processing plant, hospital, rail yard, lumber company, automotive sales and service center, highway right-of-way, and train terminal), see Diane R. Suchman, *Developing Successful Infill Housing* (Washington, D.C.: ULI, 2002).

3. *In rem* properties are abandoned properties that have liens attached, or whose owners are delinquent in paying property taxes. In some cases, they may be foreclosed upon and held for resale by the local jurisdiction. These properties have problems with their titles, and the owners often owe more in taxes than the property is worth. Programs designed to foster the reuse of such properties often involve transferring them to a community development corporation rather than to a for-profit developer.

4. Gary Binger, "Smart Growth in the San Francisco Bay Area: Effective Local Approaches" (study commissioned by the San Francisco District Council of the Urban Land Institute, June 2003), 9; available through www.uli.org/ Content/NavigationMenu22/Initiatives/SmartGrowth/ default.htm.

5. In addition to being subject to the usual site-development issues, urban infill sites are always vacant for a reason. There may be rubble, chemical contamination, lead, or asbestos remaining from previous uses. Existing infrastructure may be insufficient or in need of repair. Utilities may be inadequate. Nearby uses may be troubling. Zoning may be inappropriate for the intended use. Building codes may be unreasonably restrictive, especially for projects that involve rehabilitation. Nearby residents may oppose any change in the built environment, adding political risk for which the local government may have little tolerance. Suchman, *Infill Housing,* 13.

6. Tompkins County Planning Department, "Vital Communities Toolbox: Streamlined Permitting"; available at www.co.tompkins.ny.us/planning/vct/tool/ streamlinedpermitting.html.

7. Nancy Green Leigh, "The State Role in Urban Land Development" (discussion paper prepared for the Brookings Institution Center on Urban and Metropolitan Policy and CEOs for Cities, April 2003), v–vi.

8. For more information, visit www.bayareacouncil.org/ ppi/hlu/hlu_jhfl.html.

9. Paul C. Brophy and Jennifer S. Vey, *Seizing City Assets: Ten Steps to Urban Land Reform* (Washington, D.C.: Brookings Institution Center on Urban and Metropolitan Policy and CEOs for Cities, October 2002), 3.

10. King County Budget Office, "King County Buildable Lands: Evaluation Report 2002," September 2002; available at www.metrokc.gov/budget/buildland/bldlnd02.htm.

11. Association of Bay Area Governments, Bay Area Council, Greenbelt Alliance, Home Builders' Association of Northern California, Nonprofit Housing Association of Northern California, and California Affordable Housing Law Project, *Blueprint 2001: Housing Element Ideas and Solutions for a Sustainable and Affordable Future; Bay Area Housing* (Oakland, Calif.: 2001), 4–8.

12. For information about linkage programs, see "Housing Linkage Programs," a later section of the toolkit.

13. The HOME program, administered by the U.S. Department of Housing and Urban Development, provides formula grants to states and localities, often working in partnership with nonprofit entities, to fund a wide variety of activities related to affordable housing, including direct rental assistance to low-income households.

14. According to one account, Philadelphia now contains 31,000 vacant lots; 26,000 abandoned residential structures, of which an estimated 9,000 are in danger of collapse; and about 3,500 abandoned sites with structures for commercial use below and residential use above, for a total of about 60,000 units. Rob Gurwitt, "Betting on the Bulldozer," *Governing* (July 2002); available at www.governing.com/archive/2002/jul/philly.txt.

15. Among other means, housing authorities can raise money by issuing tax-exempt revenue bonds backed by revenue from the property; such bonds do not affect a jurisdiction's bond limits. Municipal Research and Services Center of Washington, *Infill Development: Strategies for Shaping Livable Neighborhoods,* Report No. 38 (June 1997), 54.

16. U.S. Environmental Protection Agency, "Smart Growth Policy Information: Brownfields Redevelopment,

Denver, Colorado"; available at http://cfpub.epa.gov/sgpdb/policy.cfm?policyid=745.

17. Twenty-five percent of the rental apartments will also be affordable, but the target income level is households earning 60 percent or less of AMI, which is lower than the income level for workforce housing used in this book.

18. For more information on land trusts, see "Maintaining Long-Term Affordability," a later section of the toolkit.

19. Five percent of the for-sale homes will be offered at prices between $125,000 and $150,000, but without income restrictions on buyers or long-term affordability controls.

20. Michael Greenberg, Karen Lowrie, Henry Mayer, Tyler Miller, and Laura Solitare, *Brownfield Redevelopment as a Smart Growth Option* (New Brunswick, N.J.: National Center for Neighborhood and Brownfields Redevelopment, Bloustein School, Rutgers University, January 2000), 4.

21. The Web site of the U.S. Environmental Protection Agency (www.epa.gov) provides current information on the redevelopment of brownfields. The Web site of the Northeast-Midwest Institute also offers extensive information on federal brownfields programs, resources for environmental cleanup, and financing options for cleanup and redevelopment.

22. Leigh, "Urban Land Development," 15. The act also allows federal money to be spent for the cleanup of brownfield sites (instead of just for assessment, as was previously the case) and provides liability relief for several categories of landowners who demonstrate due diligence.

23. For a more complete discussion of the potential, implications, and requirements for brownfield redevelopment, see Robert A. Simons, *Turning Brownfields into Greenbacks* (Washington, D.C.: ULI), 1998; or Todd Davis, *Brownfields: A Comprehensive Guide to Redeveloping Contaminated Property* (Chicago: ABA Publishing), 2001.

24. The Clark Group, "Fort Ord Reuse Authority Affordable/Workforce Housing Study" (report prepared for the Fort Ord Reuse Authority, March 2003), 29.

25. Leigh, "Urban Land Development," 15.

26. Ted Mondale and William Fulton, "Managing Metropolitan Growth: Reflections on the Twin Cities Experience" (case study prepared for the Brookings Institution on Urban and Metropolitan Policy, September 2003), 11–12.

27. Binger, "Smart Growth," 8.

28. Stephen Wheeler, *Smart Infill: Creating More Livable Communities in the Bay Area* (San Francisco: Greenbelt Alliance, 2002), 24, 50.

29. As defined by the Department of Housing Preservation and Development, a low-income household earns less than 50 percent of the New York City median income, a moderate-income household up to 100 percent, and a middle-income household up to 250 percent.

30. The Brownfields National Partnership highlights successful collaborative community efforts by designating them Brownfields Showcase Communities.

31. Brophy and Vey, *Seizing City Assets,* 11.

32. Westminster Square has been featured as a ULI development case study. Subscribers can access the case study through ULI's Web site (www.uli.org).

33. Treasurer, Wayne County, Michigan, "Michigan Tax-Reversion—Revisions: Questions and Answers"; available at www.waynecounty.com/treasurer/tax_reversion.htm.

34. Brophy and Vey, *Seizing City Assets,* 14.

35. Until 1988, interested parties other than the landowner were informed of the impending sale of tax-delinquent property through public notice (such as newspaper announcements), an approach that can result in title disputes. Under the 1988 legislation, all interested parties must be notified by certified mail.

36. Christina Rosan, "Cleveland's Land Bank: Catalyzing a Renaissance in Affordable Housing," *Housing Facts and Findings* 3, issue 1; available at www.fanniemaefoundation.org/programs/hff/v3i1-landbank.shtml.

37. Charles Euchner, with Elizabeth G. Frieze, "Getting Home: Overcoming Barriers to Housing in Greater Boston" (report prepared for the Pioneer Institute for Public Policy Research, Boston, Massachusetts, and the Rappaport Institute for Greater Boston, John F. Kennedy School of Government, Harvard University, January 2003).

38. U.S. Department of Housing and Urban Development, "America's Affordable Communities Initiative, HUD's Initiative on Removal of Regulatory Barriers: Proposals for Incentive Criteria on Barrier Removal in HUD's Funding Allocations; Notice," *Federal Register* 68, no. 227 (November 25, 2003): 66, 288.

39. Atlanta Regional Commission, "Jobs-Housing Balance," in *Community Choices Toolkit* (Atlanta: Atlanta Regional Commission, October 1, 2002), 6.

Notes

40. The author is grateful to Douglas R. Porter, president of the Growth Management Institute, for reviewing, editing, and adding to the inclusionary housing section. In 2004, ULI published Douglas Porter's *Inclusionary Zoning for Affordable Housing.*

41. Under New Hampshire law, each regional planning commission must prepare an assessment of family and senior housing needs for use by those local governments that include housing elements as part of their master plans; however, local governments are not required to provide the level of housing identified in the assessment.

42. Douglas R. Porter, "The Promise and Practice of Inclusionary Zoning" (draft report prepared for the Brookings Institution Symposium on Growth Management and Affordable Housing, Washington, D.C., May 29, 2003), 19.

43. Stuart Meck, Rebecca Retzlaff, and James Schwab, *Regional Approaches to Affordable Housing,* Planning Advisory Service Report 513/514 (Chicago: American Planning Association, 2003), 32.

44. Ibid., 34.

45. California Coalition for Rural Housing and Nonprofit Housing Association of Northern California, *Inclusionary Housing in California: 30 Years of Innovation* (Sacramento: California Coalition for Rural Housing and Nonprofit Housing Association of Northern California, 2003).

46. According to the *Sacramento Bee* (June 30, 2003), "In 1990, the state Department of Housing and Community Development told local governments in the Sacramento region that they needed to build 41,015 affordable apartments and houses by 1996 to provide their share of the state's housing needs for low- and very low-income people. But by 2001—11 years later—the local housing market produced only 8,998 such units."

47. Porter, "Promise and Practice."

48. "A Nod to NIMBY-ism," *Boston Globe,* October 27, 2003.

49. Philip B. Herr and Associates, *Zoning for Housing Affordability* (report prepared for the Massachusetts Housing Partnership Fund, Boston, 2000).

50. Meck, Retzlaff, and Schwab, *Regional Approaches,* 15.

51. Edith Netter, land use attorney and consultant, e-mail to author, July 10, 2003; and Nicholas J. Brunick and D. Jo Patton, *Eliminating Barriers: Letting the Market Help Meet Illinois Housing Needs* (Chicago: Business and Professional People for the Public Interest, 2003).

52. Bay Area Economics, "Affordable Housing Incentive Programs" (report prepared for the Growth Management Planning Council, King County, Washington, February 2001), vii. According to the report, "the combinations of density bonuses and parking requirement reductions can have dramatic financial impacts in areas where parking garages or other costly forms of structured parking are needed to fit the project within an urban site."

53. IZ programs have drawn opposition on the basis of economic and legal issues. In the view of some observers, IZ programs pass on to the private sector the responsibility for providing decent housing for low-income households—and, since developers offset the cost of including affordable units by increasing the prices of the market-rate units, IZ programs can even be said to pass the costs on to homebuyers. It has also been argued that if incentives are insufficient to cover the cost of constructing affordable units, IZ programs can dampen housing production. Nevertheless, builders who participate in inclusionary programs say that they view the affordable-housing burden as a cost of doing business where there is a strong market—and that they do continue to build in jurisdictions with inclusionary programs. Furthermore, opponents of inclusionary programs have not initiated extensive litigation: only four cases have been tried—and, except for a 1971 decision concerning the right of Fairfax County, Virginia, to proceed without explicit state permissions, courts have found that inclusionary programs are a legitimate form of development regulation, especially if cost-offsetting incentives are provided. Douglas R. Porter, "Economic and Legal Issues of IZ," *Urban Land* (February 2004).

54. Brunick and Patton, *Eliminating Barriers.*

55. The Montgomery County program, enacted in 1973, is one of the oldest, most successful, and best-known examples of a local IZ program, though its income targets are below the those defined for workforce housing in this book. Under the program, private developers of housing projects with more than 35 units must include 12.5 to 15 percent affordable units. As an incentive, the program offers a 20 to 22 percent density bonus, depending on project size. The county's Housing Opportunities Commission (its housing authority) retains the right to purchase up to one-third of the affordable units. Ownership units are subject to affordability controls for ten years, and rental units for 20 years. As of 2001, the Moderately Priced Dwelling Unit program had resulted in the production of

11,000 units of affordable housing. About 64 percent of those units have passed the ten-year control period and are available in the marketplace. The county retains the right of first refusal for resale, which it exercises in about 60 percent of cases. Because rising housing prices have prevented the county from acquiring all resales, the total number of units in the program has dropped to 3,805. According to county staff, however, many households remain in their inexpensive units rather than put them up for sale.

56. However, even if they are allowed in the same zone, mixed-use projects may be difficult to build if residential and commercial developments have different setback and parking requirements, thus limiting the range of potential project designs.

57. Duncan Associates, "Pittsburgh, Pennsylvania: Urban Zoning Code"; available at www.duncanplan.com/projects/pittsburgh.html.

58. Colorado Department of Local Affairs, *Best Practices in Land Use Planning and Growth Management,* Colorado Heritage Report (Denver: December 1999).

59. The U.S. Department of Commerce reports that in 2004, the average sales price of an average-sized (2,349-square-foot; 218-square-meter) single-family stick-built home, not including the cost of land, was $201,418, or $85.75 per square foot ($924 per square meter); the average sales price of an average-sized (1,750-square-foot; 163-square-meter) multisection manufactured home was $63,300, or $36.17 per square foot ($388 per square meter), including installation costs. See Manufactured Housing Institute, "Quick Facts: Cost and Size Comparisons for New Manufactured Homes and New Single-Family Site-Built Homes," available at www.manufacturedhousing.org/media_center/quick_facts2006/cost_size.htm.

60. Diane R. Suchman, "Manufactured Housing: An Affordable Alternative," ULI Research Working Paper 640 (Washington, D.C.: ULI, March 1995), 7.

61. There was a moratorium on tandem housing in one area of the city because neighbors were concerned about the large number of tandem homes that had been built there.

62. Wheeler, *Smart Infill,* 27.

63. Richard T. LeGates, "Housing Incentives to Promote Inter-Regional Jobs-Housing Balance" (report prepared for the Inter-regional Partnership Jobs/Housing Balance Pilot Program, January 2001), 22.

64. Some jurisdictions use "specific plan" and "precise plan" interchangeably; in other jurisdictions, the terms have distinct meanings.

65. Alan Ehrenhalt, "The Trouble with Zoning," *Governing* (February 1998); available at www.governing.com/archive/1998/feb/zoning.txt.

66. Association of Bay Area Governments et al., *Blueprint 2001.*

67. Department of Planning and Development, Teton County, Wyoming, "Jackson/Teton County Comprehensive Plan and Land Development Regulations," October, 2006, Article II, Section 2540, www.tetonwyo.org/plan/docs/ComprehensivePlan/LDR-ArticleII-2006Oct06.pdf.

68. Jerry W. Szatan, "The Uphill Battle," *Urban Land* (August 2002).

69. LeGates, "Housing Incentives," 23.

70. Arthur C. Nelson, "Top Ten State and Local Strategies to Increase Affordable Housing Supply," *Housing Facts and Findings* 5, no. 1: 2; available at www.fanniemaefoundation.org/programs/hff/v5i1-topten.shtml.

71. Douglas R. Porter, "Flexible Zoning: A Status Report on Performance Standards," *Zoning News* (January 1998): 2.

72. Information for these examples was obtained from Douglas R. Porter, "Flexible Zoning."

73. Wheeler, *Smart Infill,* 32.

74. Other objectives include a desire to address air-quality concerns; promote transit use and transit-oriented development; minimize stormwater runoff; encourage higher density and more compact development; and create more traditionally pedestrian-oriented neighborhoods.

75. Los Angeles Department of City Planning, "SB 1818—State Density Bonus Law Interim Guidelines," http://cityplanning.lacity.org (click on Zoning Information|Density Bonus).

76. BRIDGE is a nonprofit development entity founded in 1983 by Bay Area business leaders to build high-quality workforce housing, often in partnership with for-profit developers. According to its Web site, BRIDGE has developed over 8,500 homes housing 20,000 people, which makes it the leading nonprofit producer of affordable housing in California and a national model of successful nonprofit development. BRIDGE is unique in that it creates partnerships to build not only housing, but also shopping centers, parks, daycare centers, police and fire facilities,

Notes

libraries, community spaces, and job training centers. For more information, visit www.bridgehousing.com.

77. "Higher density" is a relative term: what is considered dense in Phoenix may not be considered dense in New York City. There is no "correct" density for a given site; within broad, location-dependent ranges, density decisions are largely a matter of preference and politics. In general, suburban densities range from four to eight (net) dwelling units per acre (ten to 20 per hectare), although densities in older suburbs may range from ten to 16 dwelling units per acre (25 to 40 per hectare). Within employment centers, such as downtowns, densities of 30 to 200 units per acre (74 to 494 per hectare) are appropriate when they are accompanied by supportive retail and amenities. In locations outside urban cores, dwelling units such as townhouses, duplexes, small apartment buildings, and even small-lot detached houses can be built attractively at 12 to 30 units per acre (30 to 74 per hectare), which is a housing density that can support public transit. See Wheeler, *Smart Infill,* 16–17.

78. Clark Group, "Fort Ord Housing Study," 30.

79. National Governors Association, Center for Best Practices, "Growth Tool Kit: Encourage Transit-Oriented Development"; available through www.nga.org. For more information on the Transit Village Development Planning Act, call the California Governor's Office of Research and Planning (916-322-2318).

80. Deborah L. Myerson, "Hard at Work for Workforce Housing," *Urban Land* 62, no. 9 (September 2003): 113.

81. Municipal Research and Services Center of Washington (MRSC), *Infill Development: Strategies for Shaping Livable Neighborhoods,* Report No. 38 (Washington, D.C.: MRSC, June 1997), 50–51.

82. Rick Pruetz, "Reinventing TDR" (paper presented at the 2002 American Planning Association National Planning Conference), 1.

83. MRSC, *Infill Development,* 39.

84. Pruetz, "Reinventing TDR," 3.

85. From 1990 through 1994, rehabilitation represented almost 80 percent of the total value of central-city construction in St. Louis, and between 50 and 60 percent in Baltimore, Cleveland, Detroit, Philadelphia, San Francisco, and Washington, D.C. David Listokin and Barbara Listokin, "Historic Preservation and Affordable Housing: Leveraging Old Resources for New Opportunities," *Housing Facts and Figures* 3, Issue 2, p. 2.

86. Suchman, *Infill Housing,* 80. For more information on changes in state building and rehabilitation codes, visit the National Conference of States on Building Codes and Standards, www.ncsbc.org.

87. The HUD report "Innovative Rehabilitation Provisions: A Demonstration of the Nationally Applicable Recommended Rehabilitation Provisions" (March 1999) documents the use and cost-effectiveness of the new rehabilitation provisions. Another HUD report, "Smart Codes in Your Community: A Guide to Building Rehabilitation Codes" (August 2001), provides advice and examples for communities that want to develop construction codes that encourage the reuse of existing structures. Both are available through the HUD USER Web site, www.huduser.org.

88. The rehabilitation subcode replaced a cost-based code in which the required level of compliance with new building code standards depended on the cost of the project.

89. According to Ben Forest, the New Jersey subcode can reduce rehabilitation costs by as much as 50 percent, though the average savings are about 10 percent. "New Jersey Revs Up Its Rehabs," *Planning* (August 1999).

90. David Listokin, "Housing Rehabilitation and American Cities" (draft overview paper presented at HUD conference on Housing Policy in the New Millennium), Washington, D.C., October 3, 2000.

91. Leigh, "Urban Land Development," 23.

92. National Governors Association, Center for Best Practices, "Growth Tool Kit: Encourage Transit-Oriented Development"; available through www.nga.org.

93. The model statute is available through www.planning.org/growingsmart.

94. Wheeler, *Smart Infill,* 38; and Silicon Valley Housing Leadership Council, *Towards More Affordable Homes: Streamlining the Entitlement Process in Silicon Valley* (San Jose, Calif.: Silicon Valley Manufacturing Group, Tri-County Apartment Association, and Homebuilders Association of Northern California, October 1999), 6–14.

95. Nelson, "Top Ten Strategies," 2.

96. Wheeler, *Smart Infill,* 38.

97. Kim Ilana Marschner, *Building Workforce Housing: Meeting San Francisco's Housing Challenge* (San Francisco: San Francisco Chamber of Commerce, 2003), 21. "Affordable" in this case refers to housing targeted to households earning no more than 80 percent of AMI.

98. Brophy and Vey, *Seizing City Assets,* 18.

99. Douglas R. Porter, with Anita Kramer, Terry Lassar, and David Salvesen, "Building Homes in America's Cities: A Progress Report" (paper prepared for the U.S. Conference of Mayors, the U.S. Department of Housing and Urban Development, and the National Association of Home Builders, October 2000), 14.

100. Under this program, housing is "affordable" if it can be purchased or rented by very low-income households (those who earn no more than 50 percent of AMI) or low-income households (those who earn no more than 80 percent of AMI) without using more than 30 percent of their incomes.

101. Association of Bay Area Governments et al., *Blueprint 2001*, 4-4.

102. School impact fees are not usually waived.

103. The reduction in parking requirements is 15 percent for projects located within one mile (1.6 kilometers) of a major transit corridor.

104. HUD Regulatory Barriers Clearinghouse, "City of Albuquerque Code of Ordinances, 2000"; available through www.huduser.org/rbc/search/rbcdetails.asp?DocId=83.

105. For a good general discussion of ways to finance affordable housing, see Enterprise Foundation, *Overview of Financing Mechanisms for Affordable Housing* (Columbia, Md.: Enterprise Foundation, 1995). In addition, Land-Watch, of Monterey County, California (831-422-9390), offers a good sample of affordable-housing programs in "Chapter 5: Federal, State, Local and Private Resources," Issues and Actions, Affordable/Workforce Housing Study; available at www.mclw.org/pages/issuesactions/fortord/clarkreport/chapter5.html. For information on private sector financing programs, the National Association of Affordable Housing Lenders is another good resource (www.naahl.org).

106. For detailed information on specific programs, visit the HUD Web site (www.hud.gov).

107. Income limits for HUD programs vary, but most programs that assist with housing production (as opposed to assisting home purchasers) target very low-income or low-income households (less than 50 percent of AMI or less than 80 percent of AMI, adjusted for family size). For more information, see U.S. Department of Housing and Urban Development, Office of Policy Development and Research, *FY2003 HUD Income Limits: Briefing Material* (Washington, D.C.: HUD, February 1, 2003).

108. For more information about HOPE VI projects, visit the Web site of the Housing Research Foundation, www.housingresearch.org.

109. The LIHTC program is a U.S. Department of the Treasury program administered by State Tax Credit Allocating Agencies.

110. Historic rehabilitation tax credits are jointly administered by the National Park Service and the Internal Revenue Service, working with State Historic Preservation Offices. Eligible structures include National Historic Landmarks, and buildings that are listed in the National Register of Historic Places or located within National Register Historic Districts and certain local historic districts. For more information on how federal historic preservation incentives can be used effectively with local initiatives, see National Trust for Historic Preservation, "Rebuilding Community: A Best Practices Toolkit for Historic Preservation," available at www.nationaltrust.org/housing/Rebuilding_Community.pdf.

111. Listokin and Listokin, "Historic Preservation," 3.

112. Since 1976, historic preservation tax incentives have encouraged the rehabilitation of more than 149,000 housing units and the new construction of 75,000. Of the total, 30,000 are affordable to low- and moderate-income households. For more information, call Michael Auer, National Park Service (202-354-2031), or visit www.cr.nps.gov.

113. For information on programs that might apply to a specific project, see www.epa.gov.

114. Fannie Mae is the nation's largest source of financing for home mortgages and operates a wide range of innovative programs, many in partnership with public and private entities. To learn more, visit www.fanniemae.com.

115. Mary E. Brooks, with assistance from Debbie Mingo, *A Status Report on Housing Trust Funds in the United States* (prepared for the Housing Trust Fund Project of the Center for Community Change, Frazier Park, California, September 1997), 5.

116. As a result of 1985 legislation that allows local jurisdictions to levy fees on developers for affordable housing, New Jersey alone has nearly 150 municipal trust funds. A good source of information, technical assistance, and training on housing trust funds is the Center for Community Change (415-982-0346, or www.communitychange.org). Mary Brooks, director of the center's Housing Trust Fund Project, can be reached at 661-245-0318. Mary Brooks, *Housing Trust Fund Progress Report 2002: Local Responses to*

Notes

America's Housing Needs (Frazier Park, Calif.: Housing Trust Fund Project of the Center for Community Change, 2002), 1.

117. See "Demand-Side Programs," a later section of this toolkit.

118. Mary Brooks, *Housing Trust Fund Progress Report 2002* (Frazier Park, Calif.: Center for Community Change, 1997), 26.

119. Other revenue sources include loan repayments, proceeds from the sale of public property, fees from condominium conversions, inclusionary zoning in-lieu fees, hotel/motel taxes, and interest on mortgage escrow accounts. In some cases, these dedicated monies may be augmented by city appropriations or other funds.

120. In addition to funding the SHIP program, the Sadowski Act funds several state housing programs, including the State Apartment Incentive Partnership, which provides low-interest loans to rental-housing developers for projects in which at least 20 percent of the units are set aside for households earning up to 50 percent of AMI; the Affordable Housing Guarantee Program, which insures development loans for single-family and multifamily affordable housing; the Home Ownership Assistance Program, which provides new homebuyers with deferred loans for downpayments and closing costs; and a predevelopment loan program for public and nonprofit developers.

121. Jaimie Ross, "Smart Growth and Affordable Housing in Florida," 1000 Friends of Florida, Spring 2001; available at www.1000friendsofflorida.org/housing/Smart_Growth_Afford_Housing.asp.

122. The program was initiated under interim guidelines in 1981.

123. Specific requirements are determined by formulas; for more information, see the San Francisco Planning Code, Section 313, www.municode.com/Resources/gateway.asp?pid=14139&sid=5.

124. Income categories are defined in the code according to income ceilings, rather than as percentages of AMI.

125. Housing-finance authorities are quasi-public agencies chartered by state or local governments; they are not actually part of those governments.

126. Multifamily properties funded with tax-exempt bonds must set aside 20 percent of the units for households earning no more than 50 percent of AMI, or 40 percent of the units for households earning no more than 60 percent of AMI. Developments that meet the affordability criteria

receive 4 percent LIHTCs (noncompetitive) in addition to the tax-exempt financing. "Mixed-Income Rental Housing Production Program Using Tax-Exempt Bond Financing," Millennial Housing Commission Concept Paper, 6; available at govinfo.library.unt.edu/mhc/papers.html.

127. Clark Group, "Fort Ord Housing Study," 28.

128. For rental developments, tenants must have incomes no greater than 60 percent of AMI.

129. Portland Development Commission, "Economic Development and Housing Revenue Bond Program"; available at www.pdc.us/dev_serv/finincde.asp.

130. Sam Newberg, "Finding Affordable Housing in the Pacific Northwest," in Myerson, "Hard at Work," 113.

131. MRSC, *Infill Development,* 25–26.

132. Wholly residential projects are not eligible for these grants.

133. "Public Housing Transformation TIF Program to Help Front-Fund Construction of New Mixed-Income Communities," *Business Wire,* April 11, 2003.

134. Porter et al., "Building Homes," 10.

135. According to the National Trust for Historic Preservation, 45 states provide incentives for historic preservation, either through property-tax relief or state historic tax credits.

136. Michael A. Stegman, *State and Local Affordable-Housing Programs: A Rich Tapestry* (Washington, D.C.: ULI, 1999), 111–112.

137. City of Tacoma, "Tax Incentive Program"; available at www.cityoftacoma.org/Page.aspx?nid=456.

138. As determined by HUD for the purpose of setting forth qualifications for Federal Housing Administration loans.

139. For more information, and to access the clearinghouse, visit www.hcd.ca.gov/clearinghouse.

140. Projects located in designated "urban aid" municipalities are subject to affordability controls for a minimum of ten years; all others, for 30 years.

141. As defined by the Workforce Housing Reward Program, very low-income households earn up to 50 percent of AMI, and low-income households up to 80 percent. Division of Financial Assistance, California Department of Housing and Community Development, "Workforce Housing Reward Program"; available at www.hcd.ca.gov/ca/whrp.

142. Stegman, *Rich Tapestry,* 98–100.

143. Colorado Department of Local Affairs, "Best Practices in Land Use Planning and Growth Management," Colorado Heritage Report (Denver: Colorado Department of Local Affairs, December 1999), 14. In exchange for a commitment to maintain affordability for 20 years, developers of qualified projects can defer some or all of the project's development fees until the project is ready to receive a certificate of occupancy.

144. For more information, visit the www.fhfb.gov.

145. In this case, bridge financing means providing funds to public entities that have yet to receive certain expected revenues or funding allocations.

146. Though requirements vary, lending consortia most commonly support projects that target households earning 80 percent of AMI or less.

147. National Association of Affordable Housing Lenders (NAAHL), *Affordable Housing Loan Consortia Sourcebook,* 2nd ed. (Washington, D.C.: NAAHL, 1997), 1–10. This excellent source of information includes profiles of 35 different affordable-housing loan consortia.

148. The Genesis LA Economic Growth Corporation is a nonprofit organization created in 1998 to promote economic development, job creation, and revitalization of disadvantaged low- and moderate-income communities. It operates a group of targeted private sector funding vehicles, including the Genesis Workforce Housing Fund. These funds make investments in urban development activities that yield higher returns than those typically obtained through CRA-motivated investments.

149. The two foundations recapitalized the fund with an additional $32.5 million in 2000.

150. National Association of Affordable Housing Lenders, *Sourcebook,* 41.

151. Daniel Hoffman, "A Blueprint for Employer-Assisted Housing" (white paper produced by the American Affordable Housing Institute, Department of Urban Studies and Community Health, Bloustein School of Planning and Public Policy, Rutgers University), 2–4; available at www.eahousing.com/Blueprintarticle.html.

152. Szatan, "Uphill Battle," 100.

153. According to the Military Housing Privatization Initiative Web site (www.acq.osd.mil/housing/mhpi.htm), military families have priority access to the housing developed under this program. If occupancy rates fall below a specified level, the following groups (in priority order) may rent units: federal civil-service employees, retired members of the military, members of the National Guard and the military reserve, retired civil servants, DoD employees and contractors, and the general public.

154. Myerson, "Hard at Work."

155. Rental-assistance programs are typically targeted to households whose incomes are below 60 percent of AMI, and therefore are not discussed or included as examples in this section.

156. Fannie Mae, through its Employer-Assisted Housing program, provides free technical assistance to employers interested in establishing EAH programs.

157. Jeff Bailey, "Turnover-Weary Firms Offer a Creative Benefit," Startup Journal, Wall Street Journal Center for Entrepreneurs, March 6, 2003; available at www.startupjournal.com/columnists/enterprise/20030306-bailey.html. For more information on the Illinois program, call Charlotte Flickinger, director of tax credits, Illinois Housing Development Authority.

158. "MassHousing Offers Improved Affordable Home Loans for Buyers with Modest Incomes; Enhanced Programs Are Unveiled Just in Time for Spring Buying Season," *Business Wire,* May 7, 2003.

159. Homebuyers access the CPAN program through the same application process as the New Homes program.

160. According to the HIT HOME Web site (www.aflcio-hit.com), "HIT is an open-end investment company, commonly called a mutual fund. The Trust is a national leader in the investment of union capital for the financing of housing with approximately 400 investors including major public and Taft-Hartley pension plans."

161. Michael Schubert, "Housing for a Competitive Workforce: Homeownership Models That Work," Metropolitan Planning Council, 1998; available at www.metroplanning.org/resources/119intro.asp?objectID=119.

162. An excellent general source of information on affordability controls is Peter Wermath, "Overview: Controlling Affordability Over Time in Subsidized Owner-Occupied Housing," Enterprise Foundation, June 5, 1995; available at www.practitionerresources.org/showdoc.html?id=60641.

163. Generally, to avoid triggering repayment of a second mortgage of this type, the home is required to be the owner's primary residence, and is not permitted to be rented out.

Notes

164. For example, if the control period is five years, the loan is forgiven at the rate of 20 percent per year. If the control period is ten years, 10 percent per year is forgiven.

165. "Shared appreciation" means that the agency shares in the property's appreciated value according to its share of the original purchase price. For example, if the agency provided a $20,000 second mortgage on a $200,000 home, the city would be entitled to a 10 percent share in the appreciation.

166. Wermath, "Overview," 8.

167. According to Jeanne Goldie Gura, "Resale restrictions are vulnerable to legal challenges; in some states, they are subject to the rule against perpetuities, the rule against restraint of alienation, or both. Another issue arises if the right of first refusal or option to purchase at a fixed price is exercised when the homebuyer declares bankruptcy. Because the purchase price set in the loan or deed papers is often far below the market price of the home, some bankruptcy courts could view the exercise of these clauses as a form of subterfuge. In some cases, depending on the state, the execution of this clause, even a year before the filing of bankruptcy, can be viewed as a fraudulent conveyance. In addition, some mortgage loan funds commonly used by community development groups and lenders simply do not allow resale restrictions." Gura, "Preserving Affordable Homeownership Opportunities in Rapidly Escalating Markets," *Journal of Affordable Housing* 11, no.1 (Fall 2001): 82.

168. The Enterprise Foundation makes available an excellent overview of LEHCs, "Alternative Financing Models— Hybrids of Homeownership: Limited Equity Cooperative Housing," available at www.enterprisefoundation.org/ resources/dss/large/lg&rin&rnc&ucpsff3.htm.

169. According to Section 212 of the Cranston-Gonzales National Affordable Housing Act (42 U.S.C. 12773), a "community land trust" is a community housing-development organization that is not sponsored by a for-profit organization, and that "acquires parcels of land, held in perpetuity, primarily for conveyance under long-term ground leases; transfers ownership of any structural improvements located on such leased parcels to the lessees; and retains a pre-emptive option to purchase any such structural improvement at a price determined by a formula that is designed to ensure that the improvement remains affordable to low- and moderate-income families in perpetuity." The law further requires that the corporate membership and board of directors be community based.

170. "Community Land Trusts," PolicyLink Equitable Development Toolkit; available at www.policylink.org/ EDTK/CLT/.

171. A number of CLT resale formulas are discussed in Kevin Girga, Matt Rosenberg, Vicky Selkowe, Joshua Todd, and Rachel Walker, "A Survey of Nationwide Community Land Trust Resale Formulas and Ground Leases: A Report Prepared for the Madison Area Community Land Trust" (URPL #844, Department of Urban and Regional Planning, University of Wisconsin–Madison, April 2002).

172. According to PolicyLink's Web site (www.policylink.org), most CLTs permit heirs to occupy the home if they are the children of the deceased owner, have lived in the home for a specified time, or are income-eligible themselves. Heirs can sell CLT homes but must abide by the resale restrictions.

173. "Land Trust Lets Buyers Purchase House, Not Lot," *Sunday Oregonian,* June 29, 2003, sunrise edition.

174. Additional funding has come from other governmental sources, private and philanthropic sources, and religious organizations, including the city of Burlington, the Vermont Housing and Conservation Board, the Federal Home Loan Bank of Boston Affordable Housing Program, Neighbor-Works, and the Vermont Housing Finance Agency.

175. Typically, subsidized rental housing is targeted to households whose incomes are lower than the income level for workforce housing used in this book.

176. Peter Wermath, "Overview," 3.

177. William Tucker, "How Rent Control Drives Out Affordable Housing," Policy Analysis No. 274 (Washington, D.C.: Cato Institute, May 21, 1997), 2.

178. New York State Division of Housing and Community Renewal, "Rent Control and Rent Stabilization," Fact Sheet #1; available at www.dhcr.state.ny.us/ora/pubs/html/ orafac1.htm

179. These laws also deregulated high-rent apartments occupied by tenants who earn over $250,000 for at least two years prior to the owner's application for deregulation. New York State Division of Housing and Community Renewal, "Rent Control."

180. Tucker, "Rent Control."

181. There are certain exceptions, most notably tenants in new buildings (defined as buildings constructed after 1979).

Bibliography

Adelman, Andrew A. "Streamlining the Development Permitting Process and Recent Innovations in the City of Los Angeles Department of Building and Safety." Presentation, Urban Land Institute/U.S. Department of Housing and Urban Development workshop, Washington, D.C., April 4, 2002.

Advisory Commission on Regulatory Barriers to Affordable Housing. *Not In My Back Yard: Removing Regulatory Barriers to Affordable Housing.* Washington, D.C.: U.S. Department of Housing and Urban Development, 1991.

Allred, Christopher. "Breaking the Cycle of Abandonment: Using a Tax Enforcement Tool to Return Distressed Properties to Sound Private Ownership." Report prepared for the New York City Department of Housing Preservation and Development, 2000.

Altshuler, Alan A., and José A. Gómez-Ibáñez. *Regulation for Revenue: The Political Economy of Land Use Exactions.* Washington, D.C.: Brookings Institution; Cambridge, Mass.: Lincoln Institute of Land Policy, 1993.

Association of Bay Area Governments, Bay Area Council, Greenbelt Alliance, Home Builders' Association of Northern California, Nonprofit Housing Association of Northern California, and California Affordable Housing Law Project. *Blueprint 2001: Housing Element Ideas and Solutions for a Sustainable and Affordable Future; Bay Area Housing.* Oakland, Calif., 2001.

Atlanta Regional Commission, "Jobs-Housing Balance." In *Community Choices Toolkit.* Atlanta: Atlanta Regional Commission, October 1, 2002.

Bailey, Jeff. "Turnover-Weary Firms Offer a Creative Benefit." Startup Journal, Wall Street Journal Center for Entrepreneurs, March 6, 2003. Available at www.startupjournal.com/columnists/enterprise/20030306-bailey.html.

Bartsch, Charles, and Bridget Dorfman. *Brownfields: State of the States.* Washington, D.C.: Northeast-Midwest Institute, 2000.

Bay Area Economics. "Affordable Housing Incentive Programs." Report prepared for the Growth Management Planning Council, King County, Washington, February 2001.

Binger, Gary, and Tom Miller. "Smart Growth in the San Francisco Bay Area: Effective Local Approaches." San Francisco District Council of the Urban Land Institute, June 2003. Available at www.uli.org/Content/NavigationMenu22/Initiatives/SmartGrowth/default.htm.

Boston Redevelopment Authority (BRA). *Survey of Linkage Programs in Other U.S. Cities with Comparisons to Boston.* Boston: BRA, May 2000.

Brooks, Mary E. *Housing Trust Fund Progress Report 2002: Local Responses to America's Housing Needs.* Frazier Park, Calif.: Housing Trust Fund Project of the Center for Community Change, 2002.

———. *A Workbook for Creating a Housing Trust Fund.* Frazier Park, Calif.: Housing Trust Fund Project of the Center for Community Change, June 1999.

Brooks, Mary E., with assistance from Debbie Mingo. *A Status Report on Housing Trust Funds in the United States.* Frazier Park, Calif.: Housing Trust Fund Project of the Center for Community Change, September 1997.

Brophy, Paul C., and Jennifer S. Vey. *Seizing City Assets: Ten Steps to Urban Land Reform.* Washington, D.C.: Brookings Institution Center on Urban and Metropolitan Policy and CEOs for Cities, October 2002.

Brown, Karen Destorel. "Expanding Affordable Housing through Inclusionary Zoning: Lessons from the Washington Metropolitan Area." Discussion paper, Brookings Institution Center on Urban and Metropolitan Policy, October 2001.

Brown, Michael. "The Diverse World of Community Land Trusts." Presentation, ULI workshop on Promoting and Preserving Workforce Housing in Urban Areas, Washington, D.C., April 4–5, 2002.

Builder Magazine Staff. "Special Report: Workforce Housing." Builder Online, July 11, 2003. Available through www.builderonline.com.

Burbank Housing. *Affordable Housing Strategies: Suggestions for Policy Formulation in General Plans and Housing Elements.* Santa Rosa, Calif.: Burbank Housing, 2000.

California Center for Land Recycling. *Brownfield Redevelopment Case Studies.* San Francisco: California Center for Land Recycling, 2000.

California State Treasurer's Office, California Debt Limit Allocation Committee. "Extra Credit Teacher Program." Available at www.treasurer.ca.gov/cdlac/extracredit/extracredit.asp?part=desc.

Canby, Anne. "Affordable Housing and Transportation: Creating New Linkages Benefiting Low-Income Families." *Housing Facts and Figures* 5, no. 2.

Cervero, Robert. "Jobs-Housing Balance Revisited: Trends and Impacts in the San Francisco Bay Area." *Journal of the American Planning Association* 62, no. 4 (Autumn 1996): 492–511.

Clark Group, The. "Fort Ord Reuse Authority Affordable/ Workforce Housing Study." Report prepared for the Fort Ord Reuse Authority, March 2003.

Colorado Department of Local Affairs. *Best Practices in Land Use Planning and Growth Management.* Colorado Heritage Report. Denver: Colorado Department of Local Affairs, December 1999.

Cordero, Michele. "Field Guide to Transfer of Development Rights." National Association of Realtors. Available at www.realtor.org/libweb.nsf/pages/fg804.

Cox, Corey. "When the Housing Bubble Bursts." *Planning* (June 2003): 26.

Department of Development Services, Town of Cary. *1999 Town of Cary Affordable Housing Toolkit.* Cary, N.C.: Department of Development Services, 1999.

Division of Housing, State of Colorado. *Affordable Housing Regulatory Barriers Impact Report.* Report to the Joint Budget Committee of the Colorado General Assembly, November 1, 2000.

Dodge, Shannon. *San Francisco Bay Area Housing Crisis Report Card.* San Francisco: Greenbelt Alliance, Nonprofit Housing Association of Northern California, and Nine County Housing Advocacy Network, June 2002.

Ehrenhalt, Alan. "The Trouble with Zoning." *Governing* (February 1998).

Enterprise Foundation. "Alternative Financing Models— Hybrids of Homeownership: Limited-Equity Cooperative Housing." Available at www.enterprisefoundation.org/resources/dss/large/lg&rin&rnc&ucpsff3.htm.

Euchner, Charles, with Elizabeth G. Frieze. "Getting Home: Overcoming Barriers to Housing in Greater Boston." Pioneer Institute for Public Policy Research and Rappaport Institute for Greater Boston, John F. Kennedy School of Government, Harvard University, January 2003. Available through www.ksg.harvard.edu/rappaport/downloads/gettinghome.pdf.

Forest, Ben. "New Jersey Revs Up Its Rehabs." *Planning* (August 1999).

Franklin, Robert. "Companies Upgrade Corporate Housing." *Minneapolis Star-Tribune,* October 23, 2003.

Freilich, Leitner, and Carlisle. "Parking Ratios." White paper presented to the Town of Chapel Hill, North Carolina, July 24, 2002.

Girga, Kevin, Matt Rosenberg, Vicky Selkowe, Joshua Todd, and Rachel Walker. "A Survey of Nationwide Community Land Trust Resale Formulas and Ground Leases: A Report Prepared for the Madison Area Community Land Trust." URPL #844. Department of Urban and Regional Planning, University of Wisconsin–Madison, April 2002.

"Governments Lagging on Low-Cost Housing." *Sacramento Bee,* June 30, 2003.

Greenbelt Alliance and Nonprofit Housing Association of Northern California. *Key Housing Element Strategies for Bay Area Communities.* San Francisco: Greenbelt Alliance and Nonprofit Housing Association of Northern California, August 2001.

Greenberg, Michael, Karen Lowrie, Henry Mayer, Tyler Miller, and Laura Solitare. *Brownfield Redevelopment as a Smart Growth Option.* New Brunswick, N.J.: National Center for Neighborhood and Brownfields Redevelopment, Bloustein School of Planning and Public Policy, Rutgers University, January 2000.

Gura, Jeanne Goldie. "Preserving Affordable Homeownership Opportunities in Rapidly Escalating Real Estate Markets." *Journal of Affordable Housing* 11, no. 1 (Fall 2001).

Gurwitt, Rob. "Betting on the Bulldozer." *Governing* (July 2002).

Hoffman, Daniel. "A Blueprint for Employer-Assisted Housing." White paper prepared for the American Affordable Housing Institute, Department of Urban Studies and Community Health, Bloustein School of Planning and Public Policy, Rutgers University.

Hollis, Linda. "Spreading the Wealth." *Planning* 69, no. 9 (October 2003).

"Housing Advocates, Builders Unite against Common Enemy: COAH." *New Jersey Law Journal,* July 21, 2003.

Housing Committee, San Francisco Planning and Urban Research Association (SPUR). *Secondary Units: A Painless Way to Increase the Supply of Housing.* Report No. 398. San Francisco: SPUR, 2001.

———. *Zoning for More Housing: Proposed Changes to San Francisco's Planning Code and Zoning Map.* Report No. 362. San Francisco: SPUR, 1998.

Howard, Bob. "$100 M Fund Targets Worker Housing." Phoenix Realty Group, May 1, 2003. Available at www.phoenixrg.com/news/item.php?id=6.

Kaplan, Sharon. "Housing in Commercial Neighbor-hoods." In Beth Mattson-Teig, "Housing Conversions." *Urban Land* 62, no. 10 (October 2003).

Katz, Bruce, and Margery Austin Turner. *Rethinking Local Affordable Housing Strategies: Lessons from 70 Years of Policy and Practice.* Washington, D.C.: Brookings Institution Center on Urban and Metropolitan Policy and the Urban Institute, December 2003.

Keating, Dennis, and Mitch Kahn. "Rent Control in the New Millennium." Shelterforce Online, May/June 2001. Available at www.nhi.org/online/issues/ 117/KeatingKahn.html.

"Island Seeks to Ease Housing Crisis for Workers; Local Hospital, Schools Offer Cheaper Options." *Boston Globe,* August 17, 2003, 3rd edition.

King County Budget Office. "King County Buildable Lands." Evaluation Report 2002: Recent Growth and Land Capacity in King County and its Cities, September 2002. Available at www.metrokc.gov/ budget/buildland/bldlnd02.htm.

Kingston, Allan. "Housing Our Workforce." Multifamily Executive, May 2003. Available through www.multifamilyexecutive.com/.

Kromer, John. "Vacant-Property Policy and Practice: Baltimore and Philadelphia." Discussion paper pre-pared for the Brookings Institution Center on Urban and Metropolitan Policy and CEOs for Cities, October 2002.

"Land Trust Lets Buyers Purchase House, Not Lot." *Sunday Oregonian,* June 29, 2003, sunrise edition.

LandWatch Monterey County. "Chapter 4: Models and Case Examples." Issues and Actions, Affordable/ Workforce Housing Study. Available at www.mclw.org/pages/issuesactions/fortord/ clarkreport/chapter4.html.

———. "Chapter 5: Federal, State, Local and Private Resources." Issues and Actions, Affordable/ Workforce Housing Study. Available through www.mclw.org/pages/issuesactions/fortord/ clarkreport/chapter5.html.

LeGates, Richard T. "Housing Incentives to Promote Inter-Regional Jobs-Housing Balance." Report pre-pared for the Interregional Partnership Jobs/ Housing Balance Pilot Program, January 2001.

Leigh, Nancy Green. "The State Role in Urban Land Development." Discussion paper prepared for the Brookings Institution Center on Urban and Metro-politan Policy and CEOs for Cities, April 2003.

Leinberger, Christopher B. "Building for the Long Term." *Urban Land* 62, no. 11–12 (November–December 2003).

Listokin, David. "Housing Rehabilitation and American Cities." Draft overview paper for HUD Conference on Housing Policy in the New Millennium, Washington, D.C., October 3, 2000.

Listokin, David, and Barbara Listokin. "Historic Preservation and Affordable Housing: Leveraging Old Resources for New Opportunities." *Housing Facts and Figures* 3, issue 2, p. 2. Available at www.fanniemaefoundation.org/programs/hff/ v3i2-histpres.shtml.

Marschner, Kim Ilana. *Building Workforce Housing: Meeting San Francisco's Housing Challenge.* San Francisco: San Francisco Chamber of Commerce, 2003.

"MassHousing Offers Improved Affordable Home Loans for Buyers with Modest Incomes; Enhanced Programs Are Unveiled Just in Time for Spring Buying Season." *Business Wire,* May 7, 2003.

Meck, Stuart, Rebecca Retzlaff, and James Schwab. *Regional Approaches to Affordable Housing.* Planning Advisory Service Report 513/514. Chicago: American Planning Association, 2003.

"Mixed-Income Rental Housing Production Program Using Tax-Exempt Bond Financing." Millennial Housing Commission Concept Paper, n.d. Available at govinfo.library.unt.edu/mhc/papers.html.

Mondale, Ted, and William Fulton. "Managing Metro-politan Growth: Reflections on the Twin Cities Experience." Case study prepared for the Brookings Institution Center on Urban and Metropolitan Policy, September 2003.

Morris, Marya. *Incentive Zoning: Meeting Urban Design and Affordable Housing Objectives.* Planning Advisory Service Report 494. Chicago: American Planning Association, 2000.

Moulton, Jennifer. "Ten Steps to a Living Downtown." Discussion paper prepared for the Brookings Institution Center on Urban and Metropolitan Policy, October 1999.

Municipal Research and Services Center of Washington (MRSC). *Infill Development: Strategies for Shaping Livable Neighborhoods.* Report No. 38. Washington, D.C.: MRSC, June 1997.

Myerson, Deborah L. "Hard at Work for Workforce Housing." *Urban Land* 62, no. 9 (September 2003).

Bibliography

————. *Mixed-Income Housing: Myth and Fact.* Washington, D.C.: ULI, 2003.

National Association of Affordable Housing Lenders (NAAHL). *Affordable Housing Loan Consortia Sourcebook.* 2nd ed. Washington, D.C.: NAAHL, 1997.

National Association of Home Builders, Economics, Mortgage Finance, and Housing Policy Division. *Producing Affordable Housing: Partnerships for Profit.* Washington, D.C.: Home Builder Press, 1999.

National Governors Association. "Growth Tool Kit: Modernize Zoning Regulations and Building Codes." June 1, 2001.

National Trust for Historic Preservation. *Rebuilding Community: A Best Practices Toolkit for Historic Preservation and Redevelopment.* Washington, D.C.: National Trust for Historic Preservation, 2002.

Nelson, Arthur C. "Top Ten State and Local Strategies to Increase Affordable Housing Supply." *Housing Facts and Findings* 5, issue 1. Available at www.fanniemaefoundation.org/programs/hff/v5i1-topten.shtml.

New York City Department of Housing Preservation and Development. "Mayor Michael R. Bloomberg's Housing Initiatives: Program Descriptions from 'The New Housing Marketplace: Creating Housing for the Next Generation' Plan Issued on December 10, 2002."

New York State Division of Housing and Community Renewal. "Rent Control and Rent Stabilization." Fact Sheet #1. Available at www.dhcr.state.ny.us/ora/pubs/html/orafac1.htm.

Percy, Stephen L., and Leslie J. Singer. "The State of Employer-Assisted Housing in Milwaukee." Report prepared for the National Housing Conference, January 22, 2003.

Peterson, Tom. "Community Land Trusts: An Introduction." *Planning Commissioner's Journal* (Summer 1996).

Pill, Madeline. *Employer-Assisted Housing: Competitiveness through Partnership.* Cambridge, Mass.: Neighborhood Investment Corporation and Joint Center for Housing Studies, Harvard University, September 2000.

Pitcoff, Winton. "Affordable Forever: Land Trusts Keep Housing within Reach," *Shelterforce* (January–February 2002).

Porter, Douglas R. "Flexible Zoning: A Status Report on Performance Standards." *Zoning News* (January 1998).

————. "The Promise and Practice of Inclusionary Zoning." Draft report prepared for the Brookings Institution Symposium on Growth Management and Affordable Housing, Washington, D.C., May 29, 2003.

Porter, Douglas R., with Anita Kramer, Terry Lassar, and David Salvesen. "Building Homes in America's Cities: A Progress Report." Paper prepared for the U.S. Conference of Mayors, the U.S. Department of Housing and Urban Development, and the National Association of Home Builders, October 2000.

Pruetz, Rick. "Reinventing TDR." Paper presented at the American Planning Association National Planning Conference, April 16, 2002.

Regional Housing Authority Initiative. "Housing Trust Fund Models." In "Regional Housing Authority Workbook." Available at www.hmcnews.org/housing/workbook.htm.

Rosan, Christina. "Cleveland's Land Bank: Catalyzing a Renaissance in Affordable Housing." *Housing Facts and Findings* 3, issue 1. Available at www.fanniemaefoundation.org/programs/hff/v3i1-landbank.shtml.

Shartin, Emily. "Downpayments toward Affordability." *Boston Globe,* July 13, 2003, 3rd edition.

Shubert, Michael. *Housing for a Competitive Workforce: Homeownership Models That Work.* Chicago: Metropolitan Planning Council, 1998.

Silicon Valley Housing Leadership Council. *Towards More Affordable Homes: Streamlining the Entitlement Process in Silicon Valley.* Silicon Valley Manufacturing Group, Tri-County Apartment Association, and Homebuilders Association of Northern California, October 1999.

Simons, Robert A. *Turning Brownfields into Greenbacks.* Washington, D.C.: ULI, 1998.

Sluis, Tom. "DMR Construction Begins." *Durango Herald,* September 24, 2003.

Smart Communities Network. "Land Use Planning Strategies—Transfer of Development Rights." September 29, 2003. Available at www.smartcommunities.ncat.org/landuse/transfer.shtml.

Staley, Samuel R. "Flexible Zoning: An Overview of the Issues." UrbanFutures.org, June 1997. Available at www.urbanfutures.org/r6897b.html.

Stegman, Michael A. *State and Local Affordable-Housing Programs: A Rich Tapestry.* Washington, D.C.: ULI, 1999.

Stewart, Jocelyn Y. "State Policies Boost Affordable Housing, Study Finds; Programs That Require Low-Income Units as Part of Development Projects Stimulate Construction, Advocates Say." *Los Angeles Times,* July 15, 2003, home edition.

Strategic Economics. "Building Sustainable Communities: Housing Solutions for Silicon Valley." Report prepared for Silicon Valley Manufacturing Group and Greenbelt Alliance, November 1999.

Suchman, Diane R. *Developing Successful Infill Housing.* Washington, D.C.: ULI, 2002.

Superville, Darlene. "Employer-Sponsored Programs Turn Workers into Homeowners." *Boston Globe,* July 15, 2003.

Tompkins County Planning Department. "Vital Communities Toolbox." Available at www.co.tompkins.ny.us/planning/vct/index.html.

Tucker, William. *How Rent Control Drives Out Affordable Housing.* Policy Analysis No. 274. Washington, D.C.: Cato Institute, May 21, 1997.

Van Horn, Amy. "New Incentive for Housing Developments Approved." *Pittsburgh Redevelopment News* 1, no. 3 (Summer 2002).

Voyles, Bennett. "Operation Enduring Red Tape." Affordable Housing Finance, January 2, 2002. Available through www.housingfinance.com/ahf/articles/2002/02JanMilitaryHousing/.

U.S. Department of Housing and Urban Development. "America's Affordable Communities Initiative, HUD's Initiative on Removal of Regulatory Barriers: Proposals for Incentive Criteria on Barrier Removal in HUD's Funding Allocations; Notice." *Federal Register* 68, no. 227 (November 25, 2003).

Wermath, Peter. "Overview: Controlling Affordability over Time in Subsidized Owner-Occupied Housing." Enterprise Foundation, June 5, 1995. Available through www.practitionerresources.org/showdoc.html?id=60641.

Wheeler, Stephen. *Smart Infill: Creating More Livable Communities in the Bay Area.* San Francisco: Greenbelt Alliance, 2002.